Square Foot Gardening

by Mel Bartholomew

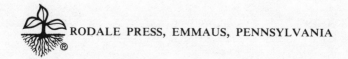 RODALE PRESS, EMMAUS, PENNSYLVANIA

To my mother, whose love of gardening
has nurtured my interest.

Project Director/Book Designer Kim Morrow

Illustrations by Erick Ingraham

Photographs by John Hamel

Project Assistant Darlene Schneck

Printed in the United States of America on recycled paper, containing a high
percentage of de-inked fiber.

Library of Congress Cataloging in Publication Data
Bartholomew, Mel.
  Square foot gardening.

  Includes index.
  1. Vegetable gardening.   2.   Square foot gardening.
I. Title.
SB321.B28   635   80–26341
ISBN 0–87857–340–2 hardcover
ISBN 0–87857–341–0 paperback

   14 16 18 20 19 17 15   hardcover
           18 20 19   paperback

Contents

Acknowledgments

Writing a book is not easy—especially for all those around the author. They tire of hearing about the book that's going to be written, but it gets worse when the writing actually starts. Then the queries change from "When are you going to start your book?" to "When are you going to finish!?"

So, to the many people who have encouraged and supported me, special thanks go out to them all not only for their interest, but mostly for their patience and understanding.

Particular thanks go to the two ladies who have helped me the most: my wife, Ginny, for her extreme patience and adaptability to an author's schedule; and our cat, Suzy, who remained a constant companion (curled up on my desk) during the long hours spent writing this book.

Chapter 1
◈ Introduction

Does anyone know the real reason people garden? Why do *you* want to garden and grow vegetables? Most surveys show that the majority of people who garden say they want that special homegrown flavor; others grow their own food to save money; and still other people garden just to have a nice hobby that provides pleasure, pride, and satisfaction. The pleasures of gardening are many—getting outdoors, exercising, putting your hands in the soil, growing things, and the special pride of accomplishment that comes with the harvest. Many gardeners want to experience the feeling of being self-sufficient or at least partly so, and to have some control over what they eat, particularly to have fresh, wholesome food without any additives or preservatives. All of these are good reasons for gardening. It is truly one of America's most popular leisure activities. Of course, for homesteaders and other people who garden on a large scale, it's a way of life and a means of subsistence.

In order to satisfy your gardening desires and goals, whatever they may be, it's important to be successful in what you're doing. For after all, the final harvest is the true goal of gardening. And growing plants in a neat, attractive, weedless garden can help lead to that harvest goal. With all of this in mind then, one must ask "How are American gardeners doing?" I'm afraid the answer is "rather poorly." Except for those belong-

1

This view of the author's garden shows the pleasing contrast of plant forms, textures, and appearance created by the many small squares of the square foot garden. A garden this attractive doesn't have to be hidden "way out back."

ing to dedicated or tireless workers, most gardens turn into unattended, weed-filled messes soon after summer is under way. If your garden stays neat and productive throughout the entire growing season, consider yourself one of the rare few. You have to remember that a very high percentage of us gardeners (probably almost half) aren't determined to have a successful garden no matter how much time and work it takes. We're mostly just people who get that tremendous urge in the springtime to till a little land and plant a few seeds. When our gardens get out of hand in August we get discouraged, and find it difficult to continue with any great interest in the garden.

This book is all about a new system for gardening, one that is so simple and easy that anyone can enjoy a weed-free garden all year, and produce a continuous harvest. I give a lot of lectures on gardening, and one of the first questions I'm asked is "Why a new method? What's wrong with the good old single-row garden that we've known for years and years?" My answer is always the same. Just look at one of those conventional gardens in mid or late season. The *average* gardener starts out each year with high hopes, great ambition and energy, and a desire for a really big, well-kept garden. But other warm-weather activities seem to get in the way of the garden work, and it soon becomes neglected, overrun with weeds and pests. By the end of the season, there might be enough tomatoes, squash, and cucumbers to make the whole effort seem worthwhile, but all the other crops that couldn't survive the neglect will have been overrun by the weeds, or bolted to seed before they could be harvested. Those tomatoes and squash seem to grow all by themselves, though, until the gardener finds he can't give them away and sets to work canning and freezing them, all the while wondering why he couldn't just grow a nice assortment of vegetables to take care of his everyday needs.

I started really noting and observing the demoralizing effects and conditions of a typical garden when I used to run the community garden in our neighborhood. Our organization had a small plot of land that we had rototilled, fertilized, and staked out into small individual plots for rental to anyone who wanted to garden. The program was very popular and well attended at the beginning of each year. In the spring, that old planting urge infected everyone and people flooded to the garden, lining up well in advance to sign up for the plots. See if this description of what I observed doesn't sound familiar. The sight of that recently tilled, rich brown soil was a tonic on a warm sunny day in early spring. People couldn't wait to get out to their plots and start raking, digging, and planting. What a beehive of activity! Actually it reminded me more of a recently disturbed ants' nest. People were everywhere, scurrying here and there, bending, digging, sitting, walking, children were running around, and there was lots of shouting and laughing—everyone was having a wonderful time! We were all returning to the bosom of Mother Earth and were loving every minute of it. Rows were laid out (this was before square foot gardening), furrows were dug, and packet after packet of seeds was poured out into the rich, damp soil. Our heads danced with visions of all those wonderful vegetables we would soon be harvesting.

By the time everyone left and I closed the gate, a glance back showed me a scene that looked like an army had just done battle there. Our carefully laid-out garden was a field of footprints, cluttered with forgotten tools and the usual debris that civilization leaves in its wake. But everyone went home happy. Some of the gardeners (the pint-sized ones), of course, stayed longer than they wanted—you know how impatient children are. "When will the seeds start sprouting?" "When are we going home?" "I'm tired." "I have to go to the bathroom." "I'm thirsty." "Can we get an ice cream cone now?" *"When are we going home?"* But nevertheless, we all did enjoy ourselves, and couldn't wait till next week!

Unfortunately, the next week brought rain and gloom. Not many of us returned, but luckily the bad weather lasted only a few days. Soon everyone came drifting back and the following Saturday the gang was out in force again. This time, they didn't stay as long and I noticed there weren't as many children in attendance. However, the following week participation and excitement were renewed because most of the seeds had sprouted and long rows of beautiful, young green leaves were visible in all the plots. Some people started thinning and transplanting; others just stood and admired all that green. Unfortunately, a lot of green was also showing between the rows, too. So some of the group started weeding, but others were busy planting transplants bought at the local nursery.

By the following week, the crowd had settled down to a more or less steady group. Oh, everyone came at one time or another during the week. But you could begin to see which gardens were going to prosper. Some people had already called me to say they were moving, doing something else on Saturday, or had developed a bad back and couldn't continue the garden. That was no problem; we had a waiting list of anxious gardeners who would be happy to take over their plots. But of 100 gardeners who started, about 20 dropped by the wayside within two months. By that time spring was well into the warm weather and *everything* grew like crazy, including the weeds.

Everyone was having trouble keeping up with the weeding, watering, and thinning. It was difficult to find time to do all three, and thinning those long rows of thickly planted seeds began to take last place on the priorities list. When we finally did get around to thinning, the crowded plants were spindly and overgrown. You couldn't pay anyone to take a few extra lettuce or cabbage plants because everyone had so many. Between our reluctance to thin out the lush green rows and the necessity of killing young seedlings that were not needed, many of us just left our rows unthinned. It was the last thing on our minds. After all, there were weeds to pull, new tomato plants to put in, stakes to pound into the ground, cucumber and squash seeds to plant. The lettuce and cabbage would just have to get thinned next week.

By early summer only the most serious, dedicated gardeners were keeping up their plots, even if they had to fight their way in at times. The others had picked some scrawny lettuce and a few overgrown radishes—only a few! Most of my colleagues planted half of a package of seeds in a 10-foot row before I could stop them. That's over 200 radishes! Of course, they were planted so close together that most didn't grow any bigger than a long, skinny root. But some of the plants, despite their crowding, managed to form nice little bulbs which grew to golf ball size before being harvested. The unharvested radishes continued to grow and soon we saw pretty white flower stalks rising above the radish rows.

Summer brought the tomatoes. What a glorious crop we were going to have! Everyone planted tomatoes. Of the 100 plots, 98 contained tomatoes. They are truly America's favorite vegetable. But you should have seen the assortment of stakes and supports everyone was using. It was a comic tragedy. The comic part (the tragedy would come later) was watching the creative-minded among us propping up their tomatoes with a motley assortment of things like old fishing poles and lines, or drapery rods tied with venetian blind cords. Other people went in the opposite direction and built the most elaborate supports you could imagine—one was constructed of long bamboo poles lashed together in a massive and complex structure that looked formidable enough to replace the Great Wall of China. But despite all the odd, elaborate supports, the tomatoes continued to outgrow whatever people installed.

I remember one plot in particular that was planted in nothing but tomatoes—enough plants for half an acre, all crowded into a tiny community garden plot. The owners reflected on how much they expected to put up in the form of sauce, soup, juice, whole and quartered tomatoes. But by August, they couldn't even get into their plot, much less try to tie up the plants. One particular weekend I remember talking to them after they had picked a bushel and a half of tomatoes and wondered what on earth they were going to do with them all. At that time of the year, all the people I knew were in the same predicament. We all found ourselves with so much harvest we were actually embarrassed, and had no idea of what we were going to do with it all.

Fortunately, for many of us that only happens for a few weeks out of the year with most vegetables. Nature has a way of helping out. Just when you're so inundated with zucchini squash that your nongardening neighbors close their curtains when you walk down the street, along comes the squash vine borer and zap go your plants. Other years, when you can't eat the cucumbers fast enough to keep ahead, the plants wilt overnight, and the season is over. And the spring vegetables have a habit of going to seed all at once. Just when you were admiring your long rows of nice lettuce heads, they all shoot up and bolt to seed within a week. When it happens you resolve that next year you'll pick them sooner, before they get full size. We all fall victim to such good intentions.

The garden writers keep telling us to be sure to thin, because the thinnings are great in salad, and picking them makes room for the other plants to grow. Unfortunately, that advice is all too seldom taken. Most gardeners don't thin until the heads are too full or the plants are too large. So the crop never develops properly. It's very difficult, if not downright impossible, to pick half-grown, half-size vegetables. It's easy to write about—I know, I've done it. But darned if it isn't almost impossible to actually do. We've all been brought up in this great country of ours to think that bigger is better. You can't make people do something that goes against what they've been taught or human nature, no matter how right it might be.

At first, I thought maybe this situation existed in just our community garden. So I asked around and started really noticing and visiting homes and gardens all around the area. I found that most of them were in the same condition, and the owners complained about the same problems I was observing. Reflecting on my own gardening experiences in various parts of the country, I realized this was par for the course. Since then, my travels and lectures in many states have convinced me that overplanting and a lack of thinning are universal problems.

Needless to say, by September our community garden was a terrible mess. It was overgrown with weeds and plants sprawled everywhere. Fewer than half of the plots were still being tended. Oh, lots of us still came around to pick whatever was ripe (or more often, overripe) but the dedicated and determined few had dwindled to less than 30 of our original 100. Then came the heavy winds and rains of September storms. Down went all the tomatoes. Over went all the peppers and eggplants. What a mess! Stakes snapped, cages overturned, unsupported stems bent and twisted. It was so discouraging that the faithful 30 dropped to 20 overnight. But we 20 were still determined to carry on. However, by the time Labor Day was over and school started, everyone became deeply involved in PTA, weekend parties, football games on TV, raking leaves, Sunday school, and all the other activities we crowd into our busy lives. After all, you only have enough time for so many organizations and activities. Then one rainy Saturday at our regular morning garden clinic, 7 people showed up. Seven! When last spring we had over a hundred and fifty!

Well, that was it for me. If gardening had such appeal that so many people wanted to try it, but less than 5 percent of them lasted the season, something was wrong. That's when I started to reflect on the past year and all of its highs and lows. After another year of the same thing I said to myself, "There's got to be a better way." I began to question all of our current gardening methods and procedures. Why do we plant an entire packet of seeds all at once and then have to go back and thin most of them out? Why do we thin plants to stand 3, 6, and 12 inches apart in the row, but then leave 2 to 3 feet between rows? Why do we plant so thickly that we have to thin at all? Why do we dig or rototill our soil to make it nice and loose, then walk all over it and pack it down? Why do we let the summer vine crops spread out and occupy so much land, land that takes fertilizing, cultivating, weeding, and watering? I spent an entire year trying to find answers to those questions.

To make a year-long story short, I couldn't find any explanation other than "That's the way we've always done it." I consulted all the experts, read all the books and magazines, and dug up all the pertinent information that I could find. What I did conclude was that most of our present home gardening methods have their origins in commercial agricultural practices.

Farmers who have had to become increasingly dependent on animals and, later, machines rather than hand labor need wide-open paths between plant rows in order to get the tractor in to plant, cultivate, fertilize, and harvest. But we poor home growers aren't farmers, and we don't have tractors. We do have a lot of hand labor available, however. In fact, that's all we have. In addition, most of us have just a small backyard garden in which to putter around and raise a few crops.

One reason those commercial agricultural practices have been and are still being taught to home gardeners is that the United States Department of Agriculture's county agriculture extension services tend to teach and promote what their big brothers, the state universities, are doing. Most academic research and experimentation is oriented toward the needs of commercial farmers. That's fine for the large-scale growers but it just doesn't meet the needs of the millions of home gardeners in this country. What we need is a simple gardening method that will produce a lot of harvest in a small space.

There have been a number of gardening systems already introduced in the United States that can do just that—produce a lot of food in a little space. But when I looked at them carefully, I found that they are still geared to a fairly large operation. The French intensive method with its broad, raised beds; scatter-seeding in wide rows; Chinese raised beds; and all the others either were derived from commercial farming in a foreign country or were designed for very large gardens using special power equipment.

Well, that was enough of a challenge for me. With my engineering background, my recent observations at our community garden, my experience teaching and writing about gardening, and the available time since my retirement from business, I set out to devise that easy, no-work, foolproof, continual-harvest garden method that would work in a small space for beginners and experts alike. And square foot gardening is the result.

If you're a beginner, you'll soon become an expert using my system. And if you are already an expert, or at least a seasoned gardener, if you try my method with an open mind you'll soon become a gourmet gardener growing the best crops with the least amount of work. In essence, I'm going to show you a way that will still allow you to get outdoors, get your hands in the soil, and produce a good harvest so you have all you want to eat, but without a lot of effort or expense. In fact, square foot gardening will save you at least 80 percent of the space, time, and money normally needed to garden, and at the same time will produce a better and more continuous harvest with less work. You're going to eliminate all of your thinning, most of your weeding, and a lot of your watering, and will do it all in only one fifth of the area you now need for gardening. It will cost much less because there are no elaborate structures, tools, or equipment to buy. It may sound fantastic, or unrealistic. But as you begin to understand this simple system you'll see that it's mostly just a lot of common sense and you'll wonder why someone didn't think of this before.

Chapter 2
What Is the Square Foot Method?

I believe that square foot gardening is more than just another new method of planning and planting a garden; it's a whole different psychological approach to gardening. The square foot garden is divided into a size and shape that gardeners of all ages, sizes, and levels of experience can understand and cope with easily. The system is simple, but versatile. It can be adapted to fit all kinds of gardening situations. Whether you want to grow all your own food or just enough for a few salads each week, whether you live alone or have a large family, whether you live in the city or the country, with a lot of land or a little, you will be able to adapt the principles of square foot gardening to meet your needs. The garden will be well organized, easy to maintain, and attractive all season long.

Like all inventors, it's been hard for me to contain my enthusiasm —I truly think the square foot method is something new and different. But before I decided to write this book I took the time to show this method to a number of respected gardening experts around the country and asked them frankly what they thought of it. Their response was very positive. To a person they all said, "You've really got something here. It's a good system that should work for most gardeners."

Old gardening habits die slowly, and I urge you to read this book with an open mind, and encourage you to drop any resistance you might have

9

to a new and different system. I'm speaking particularly to you old-timers and experts. We all get set in our ways and hate to change, but sometimes change is necessary and helpful. In the case of square foot gardening, if you're willing to change some of your gardening habits, you'll find that you really can have a better garden with less work.

Limiting the Size of the Garden

The square foot garden really is easy to maintain, basically because it sets physical limits for us ahead of time. In developing this method of gardening, I spent considerable time looking for ways to make gardening less work. In fact, the entire concept of square foot gardening is the result of that search for an easier, more foolproof way to garden. While the basic concept of growing more food in less space has been tried by many, I don't believe that anyone has ever been able to coordinate easily defined limits of space and time into a system that still makes gardening simpler and less time-consuming. Square foot gardening does just that because it sets forth definite limits, or boundaries, within which you will garden. It limits the amount of space, and thereby time, you will devote to each vegetable, chore, and step in the garden.

That's very important for most of us; we need limits to guide us in most of the things we do. For example, what would sports be if they didn't have limits? Consider how boring a football game would be if there were no sidelines or time limits, or a golf course that has no out-of-bounds. Of course, there is no sideline or out-of-bounds in gardening, and maybe that's what's wrong with it for so many people. When you don't set definite limits and goals for your garden, it's all too easy to lose control of it before the season is through. The heart of square foot gardening is the specific guidelines it sets up for all your gardening activities. If you follow the system I guarantee that your garden will be successful.

Consider how you grow one simple crop, like lettuce. Now you probably grow a whole row of it. You till the soil, plant a packet full of seeds, thin once or maybe twice, spend a lot of time weeding and watering, and still probably end up with more lettuce than you can use in the short harvest season. The square foot method will make it possible for you to grow only as many heads of lettuce as you really want or need, with less time and effort. I'll show you how to plant just 1 square foot of lettuce with exactly four seeds—no more, no less. When you have finished preparing the soil for that one square (which takes about one minute) and planting those four seeds (which takes half of a minute) you'll be all finished planting one crop. Once a week you weed the square (which takes about 30 seconds) and water that square (which takes another minute) and that's all you do until it's time to harvest those four heads of lettuce. I'll even show you how to stretch the harvest over a period of time so you are not flooded with a big harvest you wish you didn't have all at once. If you want more than four heads of lettuce (and most people do), I'll show you how to plant another square of four plants a week or two later. In fact, if you really love lettuce, you can plant a different square every week for the rest of your life but never have too much or use up too much space. That's basically all there is to the square foot method. Each crop is handled similarly, and is just as easy to care for.

The techniques involved in square foot gardening are simple. Throughout the pages of this book, I'll explain every step and every detail of the method, without going into a lot of long-winded explanations of basic gardening philosophy. But please take the time to read the text before you get started. If you understand the whole system you'll have better results.

A Garden Based on Squares Instead of Rows

Let's get right into the method, then. I call it square foot gardening because you build up your garden in a series of squares. Each square is 12 inches by 12 inches, an area of 1 square foot. Each square holds a different vegetable, flower, or herb. (I'm a firm believer in including some flowers and herbs in the vegetable garden). How many plants are placed in each square depends on the particular variety, how big the plants get, and how far apart they should be planted in order to develop properly. In general, seeds or plants are placed the same distance apart as that shown on seed packets when they recommend that you thin to so many inches apart in the row. The difference is that instead of being planted in rows with extra space between them, the plants are placed in a square, the same distance apart in all directions.

Let's consider pepper plants, for example. They grow to be fairly large, and need 12 inches of space between plants, so you place 1 pepper plant right in the center of one square. Leaf lettuce, on the other hand, needs only 6 inches between plants. So, taking advantage of all the space in a square foot, you could plant 4 leaf lettuce plants in one square. Spinach or bush beans need only 4 inches between plants, thus 9 plants will fill a square with no wasted space. Carrots, onions, or radishes take up the least amount of room. They're spaced only 3 inches apart, so an amazing 16 will fit nicely into 1 square foot, again with no wasted space. These spacings allow enough room for each plant to grow to maturity.

These small 1-foot squares are grouped together into blocks measuring 4 feet by 4 feet square. Each block contains 16 different squares, each planted with a different crop, and each square contains one, four, nine, or sixteen plants. At an average of 8 plants per square, that means you can grow almost 130 plants in that 4-foot by 4-foot block. Your garden can consist of only one block or several, depending on how many people you want to feed. One block will produce enough vegetables for salads for one person all season. Each fully planted block becomes a checkerboard pattern of contrasting colors, textures, and shapes—adding an extra visual dimension to the garden. If you have a family-size garden of at least six

This photo shows the diversity of plants you can grow in a small space. Four squares each of lettuce, cauliflower, geraniums, and cabbage grow in close proximity here.

blocks, you may wish to plant four squares of each variety at once, adjacent to each other, rather than four individual squares located among your six blocks. This still accomplishes all of the goals of the square foot method, yet looks neat and attractive.

One of the most important rules of this gardening system is that you should never walk on your growing soil! If you do, you will pack down and compact the soil, eliminating the necessary air spaces between soil particles and making it difficult for water and air to penetrate to the plants'

Pieces of scrap lumber can be nailed together to make neat, attractive walkways between the garden blocks. Recycling old boards means you can make the paths for free and with a minimum of labor.

roots. To make walking on the growing soil unnecessary, the square foot garden is laid out with a walking space around all four sides of each block. The blocks are small enough so that you can reach in from any direction to plant seeds, water, and harvest. How much walking space you allow between blocks will depend on how comfortable you are in a narrow path. You can make your paths 1, 2, or even 3 feet wide. There's no set rule. I use 1-foot paths in my garden. But you can make yours as broad or as narrow as you like. Your paths can be wood planks (as I use), grass (which needs mowing), or just plain soil (which needs weeding). A path thickly lined with hay mulch looks nice, keeps your feet clean, and needs no weeding.

What you plant in your garden blocks is determined solely by what you like to eat; how much you plant is limited by how many plants fit into a square of that particular variety and how many squares you decide to plant. As you can see, this is going to be very different from a conventional garden where you go down a 20-foot row sprinkling seeds out of the packet till the end of the row or an empty packet compels you to stop. The number of seeds and plants you put in each square establishes your stopping point for you, so you can't overplant. The number of squares in the garden block is also controlled. This entire process is what I call controlled planting. Without such control, most of us would plant much more than we really should.

Large Plants in the Square Foot Garden

You may be wondering if this sort of limited planting means you can't grow big, sprawling plants like zucchini and tomatoes. Zucchini is one favorite vegetable that takes a *lot* of room! In fact, you'll need a 3-foot by 3-foot space, or nine squares, to accommodate each plant. So if you want zucchini, it will take up over half of a full block. But it can be grown just as successfully as the smaller vegetables in the square foot garden.

Tomatoes and all other vining or climbing crops are grown vertically to save space—a much more efficient method than allowing them to sprawl over the ground. With the help of a few sturdy frames that are easy to build and erect, you can grow tomatoes, cucumbers, summer and winter squash, pole beans, melons, and other vining crops up off the ground. That eliminates stooping and bending over to harvest—you can do it standing up. The ground space needed for four tomatoes, eight cucumbers, or two squash plants is only 1 foot wide by 4 feet long—it's

Cucumbers and other vining crops are trained to grow vertically, saving space in the garden and creating an attractive living screen along its north edge.

even more space-efficient than the rest of the square foot garden. To get a better idea of the amount of space that's saved, you might compare vertical crops to tall buildings. If the Empire State Building in New York City was all on one floor it would take up many city blocks in an area where space is at a premium. For vining crops, as for buildings, the idea is to provide a good foundation and then save space by building upward.

Growing crops vertically also results in better sunlight and air circulation for plants and reduced pest damage. And the effect is visually pleasing. Training your vining crops to grow up vertical frames will let you enjoy a living wall of greenery and vegetables neatly enclosing the garden perimeter.

Single-Seed Sowing

Chapter 10 contains the details of how to start seeds both indoors and outdoors. But I'd like to elaborate here on the concept of sowing single seeds, which is the basis of all planting done in the square foot garden. The old practice of tearing open a packet of seeds, sprinkling them along a 20-foot row in the garden until the packet is empty, and then staking the empty packet at the end of the row has been with us for so long it's hard to know how it originated. As I watched hundreds of packets being emptied this way at our community garden, I began to ponder the wisdom of this practice. After all those seeds sprout, the gardener is faced with the laborious chore of thinning out all of the seedlings until a single plant remains every 4, 6, or 12 inches, depending on the variety.

Most gardeners I've known hate to thin; it goes against the grain to tear out and destroy hundreds of young plants you would like to raise. Usually the majority of seeds are planted in the spring, a time when we are so longing for something green. When the little plants come up, we somehow can't bring ourselves to thin them, so we put off the chore as long as possible. Usually we wait too long. When we do finally get ready to thin, we find to our dismay that the row is filled with hundreds of tall, lanky plants. They are big enough to consider replanting somewhere else, and most of us end up trying to transplant them wherever we can find room. I used to do this, too, and it's a real chore.

When I started to ask why we continue this practice in the garden, there didn't seem to be any logical answer. None of the books, magazines, or gardening experts I consulted had any answer except "That's the way we've always done it. Besides, many seeds are too small to handle any other way." Oh, I came across some references to mixing tiny seeds with sand or coffee grounds to help thin them out when planting. And I heard the usual advice about the need to plant enough seeds in a certain space to break the hard earth crust that always forms in a wet spring soil. But these reasons didn't really seem to answer the question.

Then I began to inquire how many seeds are actually in a packet, and that's when I became convinced that there must be a better way. I always have fun when I'm giving a lecture by asking the audience how many seeds of their favorite crop they think are in an average packet. Care to make a guess? There are, on the average, 560 cabbage, 1,550 carrot, and an astounding 1,975 lettuce seeds in a packet. I think it's safe to say that none of us could eat 560 heads of cabbage a year, or 1,550 carrots. Why then do we plant the whole packet full of seeds, only to go back later and thin 1,450 carrot plants so that we can harvest 100? (Even 100 carrots is a lot for the average garden. That's a lot of carrots every week during the normal harvest season of the home garden, probably more than most of us buy during the whole rest of the year.) It's perhaps logical to assume that all the seeds won't sprout. However, if the seeds have been stored and handled properly almost 80 percent of them *will* sprout. Another thing most gardeners don't realize is that seeds can stay good year after year, and any that aren't planted can be saved. In fact, some seeds last over five years if they are stored correctly at home (see chapter 10 for more information). At any rate, it seemed to me that with a little knowledge, care, and understanding of seed sowing and storing techniques, gardeners could easily improve their planting procedures and save money to boot.

The next assumption I questioned was whether the seeds really are too small to plant any other way. So I did some time and motion studies, drawing on my engineering background. I was amazed to find out that planting an entire packet, then going back to thin, took almost twice as long as laboriously planting one single seed at a time every 4, 6, or 12 inches, without having to thin later on. And not surprisingly, the single-seed method produces a stronger crop that matures earlier.

My first attempt at developing a new planting technique was to make a single-row furrow, then lay down a yardstick and, after getting comfortable on a kneeling board or short stool, place several seeds in one palm, and pick out one seed at a time, placing it in at the correct spacing along the yardstick. Carrots were planted 3 inches apart, lettuce at 6 inches, and cabbage at 12 inches. I then covered each seed with a little bit of vermiculite, watered the row, and placed a board or burlap strip over the row. Later, when I perfected square foot spacing, it became even easier to poke a hole in the soil with my finger at the correct spacing within each square, add vermiculite, then place one seed in the hole and cover it with more vermiculite. If you just don't trust all your seeds to sprout, you can place two or even three seeds in every hole, but then you will have to go back later to thin. Still, you will have to thin only a few plants—a lot less than in the old row method. If you do need to thin, don't do it by pulling out the seedlings and transplanting them someplace else. Snip off the extra plants with a scissors, as soon as most of the seeds have sprouted, leaving the one healthy plant in each space to grow to maturity. It won't hurt you so much to cut off a plant at this early stage.

Using the single-seed method along with block planting will enable you to limit the time usually involved in this chore to less than 10 percent of what you used to spend in a conventional row garden. That's a very dramatic difference. It comes about first, because you've limited the number of plants you're going to grow, second, because you've limited the growing area to just a few squares, and third, because you plant far fewer seeds than you used to. Working with such exact, close spacing can be a little tedious and time-consuming, but it's nothing compared to thinning. You might need your bifocals or reading glasses when planting little seeds, such as for lettuce, or a spoon might come in handy if your hands shake a little. But the little bit of extra effort initially will save lots of work later.

When explaining this careful planting method for tiny seeds to an audience, I compare it to planting large bean seeds. You wouldn't plant 500 bean seeds all on top of each other in a row, and then go back and thin out 450 to have 50 plants. That sort of wastefulness doesn't make sense, and there's no need to allow it when you plant small seeds, either. Once you get the hang of single-seed planting, you'll find that it is very

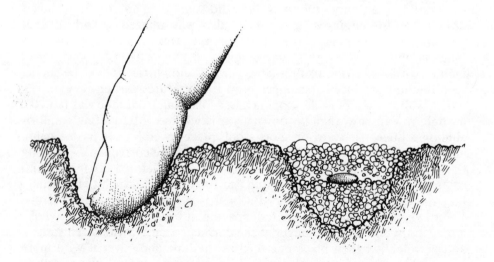

To plant a seed, make a hole in the soil with your finger, half-fill the hole with vermiculite, place in the seed, and cover with vermiculite.

easy, especially when you have a prespaced little hole for each seed to be dropped into. Seed companies have come out with numerous devices to make it easier to plant a single seed at a time. We can now buy coated or pelleted seed, and also seed tapes. All are more expensive than regular seeds, but they do help if you have trouble handling the very tiny seeds of lettuce and carrots. Although you don't get as many pelleted seeds in each packet, you still get more than enough for several years. But be careful; the two problems often reported with pelleted seeds are poorer germination rates and uncertain storage life. Pelleted seeds tend to absorb moisture and the length of time they can be stored without loss of viability is uncertain. Otherwise, they are very easy to handle and use. The problem with seed tapes is that, first of all, they are intended for use in rows, and second, seeds are not spaced along the tapes singly, but in groups of two or three or more. That means you'll still have to thin if you use seed tapes.

In summary, I want to remind you once again that overplanting is one of the biggest causes of frustration and failure in the garden. If you want to make life easier for yourself, start out by planting only a few seeds each time rather than hundreds. If you want more than one square of any vegetable, plant a new square every week until you've planted as much as you want. Staggering your planting in this way reduces the chance that pests or disease will wipe out an entire crop, and it also produces a more desirable gradual harvest.

Garden Maintenance

You'll see in chapter 5 that soil preparation, the actual first step of gardening once you have chosen your site, is going to be quick and easy simply because of the space-saving advantages of this new method. A square foot garden will yield the same harvest as a single-row conventional garden, but in only 20 percent (one fifth) of the space. That's 80 percent less—a substantial amount by any standard. Keep that space-saving figure in mind because it will affect every facet of gardening—costs, sunlight, tools, work, water, and soil amendments. Because you'll have better soil, fewer weeds, and more water per plant, your condensed garden will in effect give you more harvest in 20 percent of the area a conventional garden requires.

Regular soil improvement is another great advantage of square foot gardening. As each square is harvested you merely add a trowel full of leaf mold, rotten manure, a sprinkling of fertilizer, some lime or sulfur to correct pH, and any other material you want to add. The whole procedure takes just a minute or two, and can be accomplished with just a trowel. All this occurs almost matter-of-factly after each harvest, so you're improving your soil constantly all year without making it a major project. It's a lot easier to get a trowel full of sand or humus than a wheelbarrow full as would be required in a conventional-size garden. The advantages of soil improvement using organic materials will become more apparent as your garden progresses and you see how well the plants grow and thrive. Remember also that you're never stepping on your growing soil, so it stays loose and friable, no matter how hard and compacted it was to start.

In addition, your square foot garden will look as nice as my garden, which is shown on the cover of this book. That garden is only 15 feet by 15 feet in size, and it can feed a family of five with all the fresh vegetables they could possibly use. Your new garden will become only as big as you want it to, and it doesn't have to be located out in the farthest corner of your property. In fact, that's absolutely the worst place for it. Most vegetable gardens are "way out back" because they are unsightly and unkempt. Ironically, very often they look so messy precisely because they're so far out back that no one gets to them or sees them very often. With your garden close to the house, as I am going to recommend, you will be able to keep it weeded, watered, and cultivated. You'll have more pride in it and you'll see it more often. In fact, it can become a handsome part of your landscaping.

Special Techniques in the Square Foot Garden

A less obvious but no less important advantage of the square foot method is the incorporation of special techniques like incorporating natural pest deterrents, companion planting, crop rotation, and succession planting. I call these unseen or "hidden" advantages because you'll see that they can be accomplished virtually automatically, without the need for you to become an expert on each subject or to draw up any elaborate plans or diagrams.

Companion Planting

Let's first consider companion planting and interplanting with pest-deterrent plants. All of your vegetable and flower squares are so close together (compared to a conventional garden setup) that you can have companions in almost every combination without much advance planning. As long as you include pest-deterrent crops like onions, garlic,

Pest-deterrent crops like marigolds, front left, and onions, right rear, can be placed strategically throughout the garden to do their work. Even if your garden contains six 4-foot by 4-foot blocks, a square of marigolds will be no farther than 10 feet from any other square in the garden, and will have maximum effectiveness.

marigolds, and nasturtiums in your garden, you won't have to worry about where to put them. Because the square foot garden is so small, the deterrent effects of the plants will be felt throughout. If, for example, chives, garlic, and other members of the onion family will be used to deter various pests, you can grow a few squares of them in different parts of your garden. Each square is simply planted—you don't have to plot and plan how to tuck a plant here or there in the crop rows in order to get the desired effect. If you want to grow nasturtiums to deter aphids and several kinds of beetles, any square of nasturtiums that you plant will automatically be located within 10 feet of any other part of your garden, even when you have six blocks.

Crop Rotation

Crop rotation will also occur automatically for you in the square foot garden. It is a well-known fact that you should never grow the same crop or crops in the same botanical family in the same soil year after year. This is especially true of plants in the mustard family (cabbage, broccoli, and others) and the nightshade family (tomatoes and eggplant). But for best results you should always rotate all your plants. Disease-causing organisms gradually accumulate in soil over a period of time. Different crops are susceptible to different diseases, and growing the same crop in the same soil year after year may permit the buildup of a high enough concentration of a specific organism to cause disease in that crop. Failure to rotate the crop also makes it more likely that the soil will be depleted of the nutrients which that crop uses, and in turn the plants will be less healthy and more susceptible to pest attacks.

Most books show how to make elaborate plans and drawings of your garden, indicating when and what was planted, and the variety. But the square foot garden makes such time-consuming planning unnecessary. Consider how the squares of planting occur in your square foot garden: as soon as one crop is finished, you plant another crop in that same square. However, the season has changed and you will be planting a different crop not because you consulted a carefully drawn plan, but just because of the weather and chance. For example, after your spring spinach crop is finished the weather is too warm to plant another spinach crop, so you replant whatever is in season—perhaps bush beans. When that summer crop is harvested you can replant again for a fall crop, like carrots or beets. Thus, crop rotation becomes essentially automatic. The following spring that same square could possibly be planted in spinach again, but chances are it won't. If you have, let's say, 15 different vegetables, 2 flowers, and 3 herbs to grow in a garden that consists of six 4-foot by 4-foot blocks (or

96 small squares), the chances that one of those 20 crops will be located in the same one of those 96 squares twice in a season are fairly remote. Mathematically, there is even less chance of a given crop being in the same square the following year. So I say forget about complicated plans and concentrate on improving your soil and having fun in your garden. If you do want to keep a record of what you plant where, make a simple drawing of each of your garden blocks and write down what you plant in each square.

Succession Planting

Succession planting works much the same way as companion planting. You will find when you switch to square foot gardening that you can't stand to see a square empty, so you automatically replant as soon as the harvest is finished. Since it's not a big crop that goes in each square, the planting is quick and easy. Also, it's no big deal if you have a few too many or not quite enough squares of any one variety. You'll also find that your soil is never empty, but you seem always to have new plants started in flats or containers and waiting to be transplanted into a space in the garden as soon as one becomes available. Having new plants on hand will also encourage you to harvest sooner, while the crops are in their prime, and before the vegetables get huge and overgrown.

Interplanting

Interplanting is just as easy because you'll be more aware of how much room a plant needs if you always plant it in its final location or spacing. You know that peppers, for instance, need 12-inch spacing, so just place one plant in the center of each square. After the plant is in place, you'll see that the space around the outside edges of the square won't be needed until it grows bigger. This is an excellent place to put a fast-growing crop like radishes, scallions, Japanese turnips, or even some leaf lettuce to harvest when it's young. Tuck a few seeds of those vegetables in the corners of the square when you plant the pepper plant in the center, and you've got interplanting all taken care of. Since it's wiser not to plant an entire square of quick-growing radishes (16 is usually too many all at once), this method of planting 4 or 8 radish seeds in the pepper square makes a lot of sense. Just remember to mark where you planted the radishes so you won't pull them up after they sprout, thinking they might be weeds.

You can see how all of the advanced gardening methods fit nicely into square foot gardening. The big difference is that they become simple and

A 4-square space planted with a large, long-season crop like a bush tomato, above, can be interplanted with fast-maturing crops that will be harvested before that big plant needs the space. This space contains four Oak Leaf lettuce plants in the corners, and eight radishes were planted from seed in between them.

automatic; there's nothing to learn or study or keep records for. They happen all by themselves.

Not for Beginners Only

If you think this method might be only for beginners, you're wrong. Actually, I developed it primarily for experts who want to grow a perfect crop with little effort. The method will work well for them. And beginners will be able to have a fine garden in just a short period of time because they're starting from scratch with no old knowledge or preconceived notions. Veteran gardeners will have to change many of their lifetime habits or methods, and that isn't going to be easy. Human nature makes us resistant to change if for no other reason than that we feel comfortable and know what to expect with our present conditions and methods. With anything new, there is always the risk of failure, and most of us shy away from that. Despite the promise of success, we'd rather stay with the present situation than try anything new. If you're hesitant, let me encourage you to just try one block with this new method, even if you keep your "old faithful" row garden, too. You can't go wrong with only a 4-foot by 4-foot area. And it could easily be your first step on the road to a completely new way of gardening successfully.

Another thing to remember is that, unfortunately, each year we all get a year older. And as we get older, we don't have as much time, energy, space, or money to continue our past living standards or habits. We have to cut back a little. This method is a good step in that direction regardless of your age, experience, or desire for gardening. This new method is very practical for gardeners of all ages and situations because it does save time, space, and money.

I've explained the basic concept of this method—to plant in squares adjacent to each other rather than in long single rows—but I'd also like you to think about the psychological ramifications of this. In my studies of why people garden, what compels them to weed and succeed in the garden, I realized that when a task appears difficult or even insurmountable, 50 percent of the people don't even try it. An additional 30 percent will plan to start, but at some later time. Only 20 percent will get under way, and of them, only half will finish. Now if it's a hot, dry, sunny summer day and you know there is a 20-foot-long row of weeds between a row of onions and beans that needs hoeing, that's a lot of work. Especially if this row is just one of many in a huge garden that hasn't been weeded in over a month and the soil is dry. It's very hard to pull the weeds by hand and very difficult to hoe them. They are tough and securely anchored in the ground. What would *you* do? Are you in the 50 percent who walk away, the 30 percent who decide to do it tomorrow, or the last 20 percent who go right to it?

Now compare that 20-foot row of weeds to a situation where your garden is less than a quarter the size of the previous one and all you have to do on that hot day is go out and weed 1 square foot each of onions and beans. It might be that same hot, dusty day, but your soil in the garden isn't packed down tight because you haven't walked on it, and whatever weeds are there are easily pulled. A square foot isn't much bigger than the two pages you're reading, so you won't hesitate to go out and do that chore. It probably won't take more than about one minute to weed a square and you'll be so proud of the results that you will probably go on to weed the adjoining square. And then the next one. In the space of just five minutes, you can have weeded four squares containing an average of 32 plants. Isn't that enough for a hot day? And remember, you did it with just two fingers, rather than a big heavy tool you had to get out of the garage and then put away.

You'll see as you read this book that watering, soil preparation, planting, harvesting, and pest control take on the same proportions as this example of weeding. *And it gets done!* That's the real beauty of this method—getting the job done. You'll not only be able to reduce your garden to a manageable size, but you'll also be able to see that there's time in your busy life to take care of every square. After all, the entire philosophy behind this method is that you only have to worry about one little square at a time. The rest comes tomorrow. Moreover, in effect, just one square becomes so easy to work on that you usually go on the same day to at least a few more squares, and your entire garden gets constant and continuous attention. The end result is an almost perfect garden worthy of a magazine cover. You'll harvest more, work less, and you'll enjoy an experience you never thought possible, whether you're a beginner or an old-time veteran gardener.

Chapter 3
⧉ Garden Sizes and Basic Layouts

How large the garden should be is often hastily decided while the gardener is in the flush of spring fever. That's a bad time! It's like going grocery shopping when you're hungry. In such a case human nature causes all of us to buy more food than we intend to, and similarly, to plant a bigger garden than we need. That burst of springtime enthusiasm has a way of overwhelming the best-laid garden plans (if, indeed, we planned at all!).

Here are some of the ways people I've talked to have "planned" the size of their gardens. Maybe you can find your garden in this list: "As much room as I can spare from my small backyard." "All of the side yard." "A nice big area way out back." "That spot we could never grow grass in." "An area as large as we could rototill in the one hour we rented the machine." "Just a little larger than my next-door neighbor's."

So often, the size of the garden has nothing to do with how much space is needed to grow the amount of food the gardener is likely to need. And no one actually sits down and says "We'll eat about three cucumbers a week, so two vines are all we need to plant." Instead, you go ahead and plant three seeds every couple of feet until the packet is used up or you run out of room, whichever comes first. Similarly, you don't say we will need, or would like, only one head of cabbage a week. And somehow you

27

don't remember that the spring cabbage-harvesting season is only three or four weeks long before all the heads split or go bad. What gardener is going to plant just four cabbage plants? If you started your own seeds, you probably sprinkled out at least 40 of those tiny round seeds. When transplanting time comes you find yourself with more than 30 nice little plants to put out. Well, no matter; when you run out of space in the garden you just line them up along the walkway. On and on it goes, until your property is overflowing with more plants than you could ever possibly use.

One consideration when selecting a garden size should be (but never is) maintenance time. A conventional, single-row garden needs approximately 2 hours of maintenance per week for every 100 square feet, and that work has to get done every week from March to October, or as long as your season runs. A recent national survey showed that the average "small" garden in America is approximately 20 feet by 20 feet, or 400 square feet, while most large gardens are 40 feet by 50 feet, or 2,000 square feet. This means that the time needed for maintenance and upkeep of the average garden is from 8 hours to almost 40 hours per week. Of course, power equipment can help tremendously in reducing the number of hours needed to weed and cultivate by hand, but not everyone can afford power machines.

Further, power equipment contributes to our tendency to plant too large a garden. If you own a tiller or rent one in the spring, it's so easy to till just a little more. When it's freshly turned over in early spring, it's very hard to imagine what the garden is going to look like and how big the plants and weeds are going to grow by midsummer. The tomato plants never seem to stop growing. And those squash plants—what a sight! And the weeds can outgrow them all. Why, a small child could disappear if he walked into the garden in August—it can get to be such a jungle of plant life.

One of the biggest problems in limiting our planting in early spring is that we tend to think in terms of tiny seeds rather than full-size harvests. Think back to the cabbage example. If you made your decision on how many seeds to plant based on the number of heads you wanted to harvest, you would think more in terms of those four heads—not 20, or even 30 transplants or 40 seeds.

Picturing the harvest is the secret behind my method of deciding how much to plant. If you can only use four heads of cabbage, lettuce, or whatever during its four-week harvest period, then plant only four seeds. If you're unsure of their possible success, add a few more for extra protection (but never more than twice as many as you want to harvest).

Remember our human nature when it comes to gardening. If you start 40 seeds indoors and 35 sprout—you're going to transplant all 35 into little containers. When 30 of those grow into healthy transplants, you're going to have to plant all 30 of them in the garden—somewhere. How could anyone throw away a good plant? Then 20 of those 30 transplants are going to grow into giant cabbages. Now what on earth are you going to *do* with 20 heads of cabbage? Wouldn't it have been so much better to plant only 8 seeds and grow 4 good heads?

Planting Problems Solved

The square foot system will help you put a stop to most of these planting problems, because it's going to prevent you once and for all from overplanting. And when you do want to plant a lot of one thing, it will force you to plant the crop in staggered steps, one small square each week, so that the harvest follows automatically in the same spread-out time sequence.

Every garden book advises to start "small," but small is never defined exactly. The word means something different to an urbanite with a small yard than it does to a country dweller with 2 or 3 acres of available land. Your first square foot garden should be small, of course, but I'll be very specific about what I mean by "small." Whether you are a beginner or an expert just wanting to try this method, your very first garden should consist of only one block for each person in your family. That's a 4-foot by 4-foot area, only 16 square feet.

My suggestion that you start with only one 4-foot by 4-foot block per person is often met with disbelief, until it is actually tried. Before you scoff, take a moment to consider what can be grown in just one block with a vertical frame at one end. For example, if you started in early March, by the time the weather is warm enough to plant tomatoes, peppers, and squash, you could have already grown and harvested the following:

> 4 heads Oak Leaf lettuce
> 16 standard-size carrots
> 9 bunches spinach
> 32 radishes
> 16 scallions
> 4 heads Salad Bowl lettuce
> 16 beets, plus 4 bunches beet greens
> 5 pounds sugar snap peas
> 4 heads Ruby lettuce
> 9 Japanese turnips
> 8 bunches Swiss chard

1 head cabbage
4 heads romaine lettuce
1 head cauliflower
1 head broccoli
16 small, round carrots

Not bad for two months and 16 square feet, is it?

When the spring crop is harvested, you can replant in the same space for a new summer crop. In addition, if you find the square foot method to be as simple and productive as I've promised, and if you really are going to have the time to take care of a bigger garden, another block can easily be added at this time. One block will produce enough vegetables to feed one person, if you're growing the smaller salad crops. Two blocks will satisfy all that person's vegetable needs. If you want to grow only salad vegetables for two or more people, multiply the block recommended by the number of people you want to feed. If you want to include larger plants, like zucchini or corn, add another block. If you want to have enough to can or freeze, plant additional blocks as shown in the chart on A Garden for Canning or Freezing. But always remember that someone has to take care of all those additional blocks. Keep the garden at a size you'll be able to take care of conveniently all summer. If no one is going to help you with the garden work, and you aren't going to have the time later to keep up enough blocks for several people, *don't plant them!* Just plant one or two blocks and concentrate on growing only salad vegetables for the family.

If your garden doesn't produce quite as much of a harvest as you would like, at least you have the satisfaction of knowing that it stayed neat, clean, and attractive, and did yield a good harvest. It will be easy enough to expand your garden in subsequent years. In fact, it will be easier after your first season because then you will have a better idea of what you can handle and how much each block will produce. Additional blocks can be added to the garden any time during the season. Remember there are really three growing seasons in each year—spring, summer, and fall. Each has its own crop and harvest.

Maintenance Time in the Square Foot Garden

Plan on spending almost one hour per week per block to perform all the necessary weeding, watering, cultivating, and pest control chores as

A GARDEN FOR CANNING OR FREEZING

Gardeners who want to grow extra food for canning or freezing can plant an additional block entirely in one crop for a maximum harvest. Since you will probably want to put up the whole crop at once, plant the entire block at one time so the whole harvest will be ready at the same time.

Crop	No. of Plants	Harvest to Expect	Spacing
Bush beans	144	35 lbs.	4″
Carrots	256	30 lbs.	3″
Cauliflower	16	14 heads	12″
Corn (Short, early variety)	25	25 ears	9″
Corn (Tall, late variety)	16	24 ears	12″
Onions	256	25 lbs.	3″

Spacing of Plants in Block

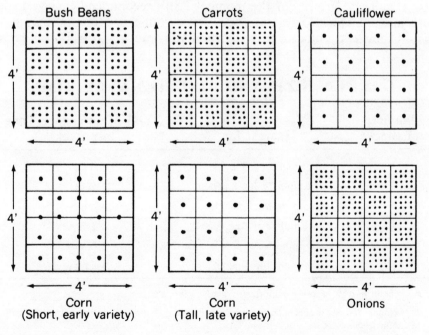

Bush Beans   Carrots   Cauliflower

Corn (Short, early variety)   Corn (Tall, late variety)   Onions

well as to replant new squares. As you add more blocks to the garden, the additional ones don't take quite as long because you're already there working and have assembled whatever tools and supplies you'll need. For a larger garden, let's say one containing six blocks, you can plan on spending about three hours per week on gardening (see the chart on Garden Size and Maintenance). This time does not include harvesting, cooking, or eating except for little snacks while you're gardening (a carrot here, a radish there, sugar snap peas all the time). One of the nice things about not spraying or using harsh chemicals in your garden is that you can pop a vegetable or two right in your mouth as you pick them (some need just a quick dunk in a bucket of clean water), and you can enjoy some tasty snacks right while you're working—a tiny beet leaf, perhaps, or a freshly pulled scallion.

You may find my method of selecting your garden size to be quite different from the conventional way—and it is! But I think you'll have to agree it makes sense. Try approaching your garden planning with the attitude that your selection is going to be based not on how much you would like to see, but on how much you can take care of and really eat.

How much space your garden will take up (actually the number of blocks you're going to have) does depend to some extent on what plants you're going to grow. For the moment I still recommend that you start with just one block for each person. After your first crop you may want to add some extra blocks, particularly if you want to grow a lot of larger

GARDEN SIZE AND MAINTENANCE TIME

Number of Blocks	Harvest for	Total Maintenance Time (per week)
1	minimum* for 1 person	1 hour
2	maximum** for 1 person	1½ hours
3	minimum for 2 people	2 hours
4	maximum for 2 people	2½ hours
6	minimum for 4 people	3 hours
8	maximum for 4 people	4 hours

*Minimum harvest means enough fresh vegetables for salads.

**Maximum harvest means enough fresh vegetables for all kinds of dishes, but not enough to can or freeze.

plants like eggplant, peppers, and cabbage. Then you may need one extra block per person as compared to the number you would need if you were growing mostly the smaller salad (leaf and root) crops.

I must caution you once again not to be overly optimistic and start more blocks than suggested, thinking that these recommendations are too conservative for you. They will produce plenty of harvest if you have the time to take care of them. Remember the pitfalls of big gardens: the more you plant, the harder the garden is to take care of, and subsequently the weeds may steal most of the moisture and nutrients, leaving the plants with a poorer harvest. Pests also get a larger portion of the harvest because you don't spot them early enough, and can't provide all of the necessary protection. To make up for this decreased harvest, you find yourself making the garden even bigger and planting extra to compensate. Remember the old rhyme about how to plant?

> One for the black bird,
> One for the mouse,
> One for the rabbit,
> And one for the house

That's overplanting if I've ever heard of it, actually four times what you want to harvest. My advice is to plant only one fourth as much and you'll have time to protect and take care of what you did plant so it's all yours.

Some Sample Garden Plans

Here are some charts to help you plan a garden for one, two, or four people.

You can mix and match crops as you choose. Each 1-foot by 1-foot square will hold any of the following crops:

Small Plants	Large Plants	Vertical Plants
16 radishes	1 cabbage	1 tomato
16 carrots	1 broccoli	2 cucumbers
16 onions	1 cauliflower	8 pole beans
9 spinach	1 pepper	
9 beets	1 eggplant	
4 Swiss chard		
4 lettuce		
4 parsley		
4 marigolds		

If you want to grow corn or zucchini squash, add one additional 4-foot by 4-foot block to the garden for every two people you're going to feed.

A One-Person Garden

For a small garden with mostly small plants, you'll need one block with a vertical frame:

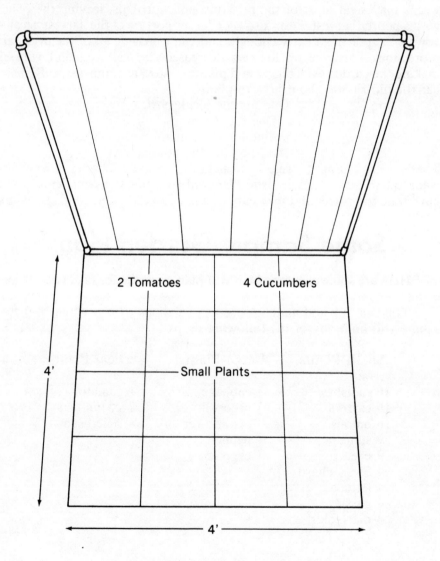

2 Tomatoes   4 Cucumbers

4'

———Small Plants———

4'

For a larger garden with more large plants, you'll need two blocks with two vertical frames:

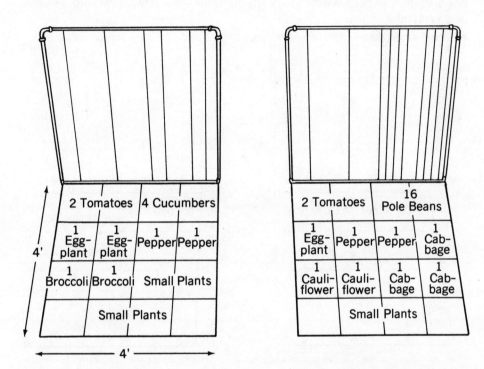

2 Tomatoes	4 Cucumbers
1 Egg-plant	1 Egg-plant	1 Pepper	1 Pepper
1 Broccoli	1 Broccoli	Small Plants
Small Plants

2 Tomatoes	16 Pole Beans
1 Egg-plant	1 Pepper	1 Pepper	1 Cab-bage
1 Cauli-flower	1 Cauli-flower	1 Cab-bage	1 Cab-bage
Small Plants

Note: By replanting immediately, two to three different crops can be grown in each square during the year. Example: 4 lettuce plants can be followed by 1 pepper; or 16 radishes followed by 1 tomato; or 16 carrots followed by 9 bush beans followed by 4 spinach plants.

A Two-Person Garden

For a smaller garden with mostly small plants, you'll need two blocks with
two vertical frames:

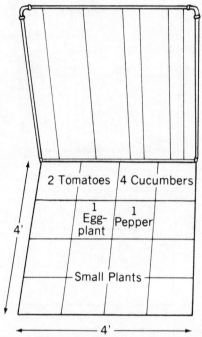
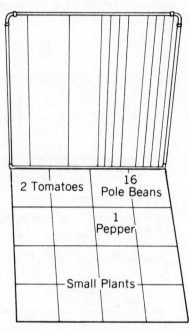

For a larger garden with more large plants, you'll need three blocks
with three vertical frames:

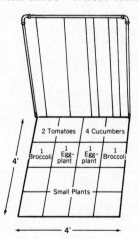
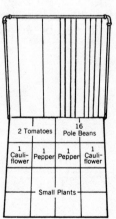
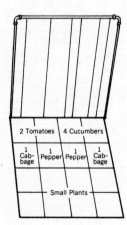

Again, you'll harvest two or more crops from each square of small plants.

A Garden for a Family of Four

For a smaller garden with mostly small plants, you'll need four blocks with two vertical frames:

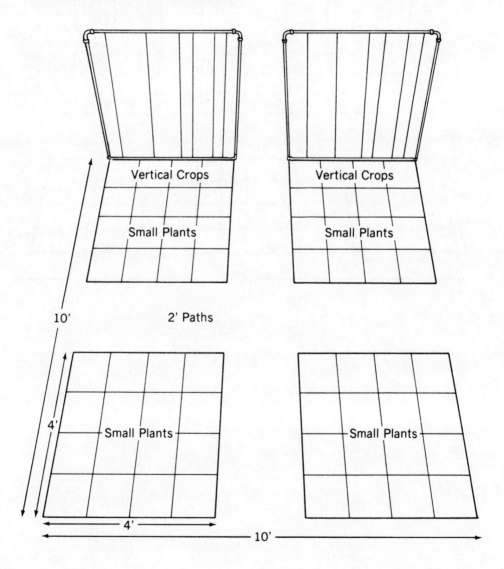

For a medium-size garden with a mixture of small and large plants, you'll need six blocks with three vertical frames:

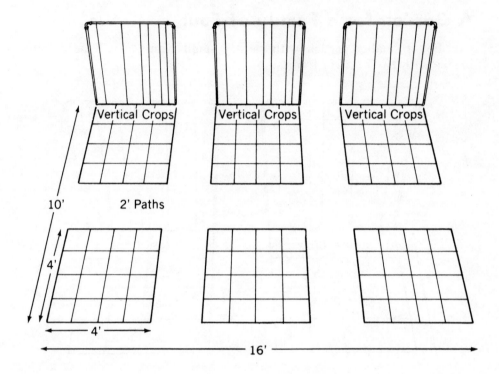

For a large garden with more of the larger plants, put in eight blocks with four vertical frames:

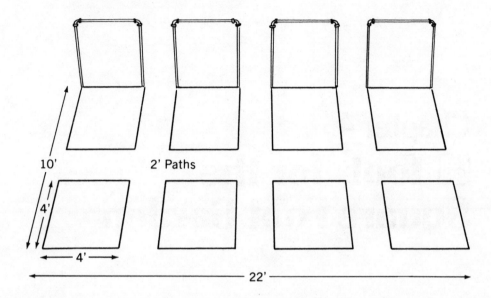

Chapter 4
🔯 Tools for the Square Foot Garden

Conventional row gardening requires not only a lot of space, but usually a lot of tools. The larger the garden, the more tools you need to work it. Once you reach the "professional-size garden," (at least 50 feet by 50 feet) you'll probably be tempted to buy a lot of expensive wheeled and power tools to help with all of the garden work, and in reality they will probably turn out to be necessary. With a big garden, you need all the help you can get to keep up with the weeding and cultivating. A good heavy-duty rototiller is almost a necessity, and you'll also need a lot of hand tools. Watering equipment will be another major investment—many rolls of hose and various types of sprinklers will be necessary. A watering system specially designed for the garden will cut down considerably on the laborious work of moving hoses and sprinklers in order to cover the entire garden, but is expensive.

You'll need literally tons of compost and manure to condition the soil in such a large area, and to move all that material around you'll need a heavy-duty wheelbarrow or a large-wheeled cart. To plant the garden, a wheeled seeder will come in handy. To make the large amounts of compost needed for a big garden you'll need either hand-cranked or power composters and shredders. Even an average-size garden requires a lot of tools and equipment. And all to produce a harvest valued at about $350.00

worth of vegetables. Of course saving money is only one of the reasons people garden.

But in a square foot garden, you need only a few trusty implements, and a lot less soil-building material. To illustrate the vast difference in size and, subsequently, in materials and equipment needed for a smaller garden, here are some examples that speak for themselves.

As you've seen in chapter 3, the average square foot garden for a family of four contains six blocks with paths between, and measures only 10 feet by 16 feet (or an area of 160 square feet). This produces the same amount of food as a conventional row garden of a size 20 feet by 40 feet (800 square feet)—five times as large.

If you bought a small truckload of manure it would spread almost 3 inches deep on your square foot garden, but would cover to a depth of less than ½ inch in the conventional garden. If you have your own compost or leaf mold pile, you would need less than 2 cubic yards of compost to put down a layer almost 4 inches thick over your square foot garden, but you would require almost 10 cubic yards to apply the same thickness to a conventional garden.

In watering, to provide 1 inch of water per week over the square foot area requires only 95 gallons, and would take less than 20 minutes to water, while the conventional garden would require 500 gallons and take over an hour and a half. (See chapter 12 for an explanation of the best watering techniques to use in the square foot garden.)

Since everything except the harvest is five to ten times smaller in the square foot garden, you can appreciate that few if any tools will be required. What tools you will need are relatively small and certainly inexpensive. You'll need either a shovel, spade, or fork (depending on your preference) for turning over the soil, a good sturdy bucket for watering, and a small hand trowel for planting. No other tools are needed! Only in the very beginning, when you first lay out your garden and turn the soil over for the first time, will you need to use a rototiller, rake, or heavy-duty shovel. After you've finished that first step and laid out each 4-foot by 4-foot block, you'll never have to do any heavy digging or rototilling again. Your soil will stay soft and friable no matter how poor it was to begin with, mainly because you're never going to walk on it and pack it down or run heavy equipment over it. Only your paths will get traffic.

Turning over the soil after each crop's harvest becomes a simple hand operation that can be performed with a trowel because the area is so small. (Remember, each little square is only 1 foot by 1 foot, and even turning over a full block, 4 feet by 4 feet, will take you less than five minutes with a spade.) Thus, soil preparation requires only two digging tools.

The only tools needed in the square foot garden are a trowel, a spade, and a sturdy water bucket.

Seeding is all going to be done by hand, and the same trowel you use for turning the soil will serve nicely for transplanting. Weeding is also done by hand, with your two fingers so you don't need a lot of hoes and weeders, and watering is also by hand with a cup and bucket so sprinklers and even hoses aren't necessary. You might want to use a pair of hand clippers to harvest corn, cabbages, or other crops with a tough stem or stalk, but you can just as easily use a kitchen knife.

To keep rabbits and other unwelcome visitors out of the garden, you're going to need 50 feet of fencing, rather than the 120 feet it would take to enclose a conventional garden. If you'll follow my advice in chapter 13, you'll do all your pest control by hand and won't need to buy a sprayer.

For the few tools you do need, I recommend you buy whatever you can afford. I don't always agree with the often-given advice to buy the best so that it lasts your lifetime. That's good advice when you have a lot of heavy work to do, and inexpensive equipment or tools will break or bend under the strain of tough, unyielding soils. However, after you've done the initial soil preparation in your garden, yours will be easily dug, almost with a child's spade. That's perhaps a slight exaggeration, but I would definitely advise against any heavy, large tools of any sort. For the square

After a square is harvested, all you need do to prepare for the next planting is to add a trowel full of compost, manure, and a sprinkling of fertilizer, then turn over the soil with a trowel.

foot garden they are out of place and not needed. Pick small, lightweight but strong tools. If you are a beginner, don't spend a lot of money; buy the medium-priced brands. Try to pick something that is sturdy and not terribly expensive.

To do the initial groundbreaking and digging of your garden area, rent a rototiller, or hire someone to do the tilling. An even better idea is to rent a shovel and rake along with the rototiller at a rental store. Such heavy-duty tools are very inexpensive to rent for one or two days, and most rental companies carry the strong, tough tools. Once your plot is turned over, and your walking planks or paths are set down, you'll never need these heavy tools again.

If you are an experienced gardener, you probably have a garage full of garden tools now—at least several rakes, and shovels of many sizes and kinds. My advice to you is to have a garage sale in the spring. Keep your favorite small spade or a fork and your very favorite trowel, and sell all the rest! Hose them down, clean them up, sharpen the cutting edges, wipe the handles with an oily rag, and then put an ad in the paper. But don't try to sell your tools unless it's springtime. May 1 seems to be the best time throughout most of the country. Everyone wants tools then. Take the money and buy yourself a nice hammock or lounge chair; you'll need it when you switch to my methods of gardening because you're going to have a lot of spare time to relax and watch your garden grow.

In summary, here's a list of tools and equipment you will and will not need in the square foot garden:

Don't Need	Might Want	Do Need
any heavy-duty tool	shovel or fork	trowel
Rototiller	hose with	spade
scuffle hoe	attachments	water bucket
weeding and digging hoe	hand clippers	
cultivator		
iron rake		
sprinklers		
watering cans		
drip irrigation system		
fertilizer spreader		
sprayer		
wheelbarrow		
garden cart		
row markers		
wheeled or power		
equipment of any sort		

Chapter 5
▣ Getting Started— Sun, Soil, Drainage, and Location

Whether you're new to gardening or just new to the square foot method, the information in this chapter will be quite important to you. If you've had a large row-type garden in the past, you may now find that either because of the smaller size required or the new procedures used in the square foot system, you might want to choose a new site for your garden. The location of your square foot garden need not be dictated by the usual standards. Invariably the vegetable garden is "way out back," at the farthest point from the house, mostly because it takes so much room and quite often isn't very attractive (usually by July the garden is overgrown with weeds). But the methods outlined in this book will enable you to have a very productive, attractive vegetable garden in such a small space that it can fit in anywhere on the property and be an asset because of its good looks.

Sun

Of the important environmental considerations for the garden—sun, soil, drainage, and location—all can be altered or improved in some way by the gardener except sunlight. Unless you plan to cut down trees or large

45

shrubs, that's the one consideration that can't be changed. So your first priority in locating the garden should be to pick a spot that gets as many hours of sunlight a day as possible; at least six hours, but preferably eight hours a day. What time of day you get the sun is also important. The best time is from midmorning to midafternoon, the hottest part of the day when the sun is at its peak intensity—say from 9:00 A.M. to 4:00 P.M. If you get mostly early morning or late afternoon sun (from 7:00 A.M. to 3:00 P.M. or from 10:00 A.M. to 6:00 P.M.), then your garden site should receive it for at least eight hours. The sun doesn't have great power or light in those early morning and late afternoon hours. Many hours of sunlight are most important if you want to grow light-loving summer or hot-weather vegetables. The spring/fall or cool-weather crops can get by with less sunlight, and although they get a little taller or leggier than normal they will still produce a fairly good crop without eight hours of sun. Without adequate sunlight, summer crops like beans or tomatoes will still look nice, and they'll grow lots of leaves, but they will produce very little harvest.

Shade

The trees we like in our lawns have a way of growing taller as the years go by, so take that into consideration when selecting your garden spot. It's possible to have them trimmed or topped (even removed) when they create too much shade, but we seldom get around to it. It seems there's something in us all that resists cutting down a living tree, even if it is causing problems in our garden. Trees grow gradually, and we don't usually notice from one year to the next that a tree has gotten bigger and casts its shade farther over the yard. However, for every foot a tree grows, the shadow it casts on the ground becomes a little over a foot longer. It's important to consider any nearby trees when choosing a garden site. A spot that's in the sun this year may be shaded in three or four years if a tree is growing nearby. In addition, the tree roots may be creeping into the garden and stealing all the moisture and nutrients from the plants.

What do you do if you just don't have six to eight hours of direct sunlight and can't move the garden to any other spot? Aside from trimming and topping, or removing, any trees and shrubs, you're limited to concentrating on shade-tolerant vegetables such as lettuce, beets, carrots, and Swiss chard, and trying to reflect extra light onto the sun-loving tomatoes, peppers, eggplant, and squash you want to grow.

If you don't mind the appearance, one way to bounce more light onto your sun-loving crops is to line the ground around them with aluminum foil. The foil will act not only as a mulch to keep down weeds, but is said

LIGHT NEEDS OF SOME POPULAR VEGETABLES

In general, leaf and root vegetables don't require as much sun in order to produce a good harvest as do fruit and seed crops. Although all will do well in full sun, some crops can produce a respectable harvest in partial shade. Sun-loving crops will grow in partial shade, too, but they won't bear well. If you have no other choice than to locate your garden in partial shade, you can still get a good crop. The key to success lies in choosing your vegetables carefully.

Partial Sun (4 to 6 hours a day)	Full Sun (over 6 hours a day)
Beets	Beans
Carrots	Broccoli
Cauliflower	Cabbage
Swiss chard	Corn
Cucumber	Eggplant
Lettuce	Muskmelons
Onions	Summer squash
Parsley	Tomatoes
Peas	
Radishes	
Spinach	
Winter squash	

to act also as an insect repellent. It seems that the light bounced off the foil and back to the underside of the leaves confuses the insects. Aphids expect to find a quiet, dark area underneath the leaves but are confused by the increased light, and hence repelled. This extra light is said to help many shady locations. Of course, as the plants grow and bear extra leaves the advantages of the foil are cut down as the amount of light able to reach the ground surface is also reduced.

Another technique, although rather extreme, is to line a fence along the north side of the garden with foil, from the ground up to a height of 3 or 4 feet. Or you might want to make removable rigid panels by stapling or gluing aluminum foil onto lightweight, weather-resistant panels. You might use Styrofoam or some similar material. You can remove the panels when company comes, or anytime you get tired of looking at them. Of

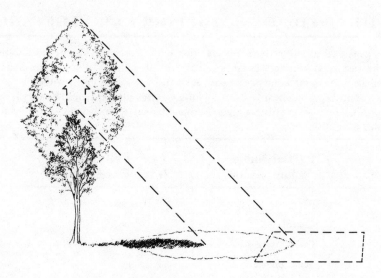

Trees grow taller each year, and shade can gradually creep into your garden before you know it.

course, even the shiny white surface of Styrofoam (which usually comes in 15-inch by 3-foot sections, or 2-foot by 4-foot panels) will also work without the aluminum foil. I admit that these are extreme measures. But if you don't have enough sunlight you may well find them worth the trouble.

Soil

The better your soil, the better your gardening results are going to be. In addition to having a larger harvest, you'll grow healthier plants which in turn will resist insect and disease attacks much better. Naturally, as your plants grow better and look better, you'll find yourself taking more pride and interest in your garden, and taking care of it more. The end result can only be a very happy and rewarding experience. Very few people are blessed with the kind of soil you read about in gardening books, the perfect soil that is well drained, loose, light, friable, rich in organic matter, and high in nutrients. To go out in your yard and find this perfect soil when you dig in the garden would be about as likely to happen as winning the million-dollar lottery.

So your goal, or your challenge, as a gardener is to keep working at your soil until it approaches a reasonable semblance of good growing soil.

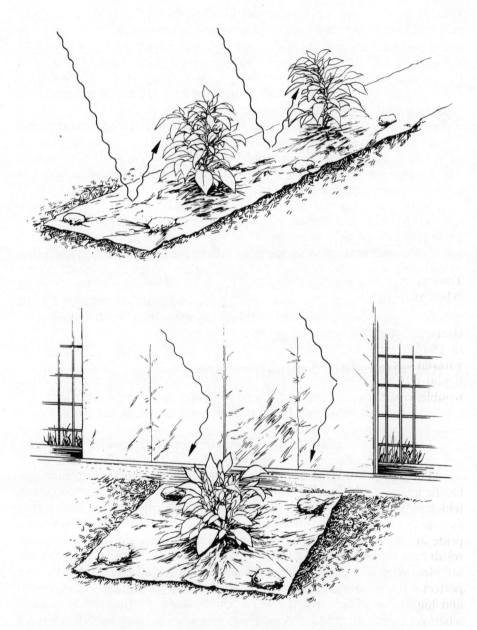

Above, aluminum foil can be used as a mulch for light-loving plants in shady areas, to bounce more light onto the plants. Below, you can also line a nearby wall or fence with foil to reflect additional light.

Usually by the time it does you find yourself having to move to another part of the country and start all over again. The average gardener takes about six years to improve his or her soil. Since no one buys a house for the garden soil (for that matter, I've never heard of anyone even digging in the yard before deciding on which home to buy), most home buyers have no idea what kind of soil their new lot has. We might notice a nice lawn or a garden growing, but we never seem to consider what type of soil we have until after we have moved in. As a result, most gardeners spend a lifetime improving their garden soil. We bring home countless garbage cans full of manure, soil, leaf mold, seaweed, sand, or what-have-you to add to our vegetable patches. Then it's dug and turned, screened and sorted, dug and turned some more.

Now, I'm not going to tell you that square foot gardening will eliminate all that; it won't. But what it will do is reduce the work by 80 percent because you'll be able to produce the same harvest in 20 percent of the space of a conventional row garden. You'll need to prepare the soil in a much smaller area. Now, instead of working six years to finally get decent growing soil, you can have it in one year. You can put all of your effort into improving the soil in your small plot, and you'll be able to get the ground in good shape in a year without any extra effort or materials, and spend the next five years growing a great garden.

Understanding Soil Structure

To really understand soil, its relationship to plant growth, and why it is so important, requires a little study of both the soil structure and what plants need to grow properly.

There's a lot of misunderstanding about soil, and especially for beginners it's a maze of sometimes contradictory terms and definitions: well-drained, loose, friable, rich, loamy, water-holding, well-graded, humusy. Other soil-related terms or phrases refer to plant needs: doesn't like wet feet, needs a firm soil, likes a fairly heavy soil; deeply rooted; likes a rich soil; demanding; likes a well-dug soil; tolerant of most soils. And when we come to pH, indicating soil acidity or alkalinity, many gardeners are ready to, excuse the expression, "throw in the trowel."

In order to easily understand soil structure and plant needs, I've always found it works quite well in my lectures to explain soil this way: Gardeners don't like to use the word "dirt"—they'd rather refer to what's in their gardens as "soil." Technically, dirt and rock can be defined as all the material making up the earth. Soil is usually referred to as the first few feet of the earth's surface, where dirt is mixed with humus. This is where most plant material grows. Healthy soil is a complex, living substance full of helpful bacteria and microorganisms that break down rock, plant, and animal matter into small particles, and make the nutrients in these materials available to plants.

All rock particles, as they are broken down by the action of weather, wind, and water, reach a certain size and are deposited over the earth as dirt. The size of the dirt particles determines how the material is classified. Most of our garden soils fall into the broad classifications of sandy, loamy, and clayey.

Sandy soil is composed of comparatively large and uniform round or angular-shaped pieces or particles and feels rough and gritty when rubbed between the fingers. Sand particles are round if it's beach sand, angular if it's quarry or inland sand. I've found that it often helps people to visualize sandy soil as if it were a pail of marbles. With lots of open spaces between the particles of soil, air can readily pass among the particles and there is plenty of room for plant roots to grow. But water also passes through very quickly. Although sandy soil is easily worked, especially in spring, and it drains well, it does not hold moisture or nutrients for very long.

At the opposite end of the scale is clayey soil, which is composed of very fine particles which lie flat and overlap each other. You might visualize clayey soil as a deck of tiny cards loosely spread out, each one lying slightly on top of the next. There is very little space between these fine particles, making it difficult for water, air, and plant roots to penetrate. Clayey soil drains poorly and dries out slowly, but when it does dry out it becomes quite hard. When wet, this kind of soil is gooey and sticky, and it is difficult to work in spring. Clayey soil feels slippery when rubbed between the fingers.

Loam is the best kind of soil for plants to grow in. It is a sort of "happy medium," halfway between sand and clay in particle size and structure. There are enough air spaces between the soil particles to allow air, water, and plant roots to penetrate, and the soil is fairly easy to work. Loam drains moderately well, but holds moisture and nutrients long enough to permit plant roots to absorb them.

If you're blessed with loamy soil in your garden, consider yourself lucky. If your soil tends to be more sandy or clayey, as is most often the case, you can improve its structure by adding organic matter.

Organic matter, or humus, consists of the decayed remains of plant and animal matter. It acts like a sponge when added to soil. Humus helps a loose, sandy soil to hold moisture (think of that bucket of marbles now with lots of little sponges mixed in), and creates more spaces between the tightly packed particles of a clayey soil. So it is perfect for both kinds of soil. If you think of clayey soil as a deck of cards, you can imagine organic

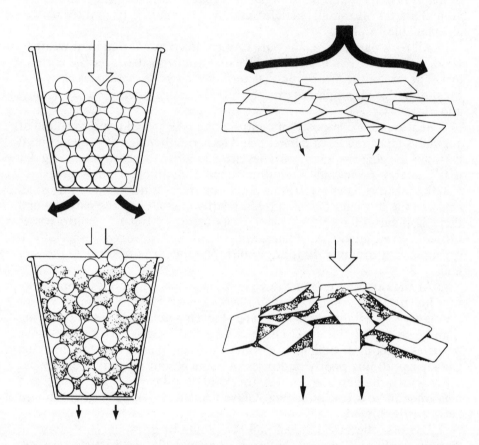

Sandy soil, left, can be visualized as a pail of marbles, with lots of space between the large particles. The addition of organic matter helps to hold moisture in the spaces between the particles. Clayey soil, right, can be visualized as a deck of cards, with few spaces between the particles. Organic matter in a clayey soil will prop apart the particles, allowing air and water to pass through more easily.

matter as little sponges that prop open those cards, and allow air to pass through while holding water and nutrients for absorption by plant roots. Organic matter is full of beneficial microorganisms so necessary to a healthy soil. Loamy soils won't need organic matter as critically as the poorer soils, but it's still a big help. I can't say enough about the importance of adding organic matter to your soil. It will make the difference between night and day in your growing conditions. Even if you disregard all of the other advantages of organic matter, the moisture-holding capacity alone is an outstanding attribute.

The only disadvantage to organic matter is that it continually breaks down and decomposes, so you must periodically add new material to your soil. Most good gardeners add it once a year, but in the square foot garden you will be adding it three to six times a year almost automatically and effortlessly. Probably the best source of organic matter for gardens is composted plant material. If you have a compost pile (see How to Make a Simple Compost Pile), you'll have a ready source of humus to add to your garden. When a compost or mulch pile (they are the same thing) is made up principally of leaves, the resulting decayed, crumbly product is called leaf mold.

The Compost or Mulch Pile

No home should be without a compost pile—even those without gardens. In fact, I feel that if every family had a mulch pile and used it to recycle their kitchen scraps (except meat and bones) and all their leaves and grass clippings, local taxes would be reduced, the price of oil would drop because we wouldn't use so much, and the balance of nature would be greatly restored.

So much has been written about composting that you'd think everyone would be doing it, but they're not. Part of the reason might be that many people are simply scared off by what they've read or heard. The procedure sounds too complicated, or they think a compost pile is messy or smelly, that it draws flies or rats, that it is expensive to construct and time-consuming to maintain. Well, you'll realize none of those things are true if you know just a few simple facts.

First, there's no difference between a mulch pile, a humus-maker, and a compost heap—they are different names for the same thing. A compost heap is, basically, a pile of plant material that was once growing and is now in the process of decaying. The time it takes for the material to decompose enough to use in the garden depends on how much work you want to do. A pile of oak leaves will decompose in a few years all by itself with nothing done to it. If you don't want to wait that long, try wetting down those leaves and adding a 2-inch layer of soil or manure between each 12-inch layer of leaves. Now your leaves will decompose in just one year. If even that is too long, you can shred all the leaves into little pieces with a lawn mower and then pile them in alternating layers with the soil and manure (wetting everything down), and turn over the pile every month. Now you will have rich, crumbly compost in just six months. Short-cut methods can produce humus in just two weeks, but these methods

A Simple Compost Pile for Your Garden

See if a compost pile isn't worthwhile for your garden. All you need is a place to dump your garden and kitchen refuse— nature will do the rest. If you are impatient or short of space, you can speed up the process of decomposition by chopping all the compost ingredients into small pieces (your lawn mower will do a good job on leaves) and turning the pile occasionally.

The secret to a successful compost pile is to not add too much of one thing at a time. Add the materials in layers, or mix several ingredients together. For example, you could start with a 6- to 12-inch layer of garden soil, add a 3- to 6-inch layer of dried grass clippings, another layer of leaves covered with a layer of soil, then a 6- to 12-inch layer of weeds and garden refuse. Dig in your kitchen refuse every day or so. Be sure to use only plant wastes, though; never add bones, grease, or other material of animal origin to your compost pile—it will not break down properly. If any of the layers are very dry, dampen them with a hose as they are added. Incorporating manure will hasten the decomposition process. You can also add some bone meal or rock powders to the heap for added nutrients.

A simple bin to hold the compost pile can be simply made from any kind of fencing. To hold a small pile that will produce about ¾ cubic yard of compost, take a 10-foot piece of fencing and bend it into a cylinder with an approximate diameter of 3 feet. To accommodate a larger pile that will produce 5½ cubic yards of compost, make the bin from 25 feet of fencing, anchored with two steel fence posts. Leave a 3-foot opening in the front of the cylinder for easier access to the pile.

To turn the pile, lift off the bin, set it on the ground next to the pile, then fork all the ingredients back into the wire enclosure. Do this once a month for best results. Keep your compost pile constantly moist, but not soggy; too much or too little water can hinder decomposition. Don't be alarmed when the pile begins to give off heat in a couple of days; this is your sign that all is well and that the microorganisms are hard at work breaking down the material.

Materials To Compost

Organic Matter

Outdoor: Straw   Shredded twigs
         Sawdust   Shredded bark
         Salt hay   Pine needles
         Corn cobs   Hedge trimmings
         Leaves   Wood shavings
         Grass clippings Old sod
           (dried)

Indoor: Coffee grounds
         Reject or spoiled garden produce
         Vegetable and fruit peels
         Tea leaves
         Eggshells

Avoid: Material thicker than ¼″ (shred or chop to speed up decomposition)
         Diseased or pest-laden materials
         Meat, bones, grease, eggs, cheese (these slow down decomposition and attract undesirable creatures)
         Seeds and fruit pits (attractive to rodents)
         Cat or dog manure (handling fresh manure and subsequent use of compost may transmit parasites harmful to humans)

Nutrients

     Stable or poultry manure
     Blood meal
     Bone meal

---

are more expensive (they require some special equipment), and a lot of work. It's up to you to decide whether or not you should have a mulch pile. But if you could see the spectacular results that a good supply of rich humus brings to any ordinary soil, you wouldn't hesitate for a minute.

If you are really serious about improving your soil and growing a great garden, you'll have a compost pile. In fact, you'll soon be out looking for more material to add to your pile. Most good garden books are filled with lists of organic materials to compost, but it takes a little searching on your part to find them free, or at a reduced cost. Many good compost ingredients are waste products from a commercial outlet or industrial process—coffee grounds, buckwheat hulls, sugar cane residue, sewage sludge, sawdust, ground bark, even manure from duck farms or horse stables. When you have found a source of organic wastes (often a job in itself), I've found the easiest way to keep adding these materials to your composting operation is to try to set up a regular pick-up schedule that allows you to bring home a little each time without taking a lot of time and trouble. Suppose you find a lumberyard, horse stable, or canning plant that's on your way home from work each day. Keep two small, sturdy, tightly covered garbage pails in your car trunk along with a short-handled shovel. Stop by on a regular basis, perhaps two or three times a week, so they will save the material for you, and you'll find you'll have a lot of material to add to your compost pile in a very short time, with very little effort.

One very good source of organic vegetable matter is the supermarket. Go to the vegetable department and ask for the manager or clerk, then explain your garden needs and your compost pile, and ask if you can have any leftover lettuce and cabbage leaves, as well as any carrot tops and other vegetable debris. They're usually glad to save it for you. In fact you'd be amazed at what supermarkets throw out—seemingly good vegetables that got mixed in with a spoiled batch, or packaged vegetables that are a few days too old. I've even found valuables that got thrown out by mistake—knives, 100 plastic bags all wrapped up, dented cans of produce, unopened boxes and bags of various kinds. This kind of scavenging is a lot of fun, but begins to take on the proportions of garbage picking. So don't start if you don't want to become addicted.

Improving Soil Texture with Vermiculite and Peat Moss

When someone asks me what they can get locally and fairly inexpensively to add to their garden soil, my answer is always the same, whether I'm talking to someone in Illinois or Massachusetts. I tell them to buy a big bag of vermiculite. I think vermiculite is a marvelous material (actually, it is mica rock heated until it explodes, like popcorn) that is lightweight, holds water better than a sponge, and works wonders when mixed with any soil. Vermiculite will help to improve the friability and water-holding capacity of both sandy and clayey soils. For best results, mix vermiculite into your garden soil at a rate of 10 to 20 percent of its volume. Vermiculite lasts forever and may well be one of the best investments you'll ever make for your garden.

Peat moss is the decomposed remains of prehistoric plants that have been compressed for thousands of years at the bottoms of bogs and swamps. Like vermiculite, it also holds a lot of water, is fairly lightweight, and is relatively inexpensive to buy. Peat moss is not quite as good as vermiculite when used as a soil builder or additive, but it still ranks high on my list. If you can't get vermiculite you can use peat moss the same way, adding an additional 10 to 20 percent in volume to your garden soil.

To cut costs, don't buy the small bags of peat and vermiculite usually sold in garden centers—they cost two to four dollars each depending on their size. If you search a little and make a few phone calls, you can usually find a local nursery or even a wholesale supplier that will sell you the extra-large commercial bags or bales of the same material which are much cheaper. You'll get twice the amount for about half the price as compared to the small-size bags. So shop around and bargain a little. Call ahead if at all possible, to save time and gas. Another nice thing about buying in the large economy size is that you can usually get different grades or sizes of the material. For example, vermiculite in large, 4-cubic-foot bags comes in either fine, medium, or coarse grade. Coarse vermiculite is particularly nice for mixing with your garden or potting soil, and I like it for starting many of the larger seeds. It has more air spaces and seems to help a poor soil much better than the fine or medium grades. However, this coarse grade is usually available only in those 4-cubic-foot bags. The vermiculite usually sold in smaller bags in hardware and garden centers is always the fine or medium grade.

Understanding pH

The concept of pH is often confusing to the gardener because it's hard to understand exactly what pH is and how to change it. In addition, all plants seem to need different levels. Actually they don't. The pH scale is actually a method of measuring the acidity or alkalinity of any substance. It is reported on a scale of 0 to 14, with 0 indicating the greatest degree of acidity, 7 being the neutral point, and 14 indicating the greatest degree of alkalinity. If you look at the pH chart in this chapter, you can see that most plants will grow nicely at a fairly neutral pH between 6.0 and 7.0. Some can grow where the pH is as low as 5.5, and a few even as low as 5.0. But even those plants will do well where the pH is 6.5. If you live in the eastern part of the United States, chances are you'll have to add some lime to your soil to raise the pH to within acceptable limits. If you're in the western or southern portions of the country your soil is probably alkaline and you'll need to add sulfur to get the pH down to at least 7.0, and preferably 6.5.

pH TOLERANCE OF POPULAR VEGETABLES

←—Acid		Neutral Alkaline—→

5.5	6.0	6.5	7.0	7.5
Beans				
	Beets			
	Broccoli			
	Cabbage			
Carrots				
	Cauliflower			
	Swiss Chard			
Corn				
Cucumbers				
Eggplant				
	Lettuce			
	Melons			
	Onions			
Parsley				
Peas				
Peppers				
Radishes				
	Spinach			
Summer Squash				
	Winter Squash			
Tomatoes				

In a small garden it's almost impossible to provide a different pH level in each garden square, especially if you're rotating crops every time you replant. So rather than try to figure out and understand exactly what pH is, why it should be changed, and what plants should be grown at what pH level, it is much easier, particularly for beginners, simply to correct the overall pH to a level acceptable to most crops. Your worries are then over and all the plants will grow well. The pH level is important, because the proper pH allows plants to utilize the nutrients in the fertilizers and soil builders you add to the garden. A very acid soil is said to lock the nutrients in the fertilizer and prevent them from being taken up or used by the plants. Therefore, it is imperative that you add lime to an acid soil or sulfur to an alkaline soil to bring it closer to a neutral level. A pH of almost 7.0 also discourages club root disease in plants of the cabbage family, and also helps prevent blossom end rot in tomato plants.

Fertilizers

All gardeners want to know how much, how often, and with what to fertilize their gardens. Because the square foot garden is maintained at a level of intensive productivity throughout the season, you can be assured of consistently superior crops by fertilizing each square when it is replanted with a new crop. But let me first emphasize one very important point about soil building—add humus first, then worry about fertilizer. If you have achieved in your garden a loose, friable, humusy soil, the additional nutrients provided by a good fertilizer will give plants an extra boost, and insure healthy, rapid growth.

Trying to grow good crops in any kind of soil without constantly adding organic matter is, in my opinion, sheer folly and a waste of time, no matter how much fertilizer you add to it. On the other hand, to garden in soil that is rich in organic matter but contains no added fertilizer is not only possible but very practical. After all, Mother Nature does it all the time. Look at any woodland or open field; no one spreads bags of fertilizer around every spring, but humus is constantly added to the soil in the form of last year's fallen leaves and old plant growth. The soil in such places is black and crumbly—about the richest soil you'll ever see.

No one comes around to rototill this soil, either, or so it would seem at first glance. But if you could look beneath the soil surface you'd find industrious earthworms hard at work tilling the soil. Earthworms eat and digest all those fallen leaves, and leave behind the digested remains in the form of their excrement, or castings. The constant tunneling of the earthworms through the soil opens up air and water passages for plant roots, and turns over and mixes the soil as well. Earthworms will do the same job in your garden, helping to keep the soil loose and light, provided it contains enough organic matter for them to eat.

There are enough nutrients in most decayed organic matter to sustain next year's plant life. So let me stress again that the key to a good soil-building program is to continually add as much humus as you can to that soil.

After, and *only* after, that's accomplished should you start adding additional nutrients in the form of fertilizer. New gardeners always want to know whether they should use organic or chemical fertilizers. There is general agreement among soil scientists that a plant, as it absorbs molecules of nitrogen or other nutrients from the soil, uses that nitrogen the same way whether it comes from a chemical or an organic source. But they also agree that chemical fertilizers do nothing for the soil. In fact, overuse of chemical fertilizers can actually damage your soil. Chemical fertilizers are highly concentrated, and too great an accumulation can burn plant roots and kill beneficial microorganisms in the soil. And earthworms are driven away from areas containing heavy concentrations of synthetic chemical fertilizers.

Well then, if organic fertilizers are so good, why doesn't everyone use them? First of all, they are sometimes difficult to find premixed in a convenient package in the garden supply center. When you can find organic fertilizer blends, they usually are more expensive than chemical fertilizers; at least they have been in the past. Like many other aspects of today's society, we chose the quick and easy route with fertilizers, coming to rely on the convenient chemical types because the manufacturing processes for them were cheaper than using natural methods or materials.

Blending Your Own Fertilizers

There are three major nutrients and a host of minor ones used by most plants. Nitrogen (N) makes possible the kind of luxurious, green growth so necessary for leaf crops like lettuce, spinach, and Swiss chard. Phosphorus (P) promotes the development of strong stems and seeds, and resistance to disease. Potassium (K) is needed for both healthy stems and roots, and for improved fruit production.

The list of minor, or trace, elements used by plants is long and for our purposes here it will suffice to say that plants, like people, need a balanced diet. Although only minute amounts of these trace elements are needed, the plants will suffer without them. If you keep your soil well supplied with organic matter, you should have no problems with trace element deficiencies.

As I mentioned earlier, it is sound practice to prepare your soil with new additions of humus and fertilizer before you replant each square with a new crop in the square foot garden. You can add dry fertilizers to the soil in the form of a packaged, preblended organic mix, or you can mix your own from organic ingredients. You can also give supplemental feedings by watering plants with manure tea, fish emulsion, or seaweed solutions. Crops that are heavy feeders will especially benefit from these supplemental feedings. Light-feeding crops can get along fine without them. Chapter 18 provides information on the nutritional needs of individual vegetables.

Supplemental fertilizers to use during the course of the season need be of only two basic types: a high-nitrogen fertilizer to feed leaf crops, and a fertilizer with a higher percentage of phosphorus and potassium for root

PERCENTAGE COMPOSITION OF COMMON ORGANIC MATERIALS

Material	Nitrogen	Phosphorus	Potassium
Blood Meal	15.0	1.3	.7
Bone Meal	4.0	21.0	.2
Cattle Manure, fresh	.3	.2	.4
Cattle Manure, dried	2.0	1.8	2.2
Cocoa Shell Meal	2.5	1.5	2.5
Coffee Grounds, dried	2.0	.4	.7
Corn Stalks	.8	.4	.9
Cottonseed Meal	7.0	2.5	1.5
Dried Blood	12–15	3.0	—
Fish Emulsion	5.0	2.0	2.0
Greensand	—	1.5	5.0
Horse Manure, composted	.7	.3	.6
Horse Manure, fresh	.4	.2	.4
Leaf Mold, composted	.6	.2	.4
Maple Leaves	.5	.1	.5
Oak Leaves	.8	.4	.2
Rock Phosphate	—	39.0	4.5
Seaweed	1.7	.8	5.0
Soybean Meal	6.0	1.2	1.5
Wood Ashes	—	1.5	7.0

and fruit-bearing crops. The chart on Percentage Composition of Common Organic Materials lists NPK values for a number of organic fertilizers that are readily obtainable. Consult the chart to see which materials are good sources of the nutrients you need, and use whatever combination of the appropriate ingredients you have on hand or to which you have the easiest access.

In general, I like to feed my garden soil with a mild fertilizer fairly often (when the soil is prepared for planting, and once a month as the crops are growing), rather than applying a strong fertilizer only once at the beginning of the growing season. When mixing up a fertilizer, you must formulate it depending on the ingredients you wish to use, and how strong they are. The numerical NPK ratings in the chart on Percentage Composition give you a clue as to the strength of the materials, and can guide you when you mix fertilizer ingredients in various proportions. Since this may be a little difficult to understand at first, I'd like to give you an example of a basic all-purpose fertilizer and a high-nitrogen mix that I make up for my garden. The basic mix and the high-nitrogen mix are made from the same ingredients mixed in different proportions. The formula for the basic, all-purpose fertilizer is as follows:

Ingredients	N	P	K
1 part blood meal	15.0	1.3	.7
2 parts bone meal	8.0	42.0	.4
3 parts wood ashes	—	4.5	21.0
4 parts composted leaf mold	2.4	.8	1.6
Total: 10 parts	25.4	48.6	23.7
NPK value of 1 part basic mix	2.6	4.9	2.4

This is the fertilizer I use to prepare my soil in most squares, for all those vegetables which require a balanced proportion of nitrogen, phosphorus, and potassium. (Information on which vegetables do well with this mix is provided in chapter 18.) I also use this fertilizer for the monthly supplemental feedings, but I dilute it by 50 percent by mixing it with equal portions of compost or sand. This gives me a half-strength mix, or one with an approximate NPK value of 1.6–2.6–1.4. The exact numbers are not critical, and if you are not good at math, don't fuss over trying to mix up an exact formula. Store the fertilizer dry in a plastic bag and use it as needed for basic soil preparation and at half-strength for monthly feedings.

For those vegetables which need a high-nitrogen fertilizer (again, this information can be found in chapter 18), I use the same basic mix with two extra parts of blood meal added to the other ingredients. The high-nitrogen formula is as follows:

Ingredients	N	P	K
3 parts blood meal	45.0	3.9	2.1
2 parts bone meal	8.0	42.0	.4
3 parts wood ashes	—	4.5	21.0
4 parts leaf mold	2.4	.8	1.6
Total: 12 parts	55.4	51.2	25.1
NPK value of			
1 part high-nitrogen mix:	4.6	4.3	2.0

Use this fertilizer at full strength for initial soil preparation, then at half-strength for monthly feedings.

Rather than mixing up two separate formulas, you can just add two parts of blood meal to ten parts of the basic fertilizer mix (a one to five ratio) to make small quantities of high-nitrogen mix. To make just one cup of high-nitrogen mix, add 3 tablespoons of blood meal to 1 cup (16 tablespoons) of basic mix.

You can mix fertilizers in any proportions you want—it all depends on what ingredients you have or can get free or at minimal cost. Use the chart on Percentage Composition and these sample calculations to guide you, but remember that all of these numbers are approximate, and don't let yourself get caught up in the numbers game. The most important thing is to add humus to your soil, followed by a mild fertilizer containing balanced proportions of nitrogen, phosphorus, and potassium. Then you'll be giving your soil a balanced diet and your plants will thrive.

Preparing Your Soil

A square foot garden involves such a small area of land that there's absolutely no reason why any gardener, no matter what kind of soil he or she starts with, can't within a couple of seasons have rich, humusy, well-drained soil that is loose and friable to a depth of at least 12 inches.

Soil preparation can begin after you have laid out the number of 4-foot by 4-foot garden blocks you want. First dig a few test holes at least 12 inches deep and take a good look at the soil. If it's full of rocks or even small stones and pebbles, you can build a screen and sift the soil through it to remove them.

Next, add lots of compost or leaf mold, vermiculite, and peat moss —at least enough to equal 25 percent of the volume of your present garden soil. If your soil is in really bad shape, you might add as much as 50

If your soil is rocky, take one 4-foot by 4-foot block at a time (perhaps you might work on one block a month), build a soil screen, and sift all the soil in that block at least 1 foot deep. While sifting, add all the well-rotted manure, leaf mold, peat moss and vermiculite, ground-up leaves, lime if it's needed, and other soil builders that you can afford or get hold of. If you have a very heavy soil with a lot of silt or clay, add sand. If you have a very sandy soil, add extra humus and peat moss, and vermiculite.

percent of its volume of these soil builders. If your soil is sandy, add extra humus and peat moss; if your soil is clayey, add some sand in addition to the other materials. Since you will be adding to the volume of soil in your garden blocks, you can build them up into slightly raised beds (with or without wood sides), or you can get rid of the extra amount by removing a 4-inch to 6-inch layer of soil from the bottom of each block to some other area.

If you want to create perfect soil for positively peak growth and don't mind doing some extra work, see How to Mix the Perfect Soil for the Perfect Garden, for details. To turn your garden soil into a perfectly adequate, rich, crumbly growing medium that will support healthy, productive crops, here's the minimum amount of soil preparation you should do to get started with a square foot garden. If your garden consists of several 4-foot by 4-foot blocks, work on one block at a time. First remove

How to Mix The Perfect Soil for the Perfect Garden

Soil Volume

Area of one garden block: 4 ft. by 4 ft., or 16 sq. ft.
Soil volume at 6 in. deep: 8 cu. ft.
Soil volume at 9 in. deep: 12 cu. ft.
Soil volume at 12 in. deep: 16 cu. ft.

Ingredients

Mix thoroughly:

   1 bale of peat moss: 6 cu. ft.
   1 large bag of coarse vermiculite: 4 cu. ft.
  10 pails (2½-gallon size) of sand: 3 cu. ft.
   2 pails of wood ashes and charcoal
  10 pails (2½-gallon size) of compost: 3 cu. ft.
  *1 coffee can full of lime
   1 coffee can full of organic fertilizers
    Total volume of mixture: 16 cu. ft.

This amount will fill one garden block to a depth of 12 in., or two blocks to a depth of 6 in.

Procedure

1. Dig out a 4-foot by 4-foot garden block to the depth desired. Dig down 12 inches if you have very poor soil, or 6 inches for average soil.

2. Mix all the ingredients thoroughly with a flat-bottom shovel on a hard surface, or in a large plastic bag by carefully rolling it around. Spray with a hose to dampen the materials (don't soak them) as you mix the pile.

3. Fill the garden block with the mixture, turning it over to mix it well with the soil at the bottom of the hole. Again spray with a hose as you mix.

4. Level and add enough additional mixture to fill the hole, level again, spray once more with a hose, and the block is ready for planting.

*Note: A 1-pound coffee can (equal to 4 cups, or 1 quart) will hold approximately 2½ pounds of lime or other fine, dry material. A 2½-gallon (or 10-quart) water pail holds a volume approximately equal to ⅓ cubic foot.

Try Containers if Your Soil Is Poor

Here's a special tip for gardeners with extremely poor soil. Sink very large flower pots full of your very best soil mix into the ground, deep enough so the lip rests about ½ inch above the soil line. Plant things like peppers, tomatoes, cucumbers, Swiss chard, or any large, long-season or long-growing plant in these containers. It makes it easy to water, fertilize, even transplant if you want to bring them indoors later in the season. The roots can grow out the drainage hole in the bottom of the pot and into your soil. But if you keep the plants well watered and fertilized, the plants will do quite well right in the pots. This is just like container growing, but the soil in the pots won't dry out as quickly because they are sunk in the ground. This is a particularly good technique for people who have a very hard pan or clayey soil.

the top 4 inches of soil from the block and pile it to one side. Then with a spade, shovel, or fork turn over the soil remaining in the block. Don't dig too deeply, just loosen the first 6 inches or so. Next, add a 1- to 2-inch layer each of peat moss, vermiculite, aged manure, and compost. Sprinkle on a cup or so of one or more of the organic fertilizers described earlier, along with ½ cup of lime if your soil is at all acid. Mix all the materials by turning over the contents of the block a few times.

If you're really ambitious and want a very deeply dug soil, turn it over once more, to as deep as you can dig. This extra step is not necessary in most soils. Finally, add some more fertilizer and manure if you wish.

Remember to always work from outside the block, and don't ever walk on the garden soil.

Fall is the best time to prepare your growing soil, because at this time of year the soil is still warm and is not usually soggy. Spring is not a good time to work your soil because the opposite conditions occur—the ground then is hard and cold and still soggy after being frozen all winter. But you don't always have a choice, so prepare your soil in spring if you must. But repeat the process in fall so your garden will be in tip-top shape the following spring.

If you do need to work your soil in spring, you'll find if your soil is clayey that it is very hard to work when it's wet and cold. To make things easier, cover the garden with a sheet of clear plastic several weeks ahead of time to warm the soil and keep out the rain until you're ready to turn over the soil.

The universal test for determining if soil is ready to be dug in the spring is to squeeze a ball of soil in your palm, open your hand, and poke the ball with a finger of the other hand. If the ball falls apart into small pieces, the soil is ready to work. If your finger just makes a hole or indentation in the ball, the soil is still too wet, and you should wait another week.

But you won't have to worry about doing this sort of soil preparation after you have prepared your garden blocks the first time. In the years that follow you won't have to do any more major digging. All you'll have to do is turn over the soil in each little 1-foot square with a trowel after each crop is harvested. You'll do that at least twice each year, and more likely three or four times for some squares.

As soon as the harvest in a particular square is finished, you may pull up the plant roots to add them to the compost or mulch pile. Then sprinkle over the square a trowel full of fertilizer, lime or sulfur if needed, a trowel full of compost, and a trowel full of well-aged manure, and turn over the soil in that square. If the texture of your soil isn't as good as you would like it to be, add a trowel full of peat moss, vermiculite, or any other soil builder you might have on hand.

That's the only sort of soil preparation you'll have to do for the rest of your gardening years. All you have to do is keep renewing the humus and nutrients each time you replant a square.

Drainage

One other condition that is important when selecting a garden site is soil drainage and how it affects your garden area. Although drainage is important, you usually end up with whatever you have in the yard. There isn't always room to change locations, especially if you have a small yard. But you should be aware of the conditions of drainage and its effect on plant growth so you can do something about it. A poor drainage area is usually defined as an area where water will sit in puddles for several hours after a heavy rainfall. This may happen at the surface where it is readily apparent, or just below ground. If it's below ground, the way to find out is to dig a few holes in any area where water puddles in your future garden site. Dig a couple of holes about 1 foot across, and at least 1 foot deep. Then watch to see how long water stays in the holes after a heavy rain. If plants are to grow in that area, the water should drain off within three to four hours at the most, otherwise the plants will have "wet feet."

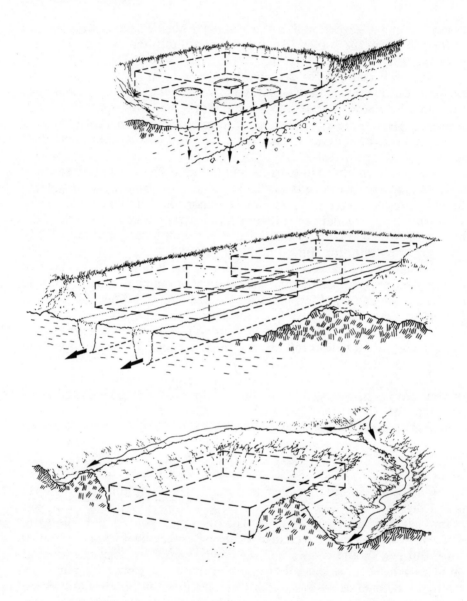

Three methods for improving drainage are to, top, sink four holes into the garden to permeate a layer of water-holding clay; middle, dig ditches through the garden every 2 feet to carry off water; and bottom, dig a ditch next to a dike around the highest edge of the garden to divert water around it.

Remember, water drives out any air from the soil spaces, meaning that plant roots can't take in air. During a heavy rainy spell that lasts over several days, the roots will be completely submerged and the plants will probably die.

If a poor drainage area is the only place you can have your garden, there are several things you can do to improve conditions. One is to build up the individual garden blocks with a sandy soil, so the upper foot of growing soil drains nicely. That's a lot of work and takes quite a bit of soil, but you might limit your garden to just a few blocks, or at least try one before you go through a lot of work. The other way is to dig deep holes every 2 to 4 feet and fill them with sand or gravel. That way you might punch through a layer of water-holding clay (called a lens) and the water will be able to drain away more quickly down the holes, leaving you with a drier growing soil. A third method of improving drainage is to dig ditches through the garden which will drain water away to a lower area. You'll need a ditch about 1½ feet deep located every 2 to 4 feet. You can lay drainage tile in the bottom of the ditches, or just fill them with sand and gravel. It's a lot of work. For a well-drained garden, the pipes or ditches must, of course, run downhill to be able to drain into a lower area. The pitch you'll need is at least a 1-foot drop for every 20 feet.

One thing you should definitely do no matter what else you try is to limit the amount of water that drains into the poorly draining garden site. You can usually do that by building a little diversion ditch and dam or dike, which is just a ridge of some soil around the garden. The idea is that when water drains down from higher parts of your property, it will run around and right past your garden. This won't improve the drainage of your garden soil, but it will keep an awful lot of water away from it. All of these actions may seem like extreme solutions, but if you don't have decent drainage you're not going to have a good garden.

Location

The last consideration in choosing a garden site is the proximity to the back door or the kitchen. When the vegetable plot is way out back, or at least out of sight, it is usually visited only when there's work to do, or a big harvest to be made. Out of sight, out of mind applies to gardens, too. This leads to less frequent visits and subsequently fewer harvests. Plants could be wilting in the sun, or bugs could be defoliating a whole crop before someone comes to notice. It's one of the prices to pay for having a large garden that can only be located where there's enough space.

But all of the opposite is true with a small, condensed garden spot. It can easily be tucked in near the house where you see or pass it daily, maybe even walk past it each time you leave the house. Both its small size and close proximity to your daily comings and goings help immensely in keeping the garden in tip-top shape. Since it's a manageable size, you can afford the time to keep it neatly weeded and watered. You'll also be able to notice any problems from pests or the effects of hot weather almost before they happen. And it will be easy for you to care for newly planted seeds and transplants. (As you'll see in chapter 10, newly planted seeds need to be kept moist, and need to be misted every day when planted directly in the garden.)

But the biggest asset is that you will begin to harvest more often, even daily. Now it becomes as easy to step out the door and pick a vegetable for dinner as it is to open a can or reach in the freezer. Fresh garden salads will become a way of life when your garden is close by. It's so easy to snip several lettuce, chard, and beet leaves, pull a few radishes, onions, and carrots, and return to the kitchen. With a small garden geared to smaller but more frequent harvests, you can begin to experiment more often in the kitchen by adding many things to your salad. Harvesting is no longer a chore, and you don't have to worry about making time to can and freeze what you can't eat. In chapter 14, you'll see how the small daily harvest will fit right into your kitchen. Menus become less complicated and more interesting with a spur-of-the-moment selection of various ingredients which is possible when the garden is close by.

For those who can't have the entire garden close by, I would suggest putting at least one 4-foot by 4-foot block for a salad garden right by the kitchen door. This is a good compromise as most of the smaller salad crops are the ones that need extra attention, and a lot can be grown in one block if you stick with all of the leaf and root crops. Put the large-growing, less demanding cabbage family and all of the summer vine and bush vegetables farther away in the main garden.

One last point: if your garden is close by and in sight to enjoy, you obviously will take better care of it. This in turn will result in a more productive garden with a larger harvest and healthier plants. Without competition from weeds, your plants can utilize all of the moisture and nutrients in the soil. All of this occurs just because you moved all or part of your garden closer to the house, so it's well worth the effort.

Another factor to consider, if you have a lot of land, is the slope of the garden site. If you have a choice, try to pick a spot that has a southern exposure (in other words, land that slopes toward the south). But avoid putting the garden on a steep slope, even if it does face south. If the land slants steeply, water that you give your plants may run off the garden before it can soak into the ground, and there is a much greater chance that a heavy rainstorm could wash away your garden. The ideal spot for a garden is one with a very slight slope to the south.

Easy-to-Grow Crops

Beans
Beets
Swiss chard
Corn
Cucumbers
Lettuce
Radishes
Squash
Tomatoes

Chapter 6
⬡ Garden Planning— What and When to Plant

Gardening, like any other activity, should follow a normal sequence of events. It should start with a little planning, and some basic decisions should be made before proceeding. All too often gardens are started without any previous planning and seeds are planted almost by whim. On the other hand, you can easily go overboard with elaborate drawings and charts. Most garden books advise the gardener to sit down in midwinter in the comfort of a cozy room to draw up an exacting garden plan all to scale. You decide where to plant everything, what seeds to buy, and review the plan and results of last year's garden. I'll admit it's a lot of fun to think about the garden in midwinter, and getting out all the seed catalogs does stimulate the desire to get going. But unfortunately, too many of us who do take the trouble to make out a plan never follow it past the first few weeks of planting. It seems a quirk of human nature to file and forget any plan. Despite all these good intentions, garden growth has a way of overwhelming any plans by midsummer.

If you've been frustrated by not being able to bring your neatly planned garden into existence, you'll be glad to know that the square foot method requires no elaborate diagrams or lists to produce a uniform, staggered harvest.

72

A Calendar of Garden Events

To get a feel for how the season will progress, let's start with a very simple one-block garden and follow its growth through one season. Assuming you wanted to try a small salad garden right next to your back door, this is how a typical year would look.

After picking the best location for the garden and preparing the soil as described in chapter 5, the next step is to divide up the area into 16 1-foot squares. To simplify this first garden, let's say it will be planted in May, mostly for salad fixings. In order to get the maximum yield, you should install a vertical frame on the north side and plant two tomato plants in the first 2 squares and four cucumber seeds in the next 2 squares. These vine crops will be supported right up the strings on the vertical frame and produce a harvest all summer. The remaining 12 squares will be planted primarily with vegetables, but it's a nice idea to include a few flowers and herbs, too. You might put some flowers in each corner of the block—dwarf marigolds in one square and nasturtiums in the other. Each can be planted from seed and should be located 6 inches apart. So mark off each of these corner squares into four small spaces and plant one seed in the center of each little space (spacing and planting details are given in chapter 7).

Next, you can plant a square each of three varieties of leaf lettuce—such as Ruby, Oak Leaf, and Salad Bowl—all at 6-inch spacings. The same planting procedure is used as with the flowers. Where to put each square of lettuce isn't too important; they are of average height so they could go just about anywhere, either all together or spread out. Just put them where you think they will look the best.

Next, you'll plant some onion sets. These can go in at 3-inch spacing, so divide the next square into fourths each way, creating 16 little spaces, then push each onion bulb into the ground just far enough so the top still sticks out a little. Another garden square will contain beets, which are also planted 3 inches apart. Divide the square as you did for the onions, but place one seed in the center of each of the 16 spaces. (Special seed-planting tips are provided in chapter 10.) Remember as you plant to never walk, kneel, or lean on your soil. Always reach in from the side.

Now plant a square of chives at 4-inch spacing, placing one seed in each hole. For the purpose of this example, we'll assume you would like some parsley, too. Because these seeds are rather slow in germinating, plant about six to eight seeds in a cup of vermiculite in the house so you can watch them closely and get them off to a better start.

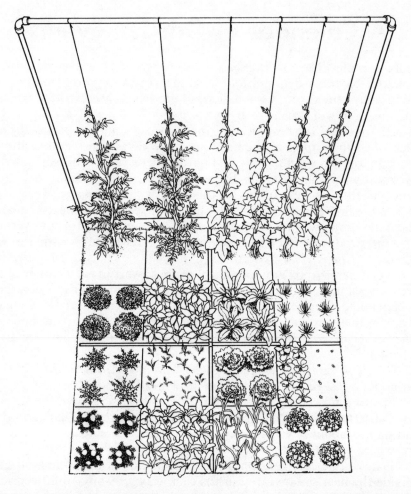

Here's a simple, one-block garden, fully planted. Tomatoes and cucumbers grow up the vertical supports. The back row contains, left to right, a square each of Ruby lettuce, bush beans, Swiss chard, and chives. The center row holds Oak Leaf lettuce, carrots, Salad Bowl lettuce, and radishes. The front row contains dwarf marigolds, beets, onions, and nasturtiums.

So far you have used up 4 square feet of garden space for vertical vines, 2 for flowers, 1 for an herb, 3 for lettuce, and 2 for onions and beets —a total of 12 squares. Three of the remaining squares will be planted with 16 carrots at 3-inch spacing, 9 green bush beans at 4-inch spacing, and 4 Swiss chard seeds at 6-inch spacing. The last square will be for radishes planted 3 inches apart. If you plant all 16 radish seeds at one time you will be inundated with too many to harvest all at once, so just plant 8 seeds now and then wait two weeks before planting the other 8 in order to stagger the harvest.

The entire 4-foot by 4-foot block is now planted and will provide a nice selection of salad fixings—enough to provide one person with a fresh salad each day, or provide a family with less frequent salads. Water the seed squares daily (with just a fine mist) until the seeds sprout. Plants should be watered once a week. The only other necessary maintenance is to pull out any little weeds once a week and to train your tomatoes and cucumbers up the vertical strings. Within three or four weeks, or as soon as your plants are about half grown, you can start harvesting. Outside lettuce leaves can be cut, individual beet leaves pinched out, the first young radishes can be pulled, and onion and chive tops snipped. The harvest will be small at first, but the idea is to start picking a little each day to add to your store-bought vegetables. Pretty soon you'll have enough for a good-size salad every single day.

Here's how much you'll be able to harvest from just that first planting:

4 plants Ruby lettuce ⎫
4 plants Salad Bowl lettuce ⎬ or 12 plants of any other
4 plants Oak Leaf lettuce ⎭ leaf lettuce
16 carrots
16 beets
24 bunches beet greens
6 pounds beans
16 radishes
16 onions
continuous harvest of Swiss chard
continuous harvest of chives
continuous harvest of marigolds and nasturtiums
continuous harvest of nasturtiums for salads
continuous harvest of tomatoes and cucumbers through the summer,
  a total of over 8 pounds of each

As soon as all your radishes are harvested, the parsley plants you started in the house should be ready to transplant into that square. First, prepare the soil in that square by adding a trowel full of leaf mold and some fertilizer if you wish, and then turn the soil over with the trowel, just in that square. Level it out and mark off the square in halves each way. Then plant your four sturdiest parsley plants, one in each small space. Give them water right away and a little shade for a few days (see chapter 11 for details).

The next square that will be harvested will probably be one of the three containing lettuce. That square could be replanted with another crop of bush beans, since the first square of beans will be harvested in about four weeks. In order to have a continuous crop of beans all summer, you should plant a new square once a month. Prepare the soil and plant the nine bean seeds in their proper 4-inch spacing. When the next lettuce square is finished, you might decide to plant another crop of carrots. They go in at 3-inch spacing after the soil is prepared. Another square might be planted in radishes. Put in four or eight at a time depending on how many you use each week. (Four per week are usually enough for each person.) As the beets are finished, you might want to try a square of summer Bibb lettuce. You can plant the seeds directly in the garden, or if you want to save time and space, you could start the seeds in a cup of vermiculite a few weeks ahead of time so that you'll be able to set out young plants.

The square foot garden employs a continuous replanting procedure all summer. As soon as a square is harvested, you simply add additional humus and fertilizer and turn over the soil, then decide what you would like to plant next. Keep up your weekly watering and weeding and you'll have a very productive garden throughout the season.

Keeping up with the continuous replanting process requires only the simplest of preplanning. Once a week, look around the garden and take notice of any squares that will be ready for final harvest in a few weeks. Decide what new crop you want to replant there, and start those seeds in a cup at that time. It's better not to replant the same crop in each square, but to rotate them. This will be accomplished almost automatically, simply by chance, but it should be kept in mind when selecting a replacement crop.

Your tomatoes, cucumbers, Swiss chard, parsley, chives, and flowers will grow all summer, right up until the fall frost. Keep picking them all —cut a little parsley and chives each week, lots of Swiss chard leaves, and remember to cut some flowers each day to brighten the dinner table. By the time the first frost occurs in fall, you will have harvested a lot of salads, and although the frost will kill many of the plants, some (including carrots, beets, Swiss chard, and parsley) can be maintained into autumn for an extended harvest.

Looking back, you can see how easy it was to keep replanting

GROWTH RATES OF SOME POPULAR VEGETABLES

Fastest-Growing Crops	Weeks to Maturity from Seed	Weeks to Maturity from Transplants
Radishes	4	—
Lettuce	7	4
Spinach	7	—
Beans	8	—
Beets	8	—
Swiss chard	8	4
Squash	8	6
Corn	9	—
Cucumbers	9	7
Carrots	10	—
Peas	10	—
Slowest-Growing Crops		
Muskmelons	12	10
Cauliflower	14	8
Broccoli	16	9
Cabbage	16	9
Tomatoes	17	11
Eggplant	19	10
Peppers	19	10
Onions	20	14 (sets)

throughout the season, and you may even be thinking about next year already. You didn't have an overwhelming amount of food, and your little 4-foot by 4-foot garden provided you with a constant supply of fresh vegetables for salad. In addition, because of its small size, it looked neat and attractive all summer. Next year you might want to try a more elaborate schedule by starting earlier in the spring and having more plants ready to go in at the proper time. More about that later.

Developing Your Gardening Expertise

One question often asked by beginners is "How do I know when to plant what?" The answer may be found by consulting the charts in this and other books showing average best planting dates for various crops. Other questions, like how to handle seeds that are difficult to sprout, such as parsley, and how to stagger the planting of a square of quick-growing radishes, are answered partly by experience, but you can also find this information in books. There are many things to learn about the best way to grow plants in the particular set of growing conditions your garden provides, but that's part of the challenge of becoming a good gardener. Don't be afraid to experiment and make a few mistakes. We learn a lot more from our own experience than any book could ever teach us. Your square foot garden will enable you to try different crops and different cultural techniques on a small scale, one square at a time. The inevitable occasional failures won't be disasters. You'll find that working or planting your garden on this smaller scale will teach you about gardening much faster than if you started right off with a large garden.

Tips for Deciding What to Plant

One of the secrets of really enjoying your garden is to plant only what you want to *eat*. Although this simple fact may seem rather obvious, it is often ignored when people plant their gardens. They choose vegetables and varieties that have captured their fancy or imagination, but when it's time to harvest they're really not too keen on eating a particular vegetable after all. Think about what you want to plant. The first step in planning your garden is to decide exactly what you want to eat from your garden, then plant only those crops, or those that you enjoy for their ornamental qualities, or that you want to grow simply for the fun or challenge of it. A good example would be peanuts. It's doubtful whether you're ever going to grow enough to really make more than a handful, but you might decide you want to include them just because they are fun to grow—a little different and rather interesting.

Conversely, don't grow anything out of sheer force of habit. For example, it seems *everyone* plants beets in their garden; they are easy to grow, very attractive, very useful, nutritious, and a tasty addition to many dishes. But lots of people grow beets even though they don't often eat them. Ask yourself how many times you buy beets in the supermarket or how often you order them when you're dining out in a restaurant. If the answer is very seldom, don't bother growing them.

What and how much to plant is also contingent upon how much time you have to spend on gardening. You need to decide just how involved you want to get in gardening, and how important an extended growing season is to you. Don't plant early-season crops unless you are willing to put in some extra work or really want an extra-early harvest. Your chances of success diminish as you go outside the normal growing season, and it involves some degree of risk. Beginners and many other gardeners are usually happier when gardening activities are confined to the normal growing season. If you are a veteran gardener or an adventuresome type who really loves to garden and wants to experiment, you may find it a rewarding challenge to raise something out of its normal growing season. This point is well taken in the fall but is especially important in the early spring. Invariably the desire to start a garden is strongest then, and after a long winter everyone is anxious to get some seeds in the ground. But because the sprouting seeds and young plants are very vulnerable and the weather is fickle during springtime, many plantings are washed away or frozen out, or just generally get off to a bad start.

After you've decided what you want to eat and how involved you want to get, the next step in garden planning is to become familiar with the requirements of each vegetable that you've chosen. You need to know its season of planting, time to maturity, spacing, any special growing requirements, pests and diseases to which the crop is susceptible, and how easy or difficult it is to grow. This kind of information is provided for a number of crops in chapter 18. An obvious bit of advice, particularly for the beginner, is to pick varieties that are easy to grow and attract few pests. Again, your chances of success are going to be increased substantially.

Once you've selected your varieties, it's time to purchase the seeds. You might want to make a shopping list before ordering; that list can be used later for other purposes. Order by mail if you want special varieties or are fond of a particular company's seeds, or shop locally if you need the seeds right away or want only popular varieties that are likely to be in stock. Don't buy too many packets of seed. Remember you're only going to plant the varieties of vegetables you want to eat.

Square foot gardening will affect your seed-buying habits in the future in a couple of important ways. First, you will plant only a small portion of the seeds in each packet every year. And second, you will learn how to properly store the remaining seeds so they remain usable the next year, and the next year, and the year after that! The only new seeds you will need to buy each year will be for different varieties you want to try. For example, you might decide to add one new variety of lettuce, carrot, and pepper to your collection each year. Your garden then takes on additional interest every season as you grow several varieties of your favorite vegetables.

Assigning the Garden Space

Assuming you've done all of the above, you are now ready with a fist full of seed packets and some high ambitions. First sort your seeds into three piles. Make one pile of vine crops for vertical growing (such as tomatoes, cucumbers, melons, pole beans, winter squash). Another pile will contain summer or hot-weather vegetables (such as peppers, eggplant, bush beans, bush zucchini). And the third pile is for cool-weather vegetables for spring/fall planting (lettuce, all root vegetables, members of the cabbage family). Now list how many plants of each you want to grow and harvest. Again, what you're really calculating is how many you want to eat. The sample layouts in chapter 3 will help you figure out how much to plant to meet your family's needs. You might add this number next to each vegetable on your shopping list.

Next assign space in the garden. To do that, some gardeners just stand in their garden and say "I'll put these here and those there." Others like to draw a simple diagram of their blocks and squares. First work on the vertical growing crops. How many frames are you going to have and what will be planted on them? Next assign your summer vegetables. Most of these crops are slow growers and will occupy the space for the entire season. Whatever room is left over can be assigned to a spring crop of cool-weather vegetables. These are usually more rapid growers so you'll be getting two or three successive crops from each square during the course of the growing season.

If you have a lot of garden space left over after designating squares for the crops you want to grow, your garden is too big. Don't plant more just to fill up the space—it's a big mistake and that's how other gardeners get in trouble. Instead, cut down on the number of blocks in your garden. On the other hand, if you find that you don't have enough room for the cool-weather vegetables that you want, your garden is either too small or you have listed too many vegetables to plant. Look over your list again and decide which is the case. By the way, don't forget to include some flowers and herbs in the garden. They should be tucked in here and there in different squares to add color, interest, and variety. If you have just a little room remaining after your crops are assigned to squares, that's just perfect. You always find you can use one or two extra squares, either for those flowers and herbs, or for some extra vegetables.

Planting Dates

Everyone wants to know "When can I get started?" The answer depends on several things, including whether the crop grows best in cool or warm weather, when the last spring frost and first fall frost occur in your area, and the length of your growing season. Planting time is also dependent upon whether you're going to raise your own transplants from seed or buy them from a local nursery.

Juggling all these variables can become quite confusing, especially for beginning gardeners, so I've boiled down the entire process to a few simple steps:

1. Estimate the date of the last spring frost (or first fall frost if you're planning a fall crop) in your area from the frost maps later in this chapter. Write down that date.

2. Look up each vegetable on the Planting Schedule for Spring and Summer Crops (or the Planting Schedule for Fall Crops) at the end of this chapter. The chart will tell you how many weeks before or after the frost date each vegetable can be planted out in the garden. (Note whether each date is for seedlings or transplants.) Look at a calendar to determine your planting dates. Add that information to your shopping list, or your garden notebook, if you keep one.

3. If you are planning to start your own transplants, look up on the Indoor Seed-Starting Schedule the number of weeks before or after the last frost they should be started indoors. Consult a calendar for the dates, and add that information to your shopping list or notebook.

The planting schedules for spring, summer, and fall crops at the end of this chapter have been designed to show you at a glance when to plant seeds indoors, when to plant seeds or transplants outdoors, and when to expect the harvest. The Planting Schedule for Continuous Harvests shows you when to replant each crop to produce a continuous harvest all season.

Since trying to determine the date of planting both indoors and outdoors has always been a little confusing, don't further complicate matters by trying to use the average dates you will obtain this way as exact dates. A week or two either way is the best you can really estimate, for a couple of reasons. First, the frost-free date is variable from year to year by at least two weeks. Second, the last frost could be a very mild one or a fairly heavy one, and obviously some plants could stand a light frost but

SPRING INDOOR SEED-STARTING SCHEDULE

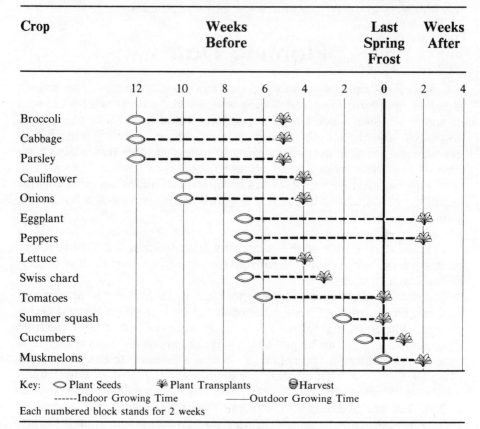

Crop	Weeks Before	Last Spring Frost	Weeks After

	12	10	8	6	4	2	0	2	4
Broccoli
Cabbage
Parsley
Cauliflower
Onions
Eggplant
Peppers
Lettuce
Swiss chard
Tomatoes
Summer squash
Cucumbers
Muskmelons

Key: ◯ Plant Seeds   ❦ Plant Transplants   ⊖ Harvest
------Indoor Growing Time   ——Outdoor Growing Time
Each numbered block stands for 2 weeks

not a heavy one. Further, the weather conditions will have a lot to do with planting times each year; a stretch of cold and cloudy weather will delay planting, and warm and sunny days will hasten it. You might ask whether the planting-out date should be different for seeds sown directly in the cool garden soil than for transplants grown indoors. For all practical purposes, I feel you can safely assume that the planting-out date is the same for seeds or transplants.

In order to simplify the difficult "when to plant" dates it was necessary to use only averages of when your area has its last frost in the spring. The frost maps show the average frost-free dates for the United States, but you must understand that they can be variable by a two-week period for each location. Also, the maps are divided into only very general climatic regions. Every area contains a range of climates due to differences in elevations and different exposures (e.g., the north side of a hill will be cooler than the south-facing slope). Also, climatic conditions are affected by whether a site is in an open field or sheltered by trees, hills, or buildings. Nearby bodies of water, such as a lake, also serve to moderate climate. There are many variables even within the same town or city. You might have a frost one night but your best friend ten blocks away may not. Any safe planting date is at best an educated guess (based on scientific data). I think you'll find it very easy to use the average frost-free dates as the basis of your planting schedule, but use them only as a general guide.

If you're adventuresome, or a little more experienced as a gardener, you might want to do your outdoor planting a week or so earlier than the safe planting date. If you're more conservative, you'll be happier if you wait a week or two past the average date to be on the safe side.

Temper your decision about when to plant by the kind of weather you're having that particular year. You have to remember you're dealing with nature and there are bound to be some disappointments every year, as well as some unexpected successes. Every vegetable won't produce a prize-winning crop every year. Some years, for no apparent reason, your

Frost Maps

Some of the most frequently asked questions at my lectures concern how early in spring gardeners can begin planting, and how late in the fall garden activities can continue. People want to know when they should start seeds indoors as well as when they can plant the crops outdoors. The answers to these questions always relate to when the last spring frost and the first fall frost occur in your area, which changes from one year to the next. All you can do is make your plans based on the average dates from past years, then carefully observe weather conditions and make an educated guess as to when to start planting.

Frost maps cannot be very detailed, as they cover the entire United States, so pinpointing your exact location on the map and approximating the actual frost date from the month-wide range shown will be a good guess at best. My advice is to estimate as best you can, but don't take that date as the final word. Understand that it is only an approximate date to be used for preliminary planning, and the actual last frost is bound to occur on a slightly different date every year.

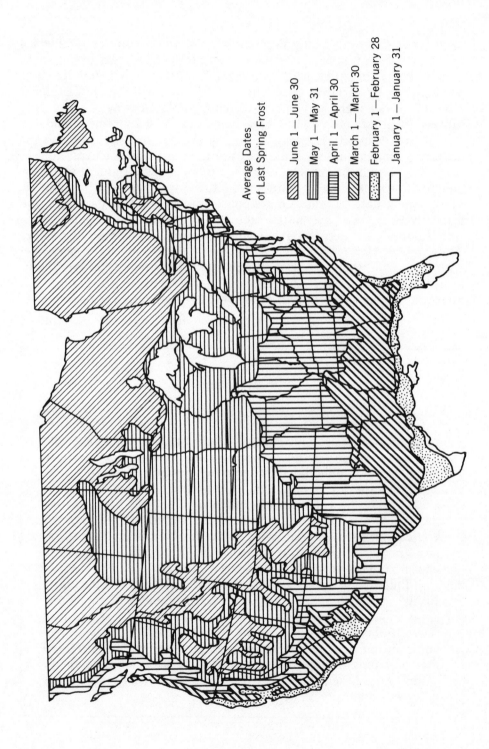

Average Dates
of Last Spring Frost

June 1 — June 30

May 1 — May 31

April 1 — April 30

March 1 — March 30

February 1 — February 28

January 1 — January 31

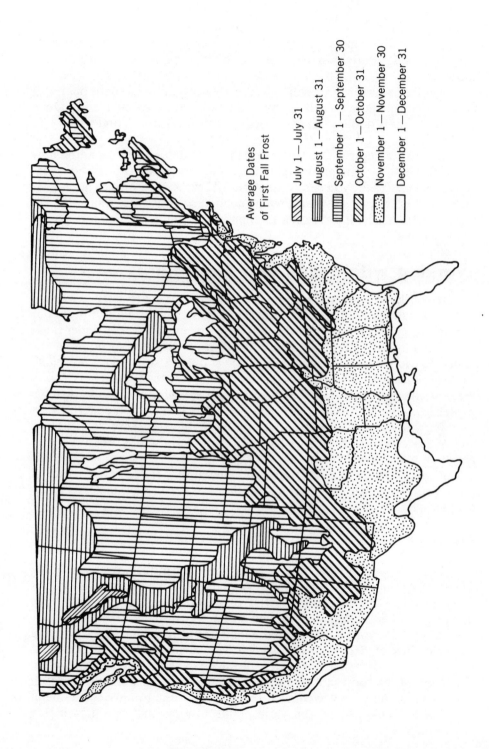

Average Dates
of First Fall Frost

July 1 — July 31

August 1 — August 31

September 1 — September 30

October 1 — October 31

November 1 — November 30

December 1 — December 31

spinach just won't grow properly; other years it will be the talk of the neighborhood. Sometimes you have to accept a poor crop and go on to the next one.

Another variable that will determine when you're going to plant, for all practical purposes, is the amount of time you have available. Quite often planting is done on the first weekend the family can find time to do it.

To further complicate the matter, planting dates depend a lot on how much protection your garden gets from chilling spring rains and wind. Now to some extent, you can control that. The easiest solution (but a little more work) is to provide your own protection so you're not totally dependent on nature (the information in chapters 10 and 15 will assure you of more success).

Working with Seeds and Transplants

If you have a greenhouse, heated sun box, or some warm spot that gets overhead sunlight, you can start your seeds according to the Indoor Seed-Starting Schedule. Seedlings will grow strong and sturdy under those bright conditions. They will also do well under fluorescent lights in the house. If you have only a windowsill, you shouldn't start your seeds quite as early because they just won't get enough light (even if it's a very sunny windowsill), and the plants will grow tall, spindly, and weak. After a winter of cold and darkness any sunny window looks great, and you start thinking you can raise almost anything there, but it just isn't so. It takes an experienced gardener to be successful at growing stocky, healthy transplants in a window.

If you're going to plant transplants make sure they are hardened-off a week or two before the planting-out date. Hardening-off is described in chapter 11.

Labels

To keep track of what you plant where in the garden, it's a good idea to put a label in each square as it's planted. To make sure this gets done you can fill in the labels when you plan your garden, leaving off the planting date. Select and buy enough wooden (painted and unpainted) or plastic labels for your entire garden. Don't spend years like I have, writing on little slips of paper, or motley leftover labels in different sizes and shapes. Treat yourself to enough large-size labels for the entire garden. Get yourself a good, wide-tipped permanent marking pen and print all your labels some snowy evening before spring. I like to have the name in big bold letters, then list the variety and date in smaller letters. Some

Good labels make a difference. The big, wood labels are easy to read, and a help to the gardener. The smaller label used in the onion square to the rear in this photograph isn't nearly so effective. The unlabeled square in the foreground leaves everyone wondering what is planted there.

gardeners like to use 12-inch-long labels, others prefer the 6-inch size. You also have a choice between horizontal and vertical labels. Look them over in the store or catalog and pick the kind that you like the best, but be sure to order them ahead of time. When you fill them out, take the time to do a nice printing job because they not only enhance the appearance of your garden, but also will be reusable year after year. Just erase or paint over the date for each year.

Calendar of Events for Advanced Gardeners

Now, let's go through the schedule for a typical garden for more advanced gardeners. Let's say you live in northern Illinois and you determine that your last spring frost date is a few days before April 30, and

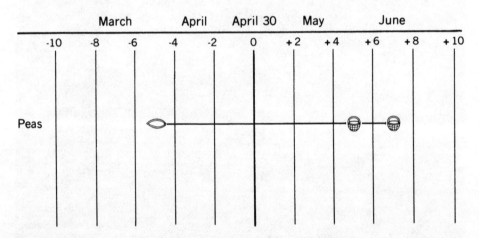

This illustration shows how you can use the planting schedules at the end of this chapter to find the planting dates for the crops in your garden. To figure out when to plant your spring crop of peas, for example, begin by finding out the average date of the last spring frost in your area. For the purpose of this example, let's assume it falls on April 30. The Planting Schedule for Spring Crops shows you that your peas can be planted five weeks before that frost date, so you can plant them on March 26. You'll be able to start picking your peas ten weeks later, on June 4. If you drew up your own planting schedule for peas, it would look something like the illustration above.

your first fall frost date is halfway between October 1 and 31. The charts were developed based on four one-week periods for every month. So, plot your spring frost date on the chart at the end of April/beginning of May and the fall date in the middle of October, with two weeks on either side.

Your list of spring vegetables to be planted might include peas, spinach, lettuce, onions, beets, carrots, and radishes. To find out how many weeks before the last frost each crop can be planted, consult the Planting Schedule for Spring and Summer Crops.

After calculating the average safe planting-out dates for each vegetable, mark it on the seed packet and in your notebook.

Your planting can begin on or about March 21, when you can safely plant out peas and spinach. Look up their spacing, divide the squares, and plant the seeds. To help them sprout more quickly and to keep the spring rains from washing them away, cover the squares with a plastic-covered cage for protection. The next week, April 1, you can plant out onions, lettuce, and cauliflower. The choices in planting onions are more varied than for most crops; you can plant seeds, seedlings, or sets. See the entry on onions, in chapter 18, to learn the advantages and disadvantages of each. If you opt for sets, go ahead and plant on that date. Space them 3 inches apart, and cover them as you did the spinach. If it's going to be seedlings you bought or raised, you might be more cautious and wait a week.

Since you're a more experienced gardener, let's assume that as an experiment you decide to plant one variety of lettuce as seeds directly in the garden, but you've also started seeds indoors four weeks earlier and the young plants are ready to move out. Rather than put them directly in the garden now if the weather has been cold and nasty, you could harden them off for one week or so in your sun box before planting them out the next week.

The next week, April 8, you can safely plant beets, carrots, and radishes. None of these vegetables transplants well, so start them all from seeds sown right in the garden. Use the same procedure you did for the onions and lettuce, remembering to fill in the variety and date on the labels when they are planted.

Along with all this planting out go the normal chores of spring cleanup, weeding, watering when necessary, and planting indoors to keep ahead of the planting-out date. It's a very hectic period but very exciting because of the promise of spring and summer garden glories to come. Now is the time to resist planting too much or making your garden too large. Once you commit yourself, you have to take care of it the rest of the year, and gardening takes work and time, even when you're using the simplified square foot method.

If you like lots of lettuce and carrots you will want to plant some every month or so in order to have a continuous harvest. You can merely look at the date of the last planting (or pick any other date you're likely to remember) and plant a new square of each crop on that date every month through the summer. The carrots will do fine, but the lettuce will need some protection from the hot summer sun and more water than normal. However, that can be provided with just a little extra effort. Shade and water can be supplied in a small garden more easily than it might seem (see chapter 15 for details).

If you would also like to harvest about six or eight radishes and scallions every week, plant only a half-square of each crop every week. This can be done by combining the radishes and onions in 1 square foot, or by planting each separately in its own square but taking two weeks to fill that square. Or, you can plant them in other assigned squares of slower-growing vegetables by "tucking in" the seeds wherever they fit (see chapter 7 for information on these special squares). Since the salad onions (scallions) and radishes will be mature enough to harvest in four to five weeks, they'll be out of the way of anything else growing.

Let's continue with the sequence of events. Once a week you should schedule a time to weed and water. At first it will only take a few minutes, but as the weather warms and the garden fills up, it becomes very important to keep ahead of the weeds and to give your plants the attention they need for maximum growth (that once-weekly session should be the same day and time each week if at all possible, so you won't forget and let it go by). Because the garden is small, though, even at the height of the season it won't take very long to do your maintenance. Once the garden is planted, it takes less than three hours per week to maintain a six-block garden (enough for a family of four).

As the weather warms it's time to plant some squares of summer vegetables. Following the same sequence as before, consult the Planting Schedule for Spring and Summer Crops to determine the best planting dates for all your summer vegetables.

When the average date of last spring frost arrives, it's safe to plant your beans, summer squash, and tomatoes. Remember to soak your bean seeds a few hours ahead of planting. Since you know that pole beans take much longer to fruit than bush beans (but produce longer once they start), you've decided to plant both varieties. So in they go with all the proper ceremony befitting a bean seed! A few more radishes and onions and a square of lettuce complete a morning's planting.

In the afternoon come the tomatoes and squash. The space for these crops has been reserved in advance, so all you need do is plant the seeds in the proper spacings. Plant your cucumbers a week after the frost-free date and keep up with the additional planting of spring vegetables if you want a continuous harvest. Don't forget your weekly weeding and watering chores. Two weeks after the last frost date it's time for the last of the summer crop: eggplant and peppers. Buy good-looking transplants at your local nursery or pick out your best homegrown plants and put them in as described in chapter 11.

By now almost all of your squares will be filled. Tuck in a few squares of flowers here and there, remembering to match their heights to those of plants growing next to them, and you're all set. Every square should look

In this photo, a square of lettuce was just harvested and is now ready for replanting. The continuous replanting process keeps every square in the garden at a high level of productivity throughout the season.

promising, although many will still look a little bare because of the small, young plants just starting. But take heart, it will all prosper in time. What you don't want to prosper are the weeds and pests, so keep after them; don't skip a week. And continue to water in order to insure lush, tender growth. As you harvest squares of lettuce, radishes, onions, and all the other spring crops as they mature, replant each square. Only one caution: don't replant any square with the same crop; always rotate your crops. After a while, your selection of what to plant in an empty square will become very easy, almost automatic. Just look around the garden and notice what needs planting. If you're new to the system, it will help you to rely on the charts included in this chapter and elsewhere in the book.

With spring now at an end and summer approaching, you have all your hot-weather vegetables planted but may still have a few extra spaces available. Looking about, you see you have only one square of green bush beans almost ready to flower. Let's assume that you decide, since you love fresh beans in a salad (cooked or raw), you'd like some more after these are finished. But this time you decide to plant a yellow variety to add color to your salads. Since your vertical frames are all taken, you buy a yellow bush variety of beans. Remember to store the leftover seeds in the refrigerator, and they'll remain viable for several years to come. The summer continues with a constant harvesting and replanting of squares. If you religiously do your few hours of maintenance work every week you'll notice right away any problems due to insects, diseases, or unusual growth conditions, and can take corrective action.

As fall approaches it's time to think again of the cool-weather crops. Although you might have successfully grown lettuce and radishes all summer, it was a lot of extra work (extra shade and water were required). Maybe it wasn't worthwhile—or maybe it was, since you were the only one on the block who did it! You have to decide.

But one thing is certain. Lettuce and radishes will all do well again in the cool fall weather. Actually August is the proper planting month for most fall crops. Although we think of August as the "dog days," the days are shortening rapidly and the longer, cooler evenings are conducive to rapid growth of new plants.

Depending on the time to maturity, some fall crops should be planted in early August, some in mid-month, and others not until late in the month or even into September. Count back from the average date of the first fall frost to determine when to plant each vegetable. Just look up the average date of the first killing frost for your area, and subtract from it the number of weeks to maturity for each crop to get your planting date. The Planting Schedule for Fall Crops will help you. If you don't have any empty garden squares at that time, or if you want to grow transplants to set out later, start the seeds in a cup and transplant them when there is room in the garden (of course assuming that crop can be transplanted).

If you are satisfied to call it quits when the first frost arrives, don't bother planting a fall crop. Your harvest will end when the frost hits. However, if you want to extend the harvest into the colder autumn and even winter months, then you'll have to do a little extra studying and figuring. Many vegetables can withstand either a light or a heavy frost (a few can even withstand a hard freeze and still be harvestable). Look these up in chapter 15, and if they are on your list of vegetables to grow, and you want to harvest them past the first frost date, then delay their planting until the calculated time. What is the calculated time? Simply decide when you want to harvest them (assuming that they will still be good at that time) and subtract their growth period to calculate your planting date.

Fall planting is a little more complicated than planting in springtime. But after a year or two of gardening it will become natural and easy to figure out. For your first few gardening seasons (at least the very first one) forget about growing out of season, and stick to vegetables that are easy to grow. Then as you're successful, expand and try new things.

Whether you grew a late-season crop or not, the last thing to do in fall is to put your garden to bed. Fall is actually the best time to prepare your soil for the next spring. Any hardy crops that can be stored right in the garden should be mulched to protect them from the cold. The techniques are described in chapters 15 and 16.

We've completed a full year's cycle now. Your garden stayed productive and busy all year, but because of its small size you were able to control the weeds and pests. Since watering was also an easy task your plants grew better and rewarded you with a lusher and more succulent harvest. But most important, I hope you stayed interested in your garden all year.

OUTDOOR PLANTING SCHEDULE FOR SPRING AND SUMMER CROPS

Crop	Weeks Before				Last Spring Frost			Weeks After					
	8	6	4	2	0	2	4	6	8	10	12	14	16
Very Early Spring (4–6 weeks before last spring frost)													
Broccoli													
Cabbage													

OUTDOOR PLANTING SCHEDULE FOR SPRING AND SUMMER CROPS

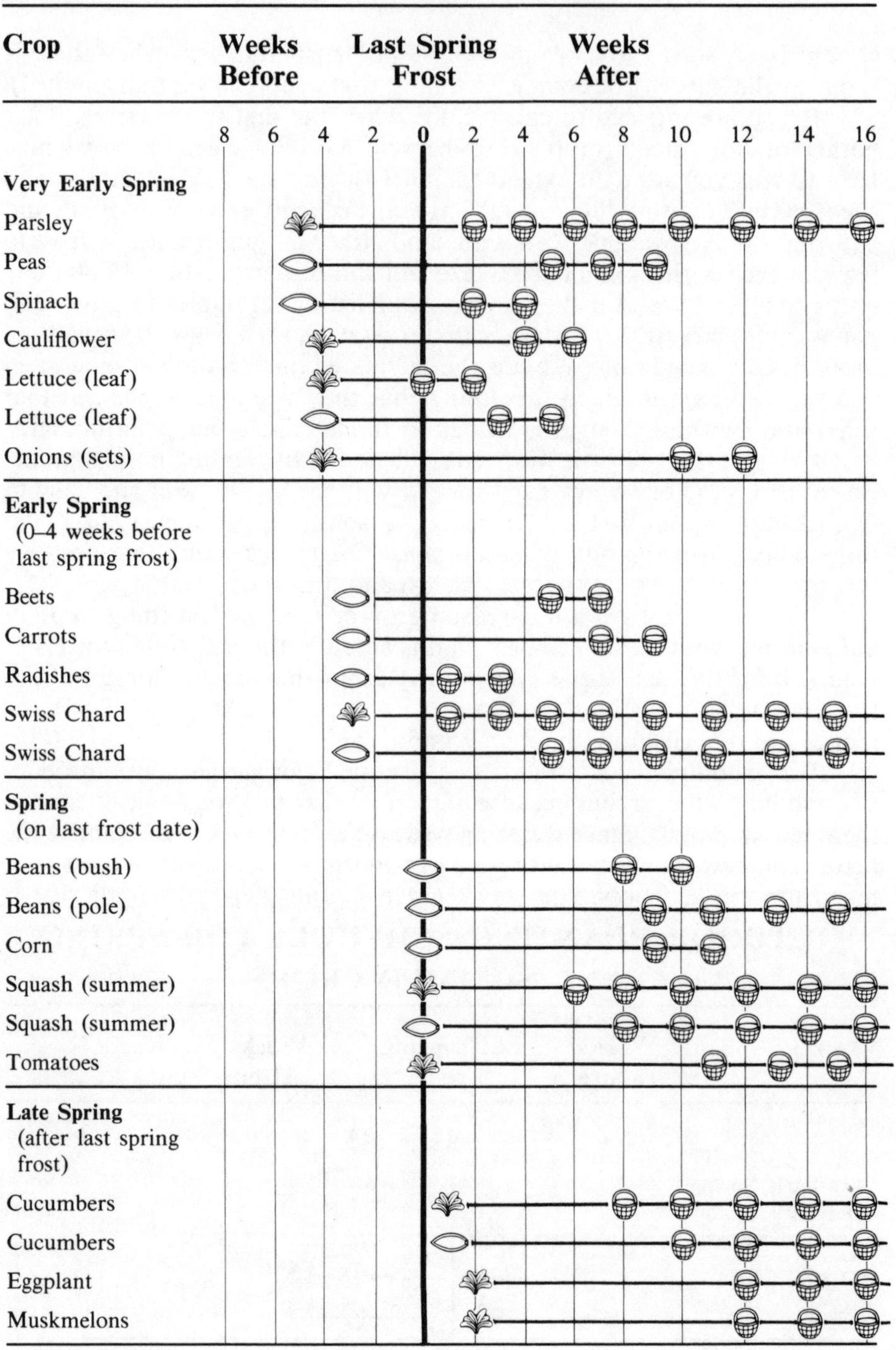

Crop	Weeks Before			Last Spring Frost		Weeks After						
	8	6	4	2	0	2	4	6	8	10	12	14	16

Very Early Spring

- Parsley
- Peas
- Spinach
- Cauliflower
- Lettuce (leaf)
- Lettuce (leaf)
- Onions (sets)

Early Spring
(0–4 weeks before last spring frost)

- Beets
- Carrots
- Radishes
- Swiss Chard
- Swiss Chard

Spring
(on last frost date)

- Beans (bush)
- Beans (pole)
- Corn
- Squash (summer)
- Squash (summer)
- Tomatoes

Late Spring
(after last spring frost)

- Cucumbers
- Cucumbers
- Eggplant
- Muskmelons

OUTDOOR PLANTING SCHEDULE FOR SPRING AND SUMMER CROPS

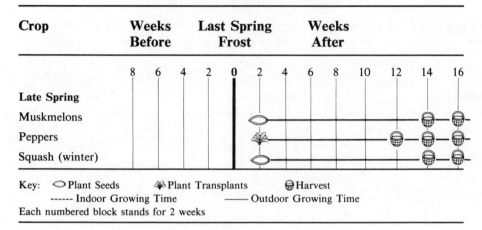

Crop	Weeks Before	Last Spring Frost	Weeks After

	8	6	4	2	0	2	4	6	8	10	12	14	16

Late Spring

Muskmelons

Peppers

Squash (winter)

Key: ◯ Plant Seds ✽ Plant Transplants ⊖ Harvest
------ Indoor Growing Time ———— Outdoor Growing Time
Each numbered block stands for 2 weeks

PLANTING SCHEDULE FOR FALL CROPS

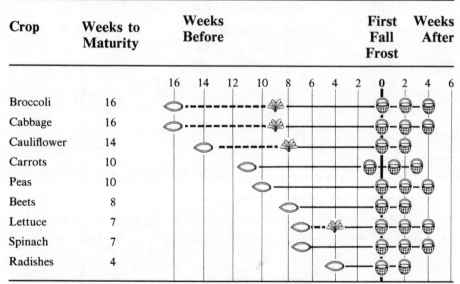

Crop	Weeks to Maturity	Weeks Before	First Fall Frost	Weeks After

		16	14	12	10	8	6	4	2	0	2	4	6

Broccoli	16
Cabbage	16
Cauliflower	14
Carrots	10
Peas	10
Beets	8
Lettuce	7
Spinach	7
Radishes	4

Key: ◯ Plant Seeds ✽ Plant Transplants ⊖ Harvest
------ Indoor Growing Time ———— Outdoor Growing Time
Each numbered block stands for 2 weeks

PLANTING SCHEDULE FOR A CONTINUOUS HARVEST

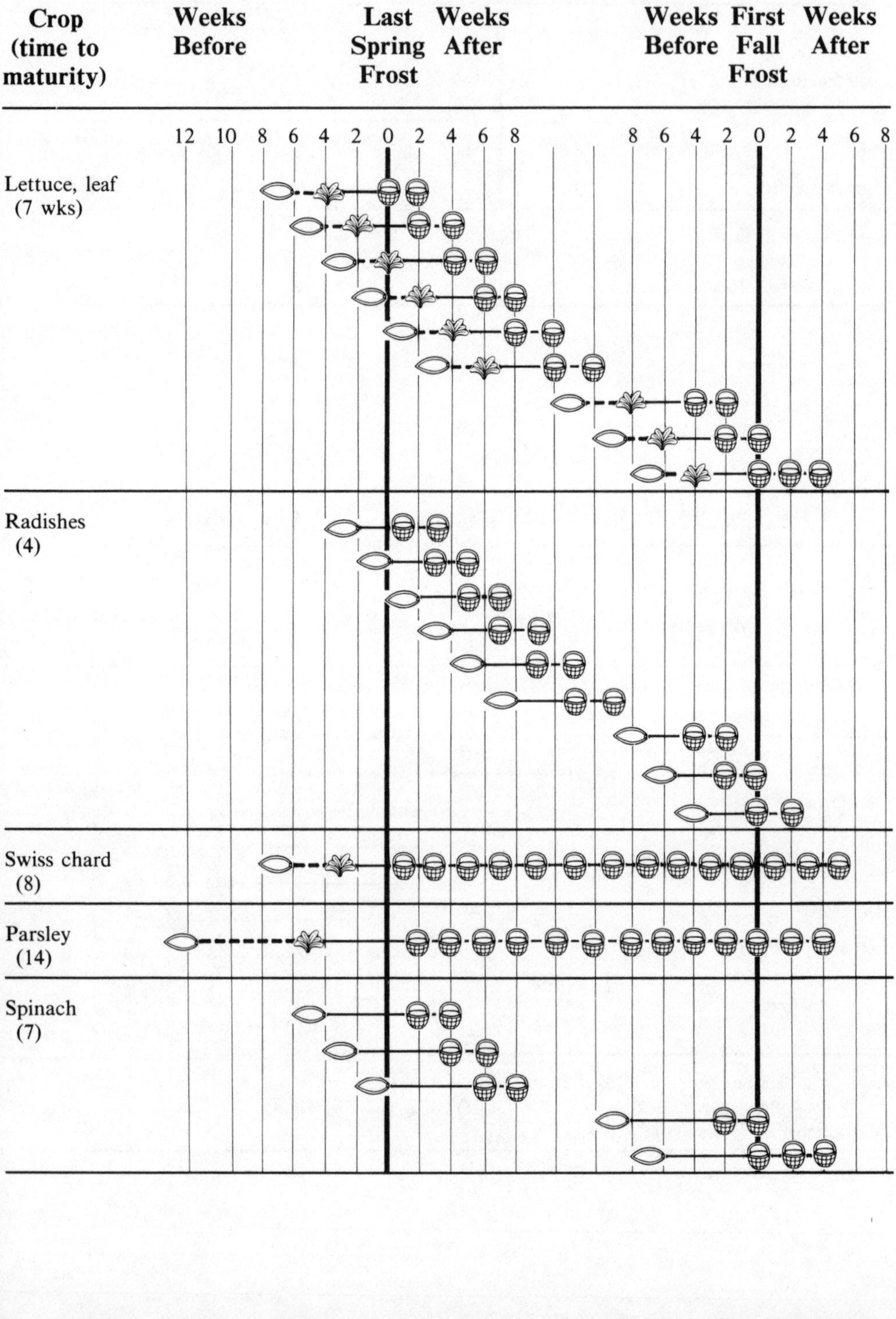

Crop (time to maturity)	Weeks Before	Last Spring Frost	Weeks After		Weeks Before	First Fall Frost	Weeks After

| 12 | 10 | 8 | 6 | 4 | 2 | 0 | 2 | 4 | 6 | 8 | | 8 | 6 | 4 | 2 | 0 | 2 | 4 | 6 | 8 |

Lettuce, leaf (7 wks)

Radishes (4)

Swiss chard (8)

Parsley (14)

Spinach (7)

PLANTING SCHEDULE FOR A CONTINUOUS HARVEST

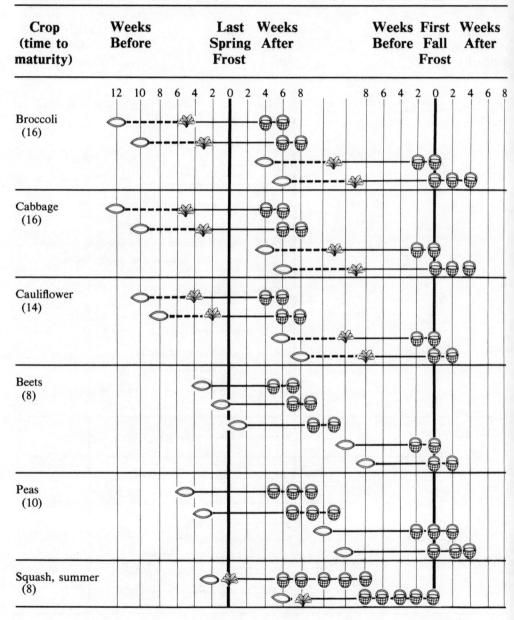

Crop (time to maturity)	Weeks Before	Last Spring Frost	Weeks After		Weeks Before	First Fall Frost	Weeks After

Broccoli (16)

Cabbage (16)

Cauliflower (14)

Beets (8)

Peas (10)

Squash, summer (8)

PLANTING SCHEDULE FOR A CONTINUOUS HARVEST

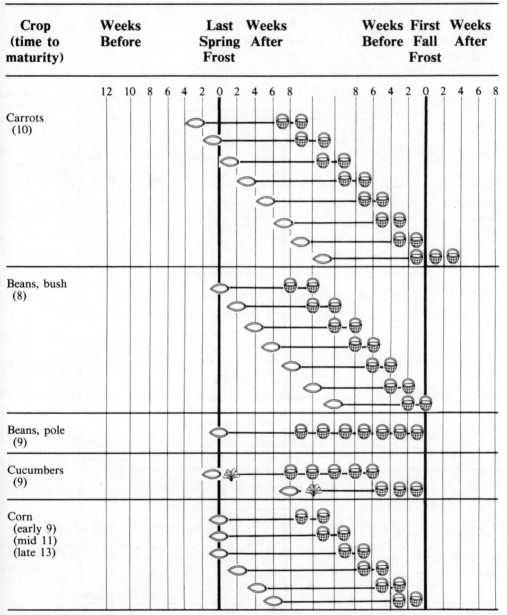

Crop (time to maturity)	Weeks Before	Last Spring Frost	Weeks After		Weeks Before	First Fall Frost	Weeks After
	12 10 8 6 4 2	0	2 4 6 8		8 6 4 2	0	2 4 6 8
Carrots (10)							
Beans, bush (8)							
Beans, pole (9)							
Cucumbers (9)							
Corn (early 9) (mid 11) (late 13)							

PLANTING SCHEDULE FOR A CONTINUOUS HARVEST

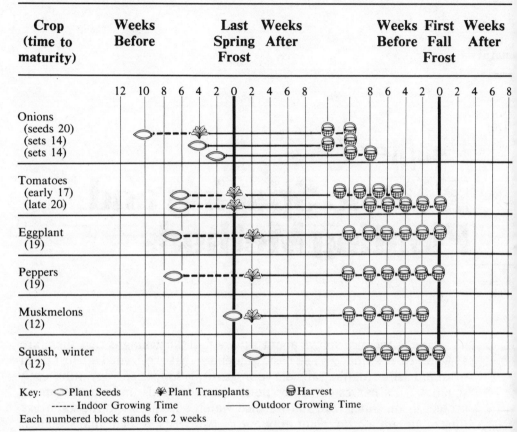

Crop (time to maturity)	Weeks Before	Last Spring Frost	Weeks After	Weeks Before Fall	First Frost	Weeks After

Key: ◌ Plant Seeds ❦ Plant Transplants ⛐ Harvest

------ Indoor Growing Time ——— Outdoor Growing Time

Each numbered block stands for 2 weeks

Chapter 7
▧ Basic Spacing and Planting Methods

One of the nice things about square foot gardening is that there are very few rules to follow. The basic guidelines that are needed are just plain common sense (don't walk on your growing soil, keep replanting each square as it's harvested, cover newly planted seeds and transplants to protect them, water with sun-warmed water, add humus to the soil every time you plant a crop, plant only one or two seeds at their final spacing). The proper spacing for each vegetable is easily looked up in chapter 18. Plant spacing is further simplified because, except for a couple of special cases, all plants fit into a 12-inch square.

How many plants of each type can fit into a square depends on how big the plants get when full grown and how far they spread. Large plants such as peppers and cabbages require a whole square all to themselves. These are the same plants that would be spaced on 12-inch centers in conventional row gardens. Smaller plants like leaf lettuce and parsley require only 6 inches between plants, so a 12-inch square is divided in half each way to create 4 plant spaces. One lettuce plant is then put in the center of each little space. The next in size are spinach and bush beans, which need only 4-inch spacing between plants. So for these crops a square is divided into thirds each way, creating 9 plant spaces, with one seed or plant placed in the center of each space. The smallest plants, carrots and

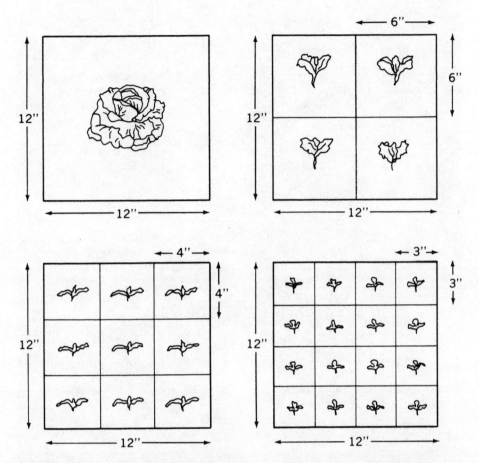

These are the basic, most frequently used spacings in the square foot garden: The 3-inch spacing accommodates beets, carrots, onions, and radishes. The 4-inch spacing is for bush beans and spinach. A 6-inch spacing is needed for Swiss chard, leaf lettuce, and parsley. A whole 12-inch square is required for each broccoli, cabbage, cauliflower, corn, eggplant, muskmelon, and pepper plant.

onions, can be planted with only 3 inches between them. So for them a square is divided into fourths in each direction so there are 16 little plant spaces, each holding a plant in the center. Vining crops are planted in front of a vertical frame, and spacing for these crops is also based on a 12-inch measure.

The easiest way to divide your planting squares is simply to draw a line in the soil with a stick or your finger. You can estimate halves, thirds, or fourths without even measuring. Once you draw the lines it's easy then

This photo shows a newly planted 4-foot by 4-foot block. The four squares in the front right contain a single eggplant surrounded by romaine lettuce plants. The four squares in the front left hold one pepper plant each. Behind them is a bush tomato plant surrounded by more lettuce, and next to that the author is planting four squares of bush beans.

to place one seed or plant right in the center of each little space you've made.

As soon as your 4-foot by 4-foot garden block is located and the soil prepared as described in chapter 5, divide that up into individual 12-inch squares using string or stakes, or by drawing lines in the soil. Then concentrate on each individual square, deciding what you want to plant in that square and then subdividing it into individual planting spaces according to the vegetable to be planted there. Of course, the larger plants are easiest since only one grows in each square. All you have to remember is to keep the taller plants to the north side of your block, and to form a shallow dish in the soil around the plant to make watering easier. The 4- and 9-plant squares are also easy to divide and plant. The only square that becomes a little tedious is the 16-space one. Some gardeners find that rather than divide the square into fourths each way to create the 16 spaces, it's just as easy and much quicker merely to divide it into halves each way to make only 4 spaces, and then to poke 4 holes in each of the little spaces, estimating their distances apart. This is readily done with two fingers; you just poke 4 holes in each quarter and end up with a total of 16 holes in the square. These can then be used for seed holes or guides to plant spacing.

Of course, one of the nice things about drawing lines in the soil with a stick or your finger is that if you make a mistake, or it doesn't look right, you can just erase the whole thing by smoothing over the soil and starting all over again. No one will be the wiser.

Sometimes you may want to increase the size of the harvest by planting several squares of the same crop all at once. For example, for a family-size garden, you might want to plant four squares adjacent to one another with a single crop. That means each vegetable will fill a 2-foot by 2-foot area, and each 4-foot by 4-foot garden block would then contain 4 different vegetables instead of the usual 16. This is the type of garden I have, and it is shown on the cover of this book and in many of the photographs. If you want an even bigger harvest because you have a big family or you want to can or freeze the crop, you can plant an entire block in one vegetable.

Spacing for Large Varieties

There's one other type of spacing that might be required in the main garden, and that would be for a distance of 18 inches between plants. Some varieties of eggplant, cabbage, and peppers grow extra large and bushy, so that they need the extra spacing for maximum production. In general,

I would recommend avoiding those large varieties because they are not the most productive for the small garden. Many experts would argue that a plant will produce its maximum harvest when given extra space all around. That is true, but it will not produce the maximum harvest per square foot of ground space. It will only produce the maximum harvest per plant. I believe it is better to space your plants closer together so that there are more plants in the same space. You may get slightly less harvest from each plant, but the total harvest will be much more for the same amount of garden space.

I've tested and grown many different vegetables and flowers in many different spacing arrangements, and the distances recommended in this book were found to be close enough so there's no wasted space, yet not too close so as to cause problems. With this in mind it's better to choose

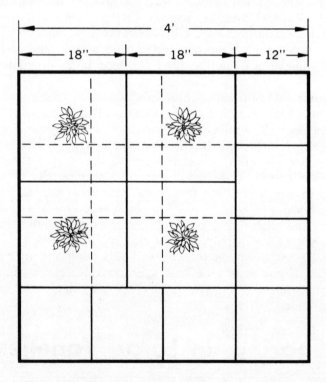

To determine 18-inch spacing for large varieties, first divide a 4-foot block in fourths each way. Erase the lines as shown by the dotted lines in the illustration and divide the remaining space into fourths. The seven squares remaining around the edges of the block can be planted with normal-size crops.

the smaller-growing varieties of each vegetable whenever you have a choice. For example, buy a Jersey or Acre variety of cabbage rather than a Danish variety, which gets so huge that it will crowd out everything within 2 feet of each plant. Using the larger variety doesn't make sense in a condensed garden. In addition, except for taking photos for the family album of Papa with a prizewinning harvest, these huge heads of cabbage are really too large for most families to use up. It would be much better to grow four smaller heads in the same space, produce a staggered harvest, and have garden-fresh vegetables over a longer period.

For gardeners who do want an 18-inch spacing for large varieties, here's how to mark it off in the garden. First, divide your block into fourths each way, creating 16 small spaces. Next, erase those lines as shown in the illustration. Then divide that new space (actually 3 feet by 3 feet) in half each way. Finally, plant one plant in the center of each of the new larger spaces (18 inches by 18 inches). This procedure takes a lot less measuring and thinking than if you tried to use a ruler and started figuring 9 inches in from the corner of the block, and so on. Of course, if you want an entire 4-foot by 4-foot block in large plants, and are willing to settle for a 16-inch spacing rather than the 18 inches previously mentioned, you can easily divide a full block into thirds each way. This would give you 3 16-inch squares along each 48-inch side, or a total of 9 plant spaces, each measuring 16 inches by 16 inches.

As you can see, then, plant spacing is very simple, even when you get away from the standard 12-inch square. But if you stick with the 12-inch spacing and just mark off each square into halves, thirds, or fourths, you've got the whole system covered.

Spacing for Extra-Large Crops

I notice that whenever I give a lecture there are several people in the audience just bursting with the question, "But what about zucchini?" Everyone is ready to accept carrots, lettuce, and even peppers in the square foot system, but they want to know how to still have zucchini and practice this method. Well, there's no other way than to assign almost an entire 4-foot by 4-foot block to each zucchini squash plant. First decide if you really want zucchini. There are other tasty summer squashes that grow as vines and can be grown vertically. If you decide you must have it in your garden, prepare a block and use it primarily for zucchini. It will take up a good portion of that entire block because it needs a 3-foot spacing. You can plant a few other smaller crops around the edges of the block. In fact, you can make good use of most of the space in the entire block for an early crop because the zucchini seeds can't be planted until after the last frost has passed and the soil has warmed up a good bit.

The other crop that takes a large amount of ground space is corn. Many gardeners think that you need a huge garden to grow corn, with row after row. It's true that corn does take up a lot of space, but actually block planting of corn is the surest way to get a good harvest. It is conventionally planted in rows with 12 inches between plants and 3 feet between rows. You don't really need that extra room between the rows; corn is much better off planted in the square with the plants 12 inches apart in both

Zucchini needs 3 feet of space to grow properly, but it will thrive like any other crop in the square foot garden. The seven squares remaining around the edges of the 4-foot by 4-foot block can be planted with other crops.

directions. This arrangement encourages better pollination, and a condensed block is so much easier than long rows to protect from the birds, raccoons, deer, and squirrels. You can select a short-growing, early-season variety that can be spaced about 8 inches apart (a total of 36 plants per block), or some of the taller, later-season varieties that require 12 inches between plants (a total of 16 plants per block). Whichever type you choose, don't plant too much of the same variety at the same time or you will end up with a big harvest all at once. Plant no more than one-half to a full block of any one variety at a time, then wait two weeks before planting another block (assuming you want two or more blocks of corn). The other way to produce a staggered harvest is to plant both an early- and a late-maturing variety at the same time.

Spacing for Vertical Crops

The last plant spacing you should know about is for vertical growing. Most of the details of vertical growing are covered in chapter 8, but you should know that you'll be planting in a straight line along your vertical frames. If the vertical frame is part of your garden block the soil will already be prepared and the spaces already divided up into 12-inch squares. However, if you're putting up frames for just vertical growing in a different part of your yard, an ideal way to provide the best growing soil is to use what I call the trench method. Dig a 12-inch-wide by 12-inch-deep trench along the entire length of any vertical support. Fill this trench with the best soil mixture you can make (lots of manure, peat moss, topsoil, and vermiculite). When the trench is almost full (leave a 2-inch depression for an easy way to water), just mark off 12-inch squares along its length, then plant according to the spacing charts provided for each crop in chapter 18.

Some Basic Planting Tips

I've tried to develop some new planting methods that will insure success, or at least make it as easy as possible for the plants to grow. Most garden advice is geared toward the gardener's ease and comfort. That's okay, but if what's convenient for the gardener is not best for the plants and the plants then have to struggle (like in a too-thickly-planted row), they won't grow well and the gardener will be disappointed and discouraged. So my method approaches gardening with the thought that healthy, productive plants are the desired result, and every procedure is

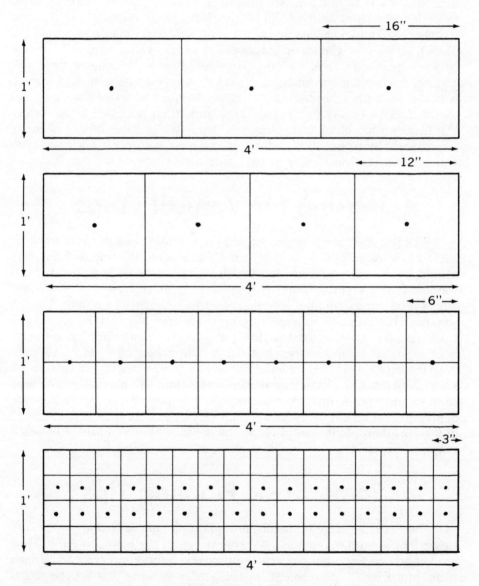

Vertical crops are spaced as shown here: vining summer squash is planted 16 inches apart in the 1-foot by 4-foot trench; tomatoes are planted one to a 12-inch square; cucumbers go in at two plants per square; and pole beans and peas are planted eight to a square.

directed toward achieving that goal. Later chapters of this book will explain in detail how to plant seeds indoors and outdoors, and how to transplant into the garden, as well as how to give each plant the ideal conditions and protection it needs to thrive. My purpose here is just to give you a general introduction into those methods.

Seeds need warmth and moisture to sprout. Once sprouted they need as little competition from other seeds and weeds as possible. In the square foot garden you plant just one seed in each hole, spaced according to the needs of the mature plants so you don't have to move or thin them. The holes are poked into the soft, rich soil with your finger. To help keep the soil moist at all times while the seed is sprouting, you're going to pour a little vermiculite in each hole, then place the seed, and cover it with more vermiculite.

Newly planted squares are sprayed daily with a fine mist of water so the soil never dries out. If even just the top 2 inches of soil dries out, the sprouting seed will die before it pokes its head up above the surface. Depending on the season, you might provide a cover to protect the young plants from drying winds, torrential rains, or hungry rabbits. When the plants are growing nicely, the cover is taken off and once-weekly waterings are usually enough. If you planted only one seed in each hole no thinning is ever required. You may want to replace any seeds that didn't sprout, or just leave a few blank spots here and there. If you can't bring yourself to put just one seed in each hole and have planted two or three, you must go back and snip off the extra plant with a scissors. Do this after the plants are up and large enough to identify. Don't try to transplant the extra plant —it will only disturb the good one.

If you're transplanting store-bought or homegrown plants into the garden the spacing is exactly the same, and the procedure is similar. Prepare your soil, then divide your square according to the crop and put each plant in its assigned space. Set it a little lower than the surrounding soil so you can form a small depression in the soil around the plant, to retain water. Then water with sun-warmed water from a bucket, and cover the square with a wire cage covered with shade material. The shade material will keep out most of the wind and rain, but will also protect the new plant from wilting in the hot sun. Water daily at first, then after a few days the cover can come off and you can start weekly watering.

In a nutshell, then, that's how to space and plant your square foot garden. The same procedures are used whether you're planting vegetables, herbs, or flowers. Seeds and plants are treated quite similarly. It also doesn't matter whether we're talking about vertically grown vine crops or large or small plants. The same spacing and planting procedures apply to all.

◈ Chapter 8
Vertical Growing

An integral part of the square foot method is vertical growing for all the vine crops. Although they take up the largest growing space, these are among the most popular of all vegetables. Who would have a garden without tomatoes, cucumbers, squash, and pole beans? Lots of people who don't even consider themselves gardeners still raise a few tomato plants every year.

Although many gardeners stake up a few tomatoes and cucumbers every year, I'd like to introduce to you a new concept for the modern garden. That is to grow all vining crops on a system of vertical supports that keeps the amount of ground space required to an absolute minimum. Although this chapter will be of special interest to gardeners who are short of space or have poor growing soil, it can and should become an integral part of every intensive or condensed garden. After all, the purpose of all intensive gardening systems is to grow more food in less space. Vertical gardening tremendously increases the space savings possible. It doesn't make sense to grow your carrots and lettuce in tightly condensed spaces to conserve room, but then to let your tomatoes and winter squash sprawl all over the yard. Get them up in the air and you'll eliminate so much of the difficult and strenuous work of preparing and maintaining a large garden space.

Vertical frames can be set up apart from the main garden in a variety of arrangements to screen off an area of property, or just for a uniquely pleasant place to sit or stroll on a warm evening.

Here's how vertical growing saves space. Just one vine-type (indeterminate) tomato plant allowed to sprawl untrained on the ground would take up an area of at least 4 feet by 5 feet, or 20 square feet. But the same plant if pruned to a single stem and trained up a vertical support would take up only 1 square foot of ground space. Now it is true that the sprawling plant will produce more pounds of fruit than the pruned vertical one, but when measuring the pounds of harvest per square foot of garden space used, the vertically grown plant comes out way ahead. In fact, in tests performed at Cornell University, the actual yield per square foot was consistently twice as much when plants were grown vertically.

Detailed information on building vertical supports can be found in chapter 9, but basically they are just tall frames having straight legs connected by horizontal top bars from which string or netting is hung. Most of the plants grow right up the strings or netting, sometimes needing a little help from the gardener. Tomato plants must be trained, but can be tied, clipped or simply twisted around the string as they grow, or pulled in and out of the netting. To make the frames tall enough for a full season's growth (at least 6 feet), and sturdy enough to support the weight of the mature plants, it is necessary to use strong material. Half-inch-diameter metal pipe works best for me. Vertical growing can also be done on fencing if the mesh openings are large enough, the fence is tall enough, and the posts are strong enough.

The reasons for vertical gardening are many and varied. They include the use of far less garden space, increased yields, improved harvests, easier soil preparation, and simplified watering methods. In addition, a vertical garden is extremely attractive and enhances the appearance of any yard or home. By midsummer you'll have a virtual living wall of greenery. This wall can be used to screen unsightly areas of the property, to give privacy to the yard, or as a backdrop or border to the main garden.

Just about any vegetable or flower that produces a vine or rambling stem can be grown vertically, including vegetables such as tomatoes, cucumbers, pole beans, peas, all melons, New Zealand spinach, most summer squash, and all winter squash; and flowers and fruit including clematis, roses, grapes, thumbellina, gourds, and morning glories. Many of these plants will climb all by themselves, grasping the support with their twisting tendrils. Others need to be attached to the strings, but you'll find more information about that under the descriptions of some individual plants provided later in this chapter.

Most experts will agree that you'll get a better harvest when the plant is up off the ground and the leaves are more exposed to sunlight and circulating air. Disease is less likely to occur, and pest damage is virtually eliminated because it will be immediately visible. Gardening chores are also a lot easier on the poor, tired gardener who doesn't have to bend over anymore to work on his or her plants or to harvest. Almost everything is done standing up, which also makes it easier to spot the ripening fruit so none is missed. Prompt harvesting is important for tomatoes, but almost critical for cucumbers and beans. If you let cucumbers grow to full size, the flesh becomes pithy and the seeds mature, telling the plant to shut down production for the year. Once this happens it takes a while for the plant to start producing new cucumbers again, even after the large fruit is picked. The same is true of beans and summer squash.

Insect control is greatly improved in the vertical garden because, first of all, when the bugs are at eye level and a foot in front of your nose you can't miss them. Knowing the pests are there at an early stage before they

When fully grown, vertical crops form a lush, green "living wall." Fruits like these cantaloupes are easy to pick when they're at eye level.

do too much damage and multiply into a horde is one of the secrets of successful pest control.

Of the three materials that can be used to support the vines, string is the least expensive and my favorite; netting is the most versatile and probably easiest for most people to use; but metal fencing seems the most durable and permanent, is usually more readily available, and is easiest to put up, especially for larger gardens. You'll see all the differences, the advantages and disadvantages of each as this discussion progresses, and you will be able to decide which is best for you.

While we're still talking in general about vertical growing and various supports, I should add that both staking and caging plants to support them must also be considered part of vertical growing. They both accomplish the same end, getting the plant up off the ground, but in different ways. For lower-growing crops, caging is a good alternative to vertical frames, but it does take up much more room. The yield per square foot is close to that obtained with vertical string and nets, but it's difficult to find adequate supports that are tall or strong enough. The tallest commercial cage on the market is just barely 4 feet tall, and in most parts of the country tomatoes and certainly cucumbers will outgrow that cage by midseason; the tops will hang over, bend, and finally break. In addition, almost all cages must also be staked down to keep them from tipping over later in the season. If you do buy cages, make sure you get the tallest ones available. Some gardeners construct their own cages out of heavy-duty concrete reinforcing wire, or hog fencing wire. Although both are tall enough and strong enough when staked down, they aren't easily obtained, are difficult to cut, and are usually too expensive for the average gardener. In addition, the reinforcing wire tends to turn rusty and unsightly.

As for wood stakes, I may offend a lot of old-timers but I can't for the life of me see why anyone would still use them. Wood stakes break and split when they are hammered into the ground, are never tall enough, warp and rot, and break under a late season's load. In addition, it's a difficult and time-consuming chore to tie a plant to a stake. Compared to vertical string or mesh growing, staking is an antiquated system that should not be perpetuated or even tolerated in today's gardens. It might have been adequate long ago when we had no other choice but to cut tree saplings out of the woods, but in my opinion gardeners would be well advised to switch to the cage or vertical frame method of supporting all vertical crops. For all those old-timers or expert gardeners who tell me, "I've been using stakes all my life and think they're great," I say, "It takes a very experienced person with an awful lot of time to be successful at growing plants on stakes."

My strong feelings about stakes come, in part, from my experiences in our local community garden, where I watched so many gardeners (both new and experienced) fail at growing tomatoes.

As I described in chapter 1, staking just didn't work well for most of my fellow gardeners. I was determined then to find a simple, easy, foolproof way for most people to grow tomatoes. I bought every conceivable contraption and device on the market for growing and supporting tomatoes. The demonstration plot in our community garden looked like a trade show. And you know what? Every single support failed. In addition to all the commercial products available, I tried all of the homemade methods written up in all the garden magazines I could find. Some were good, but not really suited to the needs of the average gardener. So the next step was to design that simple, foolproof system myself. I knew it had to be tall, sturdy, readily obtained, simple to construct, long lasting and easy to use. In addition, I wanted a space-saving device, so that ruled out the tripod or A-frame-type support. They are sturdy but take up too much room.

After experimenting with many shapes, sizes, and materials, it became apparent that two steel posts (either fence posts or pipe) should support a steel top bar. From this basic frame, string, netting, or fencing could be hung, and the tomatoes and other crops could grow right up through this sturdy support. It didn't sag, bend, or topple over at the season's end. In short, it proved ideal, and all the construction details are in chapter 9. The vertical frame is so far superior to old-fashioned stakes, there's no question in my mind as to its utility.

After I found that the frame solved our problems with tomatoes, I began to experiment with growing other vine crops on the same type of support, and found they do splendidly well, even melons and winter squash. I started to work on refining all the growing techniques for each crop, and realized that using vertical frames made easier work of both soil preparation and watering. Vertical growing using the frames proved to be extremely well suited for gardeners with poor growing soil. The reason is that the plants are not only condensed in a small area, but are also in a straight line. If one or any number of vertical frames are set up in a straight line the plants will also be planted in that same line, and soil preparation becomes very easy. In fact, I've developed a "trench" method just for planting vertical crops. Here's how it works.

The Trench Method

If the plants are going to be closely spaced along a vertical frame, the only ground you have to prepare is right in front of it. First, dig out a trench 12 inches wide by 12 inches deep, and 4 feet long. If the soil is poor, scatter it around some other area. Then loosen the soil in the bottom of the trench, and fill that trench with a 6-inch layer of well-rotted animal manure. Remember as you work not to step in the trench. On top of the manure, add 4 inches of your best growing soil. Make sure it contains plenty of humus, correct it for pH balance, and add fertilizer as described in chapter 5. You'll now have 4 inches of good growing soil in which to plant, a good layer of manure for the roots to grow down through, and a slight depression in the trench to hold water and future fertilizer. Watering will be efficient because every drop will stay in the trench and soak right down to the roots.

If you have really bad soil there are two other ways to proceed. You can, of course, just stay with the 12-inch by 12-inch trench. The roots will probably stay confined mostly in that trench, but they will be easy to water and feed. Or you can enlarge the trench sideways, and improve the surrounding soil so the roots can spread out and grow toward the rest of your garden soil. If you have hardpan, a rock ledge, less than 4 inches of topsoil, or some similar condition, you can build a raised planter box over your trench and fill it with good soil. Just nail some 1 by 12 boards into a long, bottomless, planter-shaped box to cover your trench. When it's filled with good soil, the plant roots will be able to grow down through it and can extend into the surrounding areas. If you have access to only a limited amount of humus and manure, say one wheelbarrow full, it will go much further to improve your soil if you use the trench method than if you were to add it to a large conventional garden.

Watering is one of the keys to successful growing of tomatoes and vine crops, and your depressed trench will make it almost foolproof. These vining, fruit-bearing plants like a regular but not frequent deep watering, about once a week. It takes several hours for water to soak down to a depth of 18 inches in many soils. As a result, most gardeners don't water long enough to do much good; they merely wet down the top 6 inches of soil. This is okay for lettuce, radishes, and other shallow-rooted crops, but it forces tomatoes to send their roots to the surface soil, where they can dry out more quickly than normal.

The trench method will allow a lot of water to remain in one area long enough for a deep soaking, and you'll really see great results from your plants. By containing all of the water in the trench, you also keep the surrounding area dry, resulting in nonmuddy walking paths and clean shoes. But most important, no moisture will be in the surrounding area to encourage weed seeds to sprout and grow. Water fans out as it drains down through the soil. Although it will cover only 12 inches at the surface of the trench, it will spread out over an area of 2 feet at a depth of 12

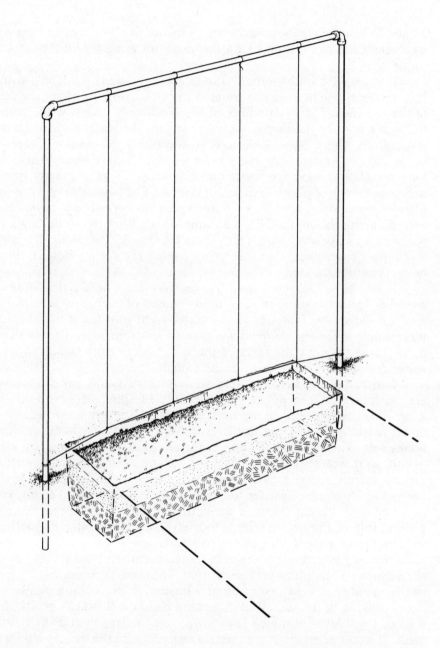

Vertical crops should all be planted in a trench 1 foot wide, 1 foot deep, and 4 feet long. The trench is filled with well-aged manure and good growing soil. The vertical frame is 6 feet tall and 5 feet wide.

inches. When the water soaks down 18 inches, it will cover an area 4 feet wide, certainly plenty to insure a thorough watering for all those tomato roots.

If you have a lot of vertical frames arranged side by side in a straight line, probably the best way to water is to run a drip hose along the center of the trenches. Then you will need to go out only once a week, connect the water hose to the drip hose, and turn on the water for one, two, or three hours. Dig a small hole next to the trench to see how deeply the water has penetrated after every hour and you'll have some idea of how long you should leave the water on each week. There are many types of drip hoses made of plastic, rubber, or canvas. The basic idea of a drip hose is to let just a small amount of water under low pressure drip out of the hose all along its length. That's accomplished either by producing a porous-wall hose or one with many small holes drilled along its length. Remember to provide warm water by coiling the supply hose in the sun before you use it.

If you have just one or two frames, you don't need a drip hose. Fill a bucket and let it stand in the sun at the end of each trench to take the chill off the water. Don't pour the water right into the trench or you'll wash a hole in the soil. Instead, lay down a short board, a piece of plastic, or anything to break the force of the water. Pour onto that, and let the water run off the sides and into the trench.

Fertilizing also becomes very simple for vertically grown plants. If you wish to give your plants a supplemental feeding, all you need to do is sprinkle the fertilizer on top of the trench. Then any watering, natural or artificial, will carry the fertilizer down to the roots. Most gardening books recommend that you scratch the fertilizer into the top few inches of soil, so it won't wash away from the plants. But it's a habit that can disturb surface roots. If you always plant in a slight depression both in your main square foot garden and your trenches for vertical crops, you'll never have to do that. Most of the vertical crops are heavy feeders. As a general rule of thumb, I recommend fertilizing them once a month and watering once a week for peak production.

Weeding your vertical crops is a snap because your trench is readily accessible and occupies a very small area. The areas surrounding the frame can be planted in grass, or covered with mulch or walking planks.

Speaking of mulch, all of your vine plants will benefit greatly from a good, thick layer of mulch laid down over the trench and surrounding areas. It won't affect watering even though it covers the trench. You'll still have a slight depression to trap the water. The mulch will conserve ground moisture as well as help to moderate soil temperatures. It's best to wait about a month after you plant before laying down your mulch, so the sun can thoroughly warm the soil for all of those heat-loving vine crops.

In fact, another good practice is to place a tunnel made of wire-reinforced clear plastic or plastic stretched on a wire frame over the trench in spring, before and after planting your crop. It will trap a lot of heat in the soil and get your plants off to a good start. Just watch out for weeds, which will also grow very fast under the plastic. Don't use black plastic; it's been finally proven that the soil temperature under black plastic is *not* raised as previously thought. Only clear plastic can raise the soil temperature; black plastic will create a lot of heat but it's stored in the plastic itself, not underneath. This heat then radiates upward at night, thereby warming the plants, but not their roots. Black plastic is often recommended for mulching all of the summer vine crops, but I don't like the look of it in the garden so I never use it. It's a matter of personal choice. You'll be so far ahead of your neighbors using the vertical method, you won't need black plastic to help you.

At this point you might be wondering if vertical gardening takes more or less maintenance time than growing the plants on cages or just letting them sprawl. In general, it's much quicker than letting plants sprawl, especially when you consider all the work needed to prepare, weed, and water the large area for the plants to roam over. But vertical growing takes about the same amount of labor time as supporting plants with cages. It really doesn't take much longer to prune off the side branches or suckers of tomatoes, and twist the top along the string or thrust it through the netting, than it does to poke the top into a cage. Of course, for climbing vines like beans and cucumbers, there's really no work to do once either the frame or cage is up, so that's a standoff.

A Vertical Garden for Patios

An interesting variation of the vertical frame is the patio planter. Many gardeners don't have room for a lot of the vine-type crops in their gardens. In fact, a lot of people don't have either a garden or a yard but would like to grow a few tomato and cucumber plants. Container or pot growing is fine up to a certain point, but it is difficult to grow and support any of the tall vining plants in standard pots.

For gardeners who would like not only an unusual but also a very attractive and functional vertical frame for the patio or rooftop, or for that matter, anywhere around the house or yard, I've designed the patio model. It is a simple 1-foot by 4-foot wood planter box with a vertical frame bolted to one side. It is lightweight, yet tall enough for most plants. In addition, it is portable so you can move it about. Directions for building a patio frame can be found in chapter 9.

I like the patio-model vertical garden because it looks good and is so much easier to take care of than individual pots or containers. Since the frame will hold four tomato plants or eight cucumber plants, your watering and fertilizing chores are concentrated into one small area.

As with any type of container growing, you should use special soil in the patio garden. Never use plain garden soil. It is not porous enough for container growing—it cannot hold enough moisture and it packs down too much. Instead, make a mix of one pail each of coarse vermiculite, peat moss, sifted compost, and good topsoil, and a cup of lime, two cups of fertilizer, and a half pail of charcoal from a fireplace or the kind sold for use in fish tanks or terrariums (don't use charcoal briquettes—they are treated with chemicals that are harmful to plants). It is very important to have a soil that drains well yet still holds enough moisture for the plants' constant use. See chapter 5 for a discussion of soil structure.

Since the soil in a shallow planter box dries out much more quickly than garden soil, you must water more often. Twice a week will usually be sufficient, but during very hot spells and especially when the plants get tall and mature, you might have to water every other day. Because you are using a soil mix with exceptionally good drainage, you will not be likely to overwater.

Because of the extra waterings and the fact that the plants' roots are confined in a small space, you should also fertilize the patio garden twice as often as you do the main garden. I usually apply about a cup of basic fertilizer mix (see chapter 5) every two weeks.

Mulching is even more advantageous in the patio frame than in the garden. Any kind of mulch that looks nice will help keep the soil at a more uniform temperature and prevent the soil moisture from evaporating so quickly. If you mulch with pieces of carpet or black plastic, just lift them up to spread the fertilizer and to check occasionally for crawling pests. One advantage of mulching with carpet is that you can water right on top and the water will soak through at an even, uniform rate. Remember to always water with warm water, as you do in the regular garden. That way, the plants can immediately start to use the nutrients that get dissolved in the water.

Plants can be spaced 12 inches apart in the patio garden if you're going to prune to a single stem, or 24 inches apart if you're going to let one or two side branches develop. I personally prefer pruning most plants back to a single stem because it means the plant's entire root system supports just one vine (making for vigorous growth). Also, since plants are more confined, several varieties can be grown in one planter box and if one plant goes bad (due to disease, pests, or accidents) you still have several others.

For example, an interesting patio garden might be planted with two different tomato plants (such as Sweet 100 and Jet Star) in the first two squares, two cucumber plants (either China or Straight Eight) in the next square, and eight pole beans (Kentucky Wonder) in the last square.

Pruning Vertical Crops

What to do when your plants climb to the top of their support is always a problem. You can let them grow until they bend over and hang down, or you can cut off the tops of the plants. Don't try to extend the frame; it will not be as stable. Four feet is about the optimum height for the patio vertical frame and 6 feet for the garden type. By going taller you just increase the chance that the whole structure will collapse or blow over in a storm. It is better to prune off the plant tops. Don't worry; you won't hurt the plant. It will continue ripening the fruit already set. In addition, pruning will force the growth of new side branches or suckers all along the main stem.

After the plants have reached the top of the frame and you've cut back the tops, you can select one or two low suckers and let them grow (assuming you want more growth from the plant). If it is late in the season —September or October—it might be better to keep all side branches cut off so each plant puts all its energy into ripening the fruit it has already set. When frost comes, all those little half-grown tomatoes won't be of much use except for pickling.

Gardeners who want to extend the growing and harvest season past the first fall frost can easily do so with the vertical frames. It's very easy to drape plastic or tarps over the tops of the frames any night that frost threatens. Or, to provide more long-term protection without having to fuss each night with putting the covers on and then remembering to take them off the next morning, try the tunnel method detailed in chapter 15. Simply cut all the strings and carefully lay the vines down in a straight line on a bed of clean mulch. Then cover the entire arrangement with a wire-reinforced plastic ("instant greenhouse") tunnel. The vines will stay alive through several frosts, allowing the fruit to continue ripening longer into the fall.

Training Plants to Grow Vertically

Tomatoes

Tomatoes are America's favorite homegrown vegetable, and with good reason. Tomatoes are very productive, easy to grow, do well in all climates and locations, and can produce a good crop with surprisingly little attention. How to improve on the performance and harvest of tomatoes is the most sought-after gardening secret.

I've often wondered, since we have rose societies, why no one has started a tomato club or society with chapters across the country. It would certainly attract a lot of attention, and enthusiastic members. Tomatoes are a popular subject for gardening magazines, and lots of articles, tips, and information are published about tomatoes every year.

Although all tomatoes are warm-weather or summer growers, there are two basic types of plants—bush types and vining types. The bush varieties are called determinate. Each stem produces a flower cluster at the end and stops growing, so these plants do not grow very tall. Being short and fairly self-supporting, they seldom need staking or trellising. Most patio tomatoes and many of the early-fruiting varieties are determinate. The majority of the popular tomato varieties, however, are of the vining or indeterminate type. These grow in a long central vine with side branches forming additional vines. All the branches continue to grow, bloom, and bear fruit until frost kills the plant. When properly supported and grown, a tomato vine can grow as high as 20 feet in a single season! However, most plants will produce a nice crop for the home grower during the normal summer growing season while reaching a height of 6 to 7 feet.

Indeterminate tomato varieties can be grown vertically if you pinch out the side-shoots and train the long, central stem to climb a string or trellis. Once you understand how they grow, you'll see the logic of eliminating the side branches ("suckers"), and you'll know what to expect from your plant.

The main or central stem grows straight up. Every 3 inches or so, a "leaf stem" grows out—first on one side, then 3 inches farther up on the opposite side, and so on. About every 9 inches, a "fruit stem" (which eventually bears the tomatoes) also grows out of the central stem. Keep in mind that the leaf stem doesn't have any flowers or fruit, and the fruit stem doesn't have any leaves (except in some unusual varieties).

So far, so good. But now, to confuse the issue (and the home gardener), another stem appears—the side stem or branch. It grows out of the main stem in the "V" or crotch where the leaf stem first appeared. If

To train tomatoes, twist the main stem around the string once a week. Pinch out the suckers that form in the leaf axils. If left unpruned, each sucker will grow into a whole new vine.

allowed to grow, this side branch—or "sucker," as it is commonly called —will become a whole new vine with its own leaf and fruit stems. When using the vertical method, you must pinch out these side branches when they're just starting to grow (1 to 4 inches long). Even if you miss some and they have extra time to grow bigger (up to 18 inches long), you can still cut them off without hurting the parent plant. In fact, you can root any large side branch in moist sand, vermiculite, or just plain water. In two weeks it will have sprouted roots, and you'll have a new tomato plant!

Pinching off these side branches serves two purposes. It creates a single central vine which is easily supported by a string—just right for the vertical method. It also channels the plant's energy along a single path. Try to visualize the plant's energy coming up from the roots. You can see that if all the side branches were allowed to grow, much of this energy would go off in many directions, leaving less for the fruit stems on the central vine. If, on the other hand, all of the plant's energy is allowed to go up the main stem, nutrients will reach the fruiting branches faster and in greater amounts. As an experiment, you might want to try growing one crop this way and another crop your usual way, then compare the results. Of course, when you pinch off the side branches you lose the potential fruit of those branches, but you'll have bigger, juicier, and earlier tomatoes on that central stem—up to two weeks earlier!

Twisting the growing plant around its string is the easiest part of the vertical method to accomplish, but the hardest to explain—it's like trying to explain how to blow up a balloon or how to kiss. Your strings are tied tightly from the top pipe down to the horizontal string at the bottom of the frame. As the plants grow upward, you just twist the top of each plant gently around its string. At first, you'll be afraid of breaking the plant, so do it very slowly and carefully. After you get the hang of it, the twisting and pinching will only take a few minutes once a week (about one minute per plant).

Cucumbers

All cucumber varieties are ideally suited to vertical growing. They climb all by themselves, bear lots of fruit, and can be pruned to a single stem or allowed to develop all their side branches. Usually just one or two plants of two or three different varieties are enough for most families since the vines are so prolific. Many gardeners are in the habit of planting at least a dozen seeds of two or three varieties each year. That many plants produce so many cucumbers, it's nearly impossible to keep up with the harvest. The result is that many are left on the vine to grow too large, and the plant starts to shut down production for the year as soon as its seeds become mature enough. Gradually the vines stop producing fruits and the harvest tapers off, ironically causing gardeners to think they underplanted.

In order to keep a cucumber plant within bounds, a good compromise method of pruning would be to train the central stem up the string and pinch back the side branches so they remain about 12 to 15 inches long.

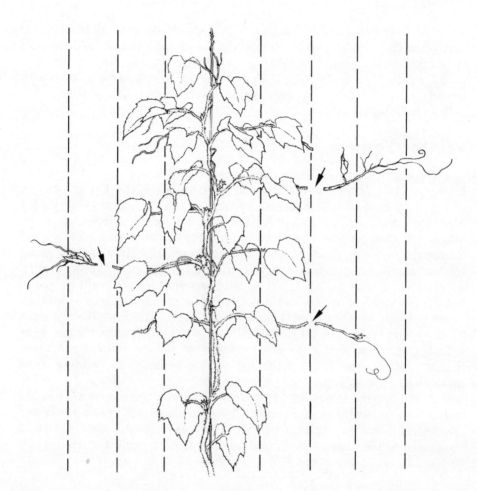

Pinch back the side branches of cucumber vines so they are not more than 12 to 15 inches long.

Summer Squash

Summer squash varieties that vine, such as yellow straightneck, will climb right up the vertical supports with just a little help. You can tie the plant at 1-foot intervals or merely twist the stem carefully around the string just like you do for tomatoes. The vine will usually stay in a single stem; if it does produce branches, just cut them back after they get to be about 6 to 12 inches long.

One interesting thing I've discovered about summer squash vines is that when they are allowed to sprawl on the ground, the fruits form only at the end of the vine. But when grown vertically, the vine continually produces blossoms and fruits all along its entire length. This gives you an abundant harvest in a very small space—and all of it straight up so it's easy to see and pick.

Winter Squash

Here's a vegetable that many people would like to grow but just don't have room for. Vertical gardening will solve that problem. I've grown just about every kind of winter squash vertically, and they all do very well. I was amazed to find that except for the huge Hubbard varieties, all of the others will grow without any extra support for the fruit. When I first tried Butternut, my family and neighbors were skeptical. "How are you going to support the squash when they form?" they wanted to know. I must admit, I certainly had all kinds of supports ready—mesh slings, panty hose, poles with horizontal platforms nailed on to hold the fruit—but they never got put up. The plants didn't need them. It seems that as each blossom faded and the fruit formed, the stem holding it grew bigger as the squash itself grew bigger. The end result was that no extra support was needed. All the fruit hung there just as nice as could be, waiting to be harvested at season's end. Most winter squashes ramble a lot and get quite heavy, and I found it was easier to grow them on large-mesh wire fencing rather than vertical strings. Plant in a 1-foot-wide trench, spacing only one plant every 4 feet for the large varieties (such as Hubbard, Butternut, and Spaghetti), while the smaller varieties (such as Acorn and Buttercup) can be placed two plants every 4 feet, or every 24 inches apart. ▸

Pole Beans

These long-time favorites hardly need any introduction—just plant them and stand back! Spacing is fairly close; I like to plant a double row of seeds 3 inches apart in each square for the most productive crop. I'd like to give you two bits of advice at the start. First, soak your seeds for one to four hours in tepid water before planting (but no longer than four hours, as they have a tendency to swell so big they split or decay in the water). This gets them off to a good, quick start once they're put into the ground. The second bit of advice is to protect those newly planted seeds from curious birds and hungry rabbits. Birds love to come and peck out the sprouting seeds (they like corn, too) and the rabbits don't even say thank you as they chomp all the tender leaves down to stumps. So—cover

Cucumbers thrive when grown vertically. As the plants grow, twist the main stems around the strings and frame supports. The China cucumbers shown here do especially well in this method, because their long, slender fruits can grow unobstructed and will be nice and straight.

your planting with a piece of 1-inch chicken wire formed into a tunnel at least 6 inches high. The plants will grow right through it with no harm done if you forget to remove it in time.

Remember that pole beans produce their harvest over a longer period of time than bush beans. In fact, did you know that bush beans were actually developed for commercial growers who wanted a plant that would mature all at once so machinery could go down the rows cutting off the plants and harvesting all the same size beans? Lots of gardeners (and I'm one of them) are convinced that a lot of flavor was lost in the process and that pole beans are way ahead of bush beans in crispness and taste.

Cantaloupes and Other Muskmelons

If you are confused because some books refer to cantaloupes as cantaloupes and some call them muskmelons, don't fret. Technically, cantaloupes are just one type of muskmelon; honeydews are another.

All of the muskmelons can be grown vertically without any special support for the fruit. One danger, though, comes when you don't harvest the fruit in time. A melon is said to be ripe when it slips easily off the stem. The usual method of harvesting is to give a slight pull or twist to each large melon—those that come off easily are ready. If a ripe melon isn't picked soon enough it will fall to the ground. Needless to say, that could be somewhat of a problem when you're growing melons 4, 5, and 6 feet off the ground. It would be prudent to spread a thick layer of straw on the ground so that any overripe melons don't bounce too high when they fall. Or you might want to support the fruit with a sling of cloth or netting.

Chapter 9
❧ Structures to Build

Gardening—like any other activity—can be a lot easier and more enjoyable if you have the right tools and equipment. Aside from the very few tools you will need for the square foot garden as described in chapter 4, there are some easy-to-build structures that will greatly enhance your chances of success and help you to save space, as well as lightening your gardening chores.

Plant Protection Cages

The first type of structures I'm going to suggest are simple devices that protect plants from the ravages of animals, insects, and adverse weather conditions. They are portable, easy to use, and adaptable for multiple reuse throughout the growing season. Keeping in mind that any accessory should be simple, easy to build, and as inexpensive as possible, these plant protectors fill the bill.

Basically they are three-sided wire mesh "cages" made from common fencing wire, to be placed over a particular garden square to support various protective coverings. There are four different protective cages, each with its own special uses. You can make a cage with a clear plastic cover for early- or late-season protection from frost; one covered with a fine screen to keep out rabbits, birds, and harmful insects; a third type covered with a shade material to protect young transplants and summer-grown lettuce; and fourth, an uncovered frame with large openings which can be used to support plants without staking.

The cage should fit over one garden square, so the top should be 12 inches square. You can make your cages either 6 or 12 inches high—the 12-inch size is more versatile. To make a 12-inch-high cage, start with a piece of wire mesh that is 12 inches wide by 36 inches long. Make a 90-degree bend in the wire 12 inches in from each end to form the sides. You may find it easier to bend the wire along the edge of a tabletop to get a straighter crease. You will now have a simple structure with three equal sides that fits over a garden square and supports the different protective covers.

Almost any kind of fencing wire can be used for the cages. It depends primarily on what you have available, and what you're going to use the

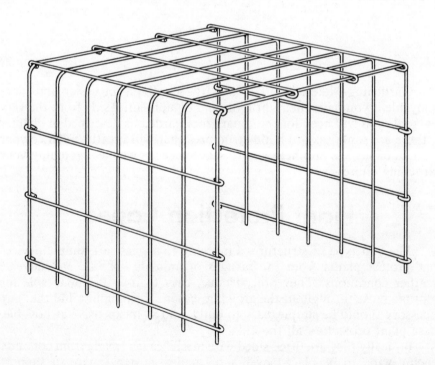

A simple, three-sided cage can be made from tomato cage wire. This protective cage measures 12 inches on each side and fits easily over a square. It can support a variety of protective coverings.

cage for. If it's intended to support plants, or if you find there will be a need to reach into the cage from above, then you should select wire with openings of at least 4 inches by 4 inches. But most fencing has openings of 2 inches by 4 inches or smaller. Chicken wire, for example, would be too small to let you reach inside, while a 6-inch by 6-inch concrete reinforcing wire would probably be too heavy, and its large openings do not offer enough support for the cage to stand on its own. An excellent wire to use for support frames would be tomato cage wire which comes in a roll 30 feet long and 4 feet high, so that it can be formed into either the small or large squares. The openings are just large enough to get your hand through, and yet small enough to provide adequate support for the frame itself. Tomato cage wire is easy to cut and pliable enough to shape into cages. The 30-foot roll length is another plus. Most fencing wire is sold in 50-foot rolls, which are bigger than you need and unnecessarily expensive just for these cages.

For protecting newly planted beans and other small plants from birds or rabbits, fencing wire with smaller openings, such as chicken wire, is

This chicken-wire cage keeps birds away from the bush bean crop.

excellent. It comes with either 1-inch or 2-inch openings, and I would recommend only using the type with 1-inch openings. Chicken wire can be cut readily and formed into the basic cage shape, and two cages can be set on top of one another at right angles to totally enclose the plants. The disadvantage of chicken wire, especially if you use two cages together, is that you cannot reach into the cages, but must remove them if you're going to work on your plants or do any weeding or watering.

Some types of wire mesh are available with a green or white plastic coating. Plastic-covered wire will last longer than bare wire, and will not scrape plants as bare wire can. These different types of wire fencing can be purchased at most hardware stores, and it's a good idea to consider carefully the uses to which you will put your cages and to shop around to find the kind that will best suit your needs.

Next, let's look in detail at the different materials with which you can cover the basic frame, and how each special kind of cage can be used throughout the growing season.

Plastic-Covered Cage

To cover the cage with plastic, wrap a 4- or 6-mil plastic sheet around the basic frame. The plastic can be secured by clipping it to the corners of the cage with clothespins. To eliminate ponding of water on the top, you can poke a drainage hole at any low point, or push the top of the cage up slightly to form a dome. Instead of covering a wire cage with plastic, you can make a comparable structure from 12-inch by 36-inch pieces of wire-reinforced plastic. This material, sometimes called "instant greenhouse," is actually a clear plastic embedded in wire mesh. It comes in rolls 36 inches wide by 20 feet long, and can be cut and shaped to whatever size you need. A cage formed from wire-reinforced plastic will be sturdy and self-supporting. Just use two pieces, bend the ends down and place them over the square at right angles to one another to provide a four-sided enclosure. This material is available in many hardware stores and garden centers.

Use either type of plastic-covered cage for early-season protection of the soil, particularly if it was prepared and ready for planting in the fall, as described in chapter 16. It will protect your soil from eroding under torrential rains, and it will help the soil to warm up more quickly. If you provide this covering one to three weeks before planting, you'll see a substantial difference in the time it takes to sprout your seeds, because of the added warmth to the soil. The clear plastic not only allows the sun and warmth to penetrate the frame, which then warms the soil, but helps in holding this warmth in at night as the cold air descends on the garden.

A plastic-covered wire cage can protect warm-weather plants, young transplants, and germinating seeds from chilly spring weather, making it possible to plant early.

Even on cloudy days you'll find a marked difference in the temperature underneath your cube. It acts just as a miniature greenhouse would. The plastic cover will also keep early insects from laying their eggs in the soil prior to your planting.

Newly planted seeds should also be covered with this kind of cage. The plastic will protect them from strong winds which will dry out the soil, and harsh rains that could wash the little seeds away. When you're planting certain seeds (like corn and beans) which birds like to eat, the plastic cage will let in the sun but keep the varmints from pecking at the ground and lifting out the seeds.

This type of cage also comes in handy when you're setting out early-season transplants. You might first cover the cages with cheesecloth or a commercial shade material so the plants don't wilt under the hot sun. After a few days when the plants are established, replace that with a clear plastic covering. This again will keep the chilling rains off the plants, prevent strong winds from drying out their leaves, and will provide a miniature greenhouse effect to get your plants off to a good healthy start. If the weather is fairly warm, wrap only the sides of the cage and leave the top open so the plants get some protection but don't overheat.

Late in the season you can use a plastic-covered cage to protect your mature plants from light fall frosts, and guard against the effects of chilling fall rains and early snowfalls. Protected by a plastic-covered cage, most of your salad crops such as spinach, lettuce, and Swiss chard will stay healthy and usable for several weeks after the first frost. Root crops will stay harvestable right up until the snow flies. Some crops, like kale, will continue to grow through the entire winter if given this extra protection.

Screen-Covered Cage

Fine window screening of metal, aluminum, or fiberglass can be placed over the basic wire cage (again secured with clothespins), to admit as much light as possible while keeping harmful insects away from your plants. At the same time, it will also protect your young seedlings or plants from hungry rabbits, birds, or anything else that could damage the plants when they are young. It's also possible under this screening to grow almost

A wire cage can be covered with netting to keep out bugs and other pests. The neighboring square in this photo is being readied for planting.

perfect vegetables which are normally subject to certain pests such as root maggots. The screening will prevent the maggot fly or cabbage moth from laying its eggs on the plant or in the soil, and you won't be bothered with the larvae pests later. You might consider the same procedure but with a larger cage and screen for a crop like summer squash, which attracts the squash borer moth. It has been found that with early protection it's possible to forestall or sometimes eliminate the squash borer if you can prevent the moth from laying its eggs on the stem when the plants are young.

Shade Cages

It's often possible to grow salad greens and other cool-weather vegetables right through the hot summer if they receive a little extra attention and protection. In hot, sunny weather lettuce normally bolts to seed, and gets tough and bitter when it doesn't get enough water, although there are some varieties of lettuce that are slow to bolt in summer. It's possible to grow many varieties right through the summer by providing a sun shield on your wire cage. Combined with a thick mulch, the sun shield keeps the

The basic wire cage can also be covered with cheesecloth or a commercial shade material (shown here on left) to shade young transplants or cool-weather crops from the hot summer sun.

soil and air temperature low enough, and it prevents the ground moisture from evaporating too fast. Radishes can be treated the same way and grown all summer long.

You can turn your wire cages into sun shields by attaching a cover of cheesecloth or one of the commercial shade film materials now on the market. These are made of nylon or plastic. Select a type with holes or slits that will allow for air circulation around the plants. Or just cover the top and south side of each cage. Shade film will also be very useful in early spring or late fall, or whenever you're setting out young plants. The shade cage will protect young plants from extremes of temperature or the vagaries of the weather at any time during the early part of the growing season. In many cases, just giving new transplants this extra bit of protection during their first two or three days in the garden will insure that they get off to a healthy start. See chapter 11 for more information on using a protective cage for transplants, and chapter 15 for some out-of-season uses.

Plant Support Cages

Your wire cages (in particular those made of a wire mesh with large openings) will be very useful in providing support for short peas, bush beans, bush tomatoes, peppers, and eggplant. Just leave the cage in place, remove any protective covering you used early in the season, and the plants will grow right through the openings. There's no need for stakes or ties, even when the plants get large and bushy and become heavily laden with fruit later in the season. Using your wire cage as a support also eliminates the chance that a stake hammered into the ground after the plant has started growing will damage the roots.

You'll also find that the wire cages make an excellent support if you've included some flowers in one of the squares of your garden. The cages are great for short dahlias, gladiolas, or some of the taller marigolds that can become quite top heavy, and are liable to be knocked over by fall rains and winds.

Protecting Root Crops from Burrowing Animals

One last structure that would be handy to have on hand is a cage made out of screening wire or hardware cloth. Two of these can be used upside down to line the bottom of a square to keep out moles or voles that tunnel under the ground and eat your vegetables from below. This is particularly useful for root crops like carrots, beets, and winter radishes that these animals find very delectable. You cannot detect the damage done by underground invaders until it's time for harvest because quite often they don't eat the entire plant but merely nibble away at it, ruining it for your use. It's very disheartening at the end of a season to be ready to harvest your carrots and find all of them chewed to pieces when it's too late to plant more. So if you've had this type of problem in your garden, it's well worth the effort to dig out a square approximately 6 to 12 inches deep, depending on what crop you're planting, and line the ground with two screen-covered cages placed at right angles. The next step is to refill the square with rich, humusy, friable soil.

If you extend the wire above ground level for about an inch or two, you might even thwart cutworms from moving into the area or discourage slugs from coming in to eat your plants. Keep in mind, though, that if the wire has been cut, the edges will be sharp and could scratch or cut your hands while working on the plants. In that case it would be best to cover the cut ends of the wire with some heavy-duty tape. Lining the garden square in this way might seem like a lot of work just to raise some carrots, but if you've been unsuccessful in the past because of rodents chewing on your vegetables, you'll appreciate all your effort at the end of the season when it comes time for harvest.

The Sun Box*

Another easy to use but very useful structure for your square foot garden is the sun box; it's a more versatile and, I've found, more useful version of the traditional cold frame. The sun box is a triple-decker cold frame made of three portable wood "frames" set on top of one another and covered with an old storm window. It resulted from several frustrated attempts on my part to build a satisfactory cold frame according to the directions given in the garden books. I designed the sun box to be portable, inexpensive, easy to build, simple to operate, expandable, and usable year-round.

The first design consideration of a cold frame is to catch as much sunlight as possible, particularly during the winter months when the sun is low in the sky. The usual solution is to cut the two sides at an angle so the top slopes toward the sun. But this design requires a difficult saw cut (have you ever cut a 12-inch-wide board or piece of thick plywood at a deep angle?). It seemed to me the obvious alternative solution for a sloping cold frame is to slope the dirt bottom or floor instead. Then the sides can all be even, but the top will be at the same slope as the bottom.

*Much of this material originally appeared in *The Avant Gardener,* vol. 10, no. 11, March 15, 1978.

As plants grow taller, more wood frames can be added to the sun box to accommodate them until it's warm enough to move them to their permanent locations in the garden.

Or better still, you can just dig in the bottom layer so one side is in the ground and the frame tilts toward the south.

How to Build a Sun Box

To simplify the cost, construction, and use of your sun box, start with a cover made from an old wood-framed storm window. These are readily available and the price is right.

The four sides of your box frame can be cut from inexpensive 2 by 4s or 2 by 6s to fit the storm window. A window measuring 2 feet by 4 feet would be a convenient size. The 2-foot by 4-foot frame will fit nicely over eight garden squares. If you can't find a storm window of those dimensions, make some adjustments to your garden squares to accommodate the sun box.

Your saw cuts should be fairly straight and square, but complete accuracy isn't very critical. Assemble the four pieces to make sure the top fits before nailing the 2 by 4s together with two nails in each corner. After you've finished one level or deck of your sun box, you can go on to cut

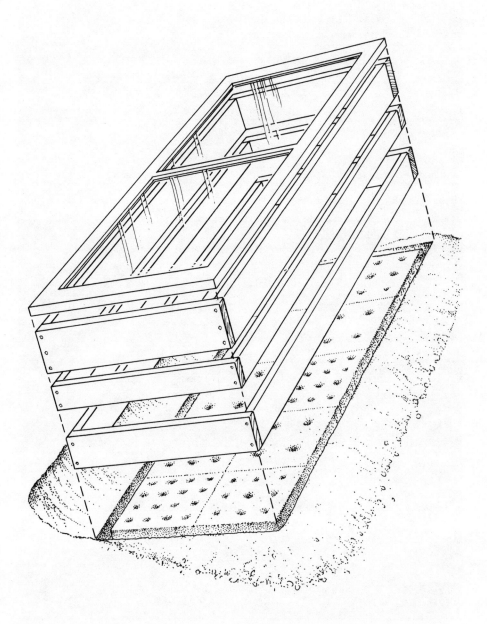

The sun box is a portable, multi-level cold frame constructed from individual wood frames. The box can be covered with a storm window for cold-weather growing, and a screen-window for summertime use.

To vent the sun box, carefully slide the cover forward. The hot air inside will naturally rise toward the opening.

and nail together as many frames as you want. Stack two or even three frames on top of each other to make a deeper box.

Since the wood frames are fairly small and light, you can easily carry them about. This adds a great deal of flexibility to the sun box, and you'll find the simplest part of this design is moving the box where it's needed in different seasons.

Most cold frames are heavy and hard to move. In fact, most books show how to anchor them into the ground. But the sun box is very portable. To move it, merely remove the glass cover and carry each section of the frame to its new location. To carry a section a long distance, step into the center and pick it up with both hands. The weight will then be distributed all around you, eliminating strain on your back or arm muscles.

Another construction advantage the sun box holds over previous cold frame designs is that you don't need expensive hinges, screws, latches, or prop sticks to hold the cover open for venting. This idea came to me after trying to find a matched pair of hinges, a handle, and enough screws all the same size in my workshop junk drawer. When I finally went to the hardware store and found out how much these items cost nowadays, I thought there must be a better way.

The simple solution to venting without an intricate hardware installation is to just lay the cover on top of the frame. When you need ventilation, slide it down slightly so the top side is open. How far you slide the cover depends on how much you want to open the box. The hot air will rise to the highest point and escape through the opening, but cold air will not enter as easily as it might in a conventional cold frame. If it gets really hot or you want to tend the plants inside the box, slide the cover all the way off the box and prop it against one side.

Variations on the Basic Design

Some gardeners ask why they can't use 2 by 8s or 2 by 12s to make the box deeper without adding layers. They can, although these are much heavier and more cumbersome to handle. But I recommend against using 1-inch lumber like 1 by 6s. It's too thin and light, and the top won't fit as snugly.

Aluminum-framed storm windows instead of the wood-framed type could be used for the top of the frame, but they provide no insulation. Even a broken storm window can be used, if you remove the glass and cover it with a piece of heavy plastic stapled all around the edge. In fact, a large piece of plastic can be wrapped around both sides of the window to create an insulating air pocket in between.

How about applying preservative paint to the wood? I never bother. First, I don't have any around or if I do it's bound to be dried up like all the cans of paint I save; second, I can never find a brush that's not as hard as a rock; and third, the wood frames won't stay in one place for more than a few months, so they won't have much of a chance to rot or be eaten by termites. To me, painting on preservative is a lot of extra work and not really necessary. Your sun boxes can and should be moved into spring, summer, and fall locations or temporary storage.

If you can find several storm windows and window screens the same size, you can have several sun boxes with interchangeable sides and tops, enabling you to do many different things. For example, you can use several single-layer boxes to start seeds or seedlings. Add a window top in spring or a screen top in summer. Later you can add more layers or decks to the sun box as the plants grow taller. You can also replace the window top with a screen top as the warm weather arrives, or conversely, the screen top with a window as the weather gets colder. The versatility of the sun

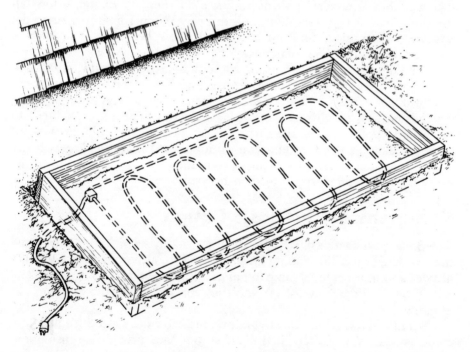

For winter growing, put a sun box next to the house and install a heating cable in the bottom. If the box is covered and insulated, the cable will provide enough heat to grow cool-weather crops throughout the winter.

box is limited only by your imagination. It's a useful structure to have in the garden in all seasons.

Some Special Sun Box Tips

Here are some ideas and suggestions for getting even more use from your sun box:

Winter and Spring

- Weatherstrip the bottom of the cover to reduce heat loss.
- Add Styrofoam panels or bank with soil, leaves, or hay around the outside for insulation.
- Protect the frame from winter winds by backing it up to a wall, hedge, or fence on the north side.
- Place it against the south wall of the house to take advantage of a surprising amount of radiated heat from the building.
- Add about 25 percent sand to the soil to make it hold warmth better.
- Add some large stones, or water-filled gallon jugs painted black, as solar storage mass to trap heat from the sun during the day and release it slowly at night.
- Use white paint or aluminum foil inside the box to reflect more light.

Summer

- Make a cover from lath strips or shade film to shade cuttings and seedlings.
- Cover the box with a window screen and use it as a solar food dryer.

Fall

- Use a deep frame to hold plants such as lettuce, endive, Chinese cabbage, and celery, that are nearing maturity when frost comes, and you'll have many weeks of salads.

Winter

- Grow hardy bulbs and other coolness-loving flowers like pansies, sweet violets, winter aconites, dwarf bulbous iris, snowdrops, and miniature narcissi, all winter.

Support Frames for Vertical Crops

The next type of structures to build are the vertical frames for all your vine crops. The specific and detailed methods of vertical growing were discussed in chapter 8. Here are some details on how to build the support frames.

I've tried just about every shape and configuration as well as all kinds of material while looking for the ideal combination to support climbing crops. A vertical support frame must be a structure strong enough to hold several tomato plants right through the season. It must be tall enough to allow them full growth, yet not so tall that it will blow down during heavy rains and winds. It should be attractive and fit into the garden, as well as being easy to construct. It would be preferable to have a structure that could be taken down and stored during the winter, and reused the following year.

First, let me caution you to stay away from wood and plastic. These materials just don't hold up for a simply constructed 6-foot-tall frame. Wood splits and breaks when you drive it into the ground, it rots easily, and is difficult to join at the corners for a strong connection. In addition, a wood frame is never very sturdy, especially if you reuse it the following year after dismantling it and storing it away for the winter. Plastic breaks, can become brittle in cold weather, and just isn't strong enough for a frame. That leaves metal, and I've found the best material for a strong and sturdy frame that can be reused year after year is steel pipe. You can use either threaded water pipe or electrical conduit with slip fittings (the ½-inch size is sturdy enough). In my experience, copper pipe and other metal pipe smaller than ½ inch was not strong enough to support the plants. Although new pipe is expensive, it will last a lifetime. It's available at building, plumbing, and electrical supply houses. To cut costs considerably, you might try shopping around for used or salvage pipe that can sometimes be found at local junk or salvage yards. Sometimes local contractors will sell used pipe, or you might even be able to get hold of some during your community's clean-up week. If you do decide to purchase new pipe, telephone ahead first to get information on prices and availability. You'll find quite a variation as you check various stores.

Water Pipe

If you're going to use steel water pipe for your vertical frames, try to have the ends threaded so that you can use standard elbow fittings. For a 6-foot-high frame, use a pipe that is 7 feet long and drive it a foot into the ground. Since a 7-foot-long leg is a little difficult to pound into the ground, you might use threaded couplings for a two-piece leg. Erect the frame by first driving the legs into the ground, 5 feet apart. Then add an elbow to one leg, screw in the top pipe, and add the last elbow to it. Last, by using a pipe wrench on the remaining leg, screw that leg up into the top pipe elbow. In effect, you just work your way up and around each joint. When it's all tight you will probably have loosened the soil a little bit around the legs, so tamp hard with your heel all around each leg to firm up the ground.

Electrical Conduit

You can buy electrical conduit in ½-inch size, in either a thick wall which can have a threaded end, or a thin wall which has a slip-on-type fitting. If you buy thick-wall conduit and have the ends threaded, you will be able to use any standard plumbing fittings, including the elbows. If you buy the thin-wall type (which is a lot less expensive), you can use standard electrical slip-on fittings and you can even bend the pipe, so the top bar

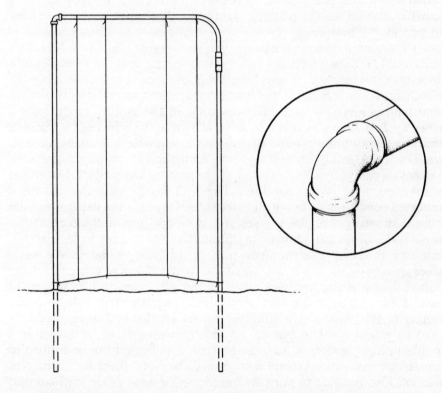

A vertical frame can be made of electrical conduit fastened with slip fittings, or ½-inch water pipe with threaded elbow couplings (detail). Strings are attached to support the plants.

doesn't need an elbow. You will have to buy a pipe bender, though, or the pipe will kink and break when you try to bend it. Pipe benders cost under ten dollars or you can rent them very cheaply, but if you don't plan to put up enough vertical frames to make the tool pay off, use the thick-wall conduit or water pipe to build the frames. Both materials are sturdy enough for a satisfactory vertical frame. It mostly depends on what materials are available to you, and at what cost.

Your plants can be supported on the frame either by strings hung from the top bar, or with a special netting sold for vertical growing. The strings are obviously less expensive, and they work quite well. Try to use a synthetic string that won't rot and break during one season. The strings do have the added advantage that they can be added later after the frame is up and the plants are in the ground. They are only needed when the plants are tall enough to require a support. It's a simple matter to tie the hanging strings to another string tied between the legs at the bottom.

If you plan to use grow netting, you should first make sure that it fits your frame. Netting is sold in a variety of materials, and in various lengths and widths starting at 3, 4, and 5 feet wide. Netting is available in plastic, nylon, and woven string, each of which has advantages and disadvantages. Prices and colors also vary. The openings in the netting range from 2 inches by 2 inches (which is a little small) on up to 6 inches by 6 inches (which is ideal). Shop around (by phone) to see what's available in your area. It's best to install the netting at the same time you put up your frame, so that you can weave it in and out of the two legs as well as the top bar before everything is put together. This will insure that the netting is supported continuously along all three sides. Once it's up, netting is easier to use than strings because it gives you more openings and directions for the plants to climb. For plants like squash that won't climb by themselves, it's a little easier to poke the stems into one of the openings once a week, rather than twist them around one of the strings if you're using the string method. But it really becomes just a matter of choice and sometimes of looks. Both methods are easy to use and require very little time for training of the plants. (Training techniques are detailed in chapter 8.)

You might want to put up several frames together, arranged in a straight line or possibly in a zigzag pattern. The frames can be connected with tee fittings, or you could leave spaces between them for a different look. It's also possible to put two frames beside each other, and connect supports over the top to form an enclosed arbor. Your plants will grow up the sides, and if you continue your netting or strings across the top, the plants will follow that support and will give you a covered, canopied effect which is very interesting and attractive in any garden.

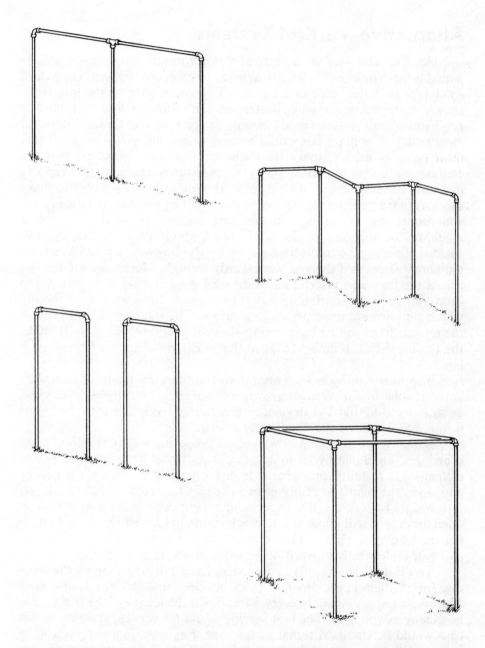

Vertical frames can be arranged in a number of ways. You can run them as a straight fence (upper left), in a zigzag pattern (upper right), with space between the frames (lower left), or as an arbor (lower right).

Alternative Vertical Systems

An alternate idea for a vertical frame without couplings or fittings would be to install two 7-foot metal fence posts as the legs, and use a third fence post or a steel pipe as a top bar. You could wire on the top bar as shown in the accompanying illustration. The frame will not be quite as rigid and strong as those made of pipe or conduit, but should suffice for most plants. The materials would be easy to get, but you must get 7-foot fence posts in order to make the frame tall enough. Do not use twine to connect the top bar, but make sure you use a sturdy, strong wire, wrapping it several times, and with a final twist. It would also be possible to make this sort of frame from plain pipe, by driving the pipe legs into the ground and connecting the top pipe in the same manner. If you do use pipe, it would not be necessary to thread the ends, which would reduce the cost. Instead of wiring the connection as previously shown, you could also form a different support if the legs were sturdy enough. Merely lay the top bar across the legs, and insert a standard steel garden stake into each leg to keep the top bar from falling out. These stakes have a hook at the top which slips around the crossbar to secure it. The stake would not prevent the top bar from sliding back and forth, so it would be necessary to make the top bar 5 feet, 6 inches long, so that it extends 3 inches beyond each leg.

For those gardeners who want to raise quite a few plants or who want a continuous line of vertical growing to screen off an undesirable view, another method that I've developed is a double fence line with the plants in the middle called the "hedgerow system."

Basically it is a system in which you prepare one long trench of good growing soil and plant your tomatoes in a continuous straight line. A row of fencing is installed on either side of the trench to contain the plants, and when the plants are fully grown the effect created is that of a large, lush hedge. Believe me, it's a spectacular sight. Use fencing with a large, open mesh that will allow you to reach inside to harvest the crop. Installing the fencing so that it starts 6 inches off the ground will allow you to reach in underneath to weed or do other work at ground level.

You'll need heavy-duty, 7-foot steel fence posts to support the fencing. Install them approximately 12 inches deep in a straight double row. Place a post approximately every 5 feet down the length of the row (it can be as long as you like). The best fencing to use for vertical growing in this case would be standard tomato cage wire. Buy a 30-foot roll, and hang it on your fence posts so the bottom is 6 inches off the ground. Unfortunately, this kind of wire fencing will be only 4 feet tall, so your vertical growing will only extend to a distance of 4½ feet. In order to allow your

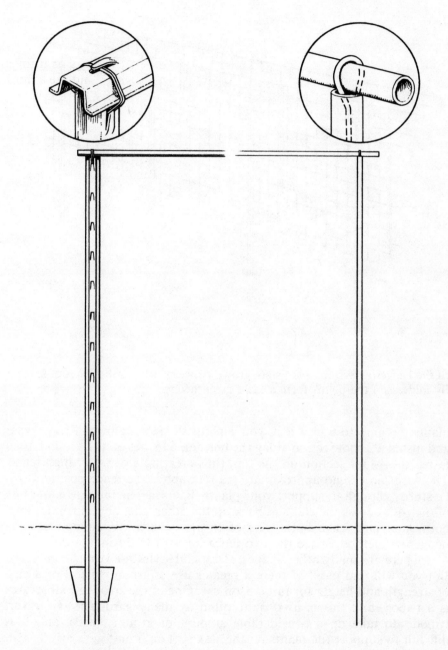

To make a vertical frame from fence posts, attach the top post to the sides with wire, as shown in the detail on the left, or with a metal garden stake, as shown in the detail on the right.

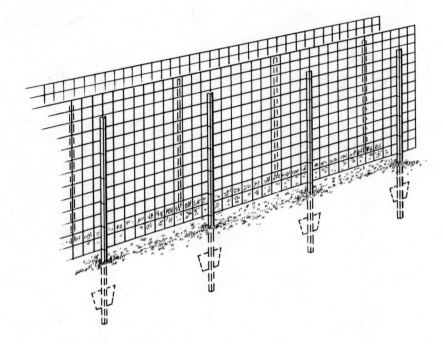

In the hedgerow system, plants are grown between two parallel lines of fencing. By midseason the plants form a lush, green hedge.

plants to climb to 6 or 7 feet, you can cut the fencing in half lengthwise and install a 2-foot section along the bottom, 6 inches off the ground, then fasten the 4-foot section on the top, thus creating a 6½-foot-high fence. The wire can extend approximately a foot above the fence post and still be sturdy enough to support your plants. Run the fencing down one side of the row, across the end and back up the other side, or just run it down both sides and leave both ends of the row open. When you use the hedgerow method, space the two fence lines 18 to 24 inches apart.

There are many other shapes, sizes, and styles for vertical supports. But you will find in all of them a greater use of ground space, or a lack of strength and height for full-season use. One of the strongest structures is a tripod, and this is used quite often by many gardeners. However, tripods do take up a considerable amount of ground space, and it is difficult to support the plants on the stakes. You'll find with any system certain advantages and disadvantages. However, I have found no disadvantages to the vertical frames other than their initial cost and the work required to assemble them. Keep in mind that you'll be able to use the frames for many years, and that they are easily removable. They make a worthwhile investment.

A Horizontal Fence

Another type of device I'd like to pass on to you is not exactly a structure but more a method of support. It combines the horizontal support idea of the open mesh wire cages, but uses the same kind of grow netting that works so well on the vertical frames. By putting four short fence posts in the corners of a 4-foot by 4-foot garden block, you can string this netting horizontally, and let your plants grow right through this support. This method is especially suitable for bush tomatoes, peppers, eggplant, bush beans, or short peas. If you use a netting with large openings (4 inches by 4 inches or 6 inches by 6 inches), you'll easily be able to reach through for weeding, watering, and harvesting. Depending on the plants to be supported, you might string the netting at 9 inches, 12 inches, or even 18 inches above ground level. In the case of very tall-growing plants or flowers, you might consider two levels for full-season support of these plants. The only caution to bear in mind is that the edges of the fence stakes sometimes can be sharp, especially after pounding them into the ground with a hammer. Cover them with a little waterproof tape so you don't scratch your legs or knees when walking past.

A Vertical Garden for Patios

You don't have to have a big backyard or even a garden at all if you want to raise some tomatoes, cucumbers, or even squash. You can build a simple 1-foot by 4-foot planter box with a vertical frame attached and enjoy the same rewards as someone with a backyard. The directions are simple and the materials are fairly inexpensive.

You'll need two pieces of 1 by 6 lumber, 48 inches long, for the sides of the box; and two pieces of 1 by 6 lumber, 10 inches long, for the ends. The bottom can be made of a sheet of ½-inch plywood, 12 inches by 48 inches (or use a sheet of plastic if you won't need to move the planter). The legs of the vertical frame are two pieces of pipe, 48 inches long. Use a piece of pipe 44 inches long for the top of the frame. You'll also need two brackets, four screws, eight nails, and two elbows to build the planter. The only tools necessary are a hammer, a saw, and a screwdriver.

On a hard work surface, such as a sidewalk or patio, nail together the wood planter box. Assemble the three pieces of pipe to form the vertical frame, connecting the sides to the top with the elbows. Stand the frame next to the wood box to mark the locations for the two brackets and the screw holes. Predrill the holes or tap in a nail to start the screw holes. Then screw in the brackets (almost tight) and staple or tack the plastic to the bottom, or nail on the plywood bottom.

Place the planter box in its final location and attach the vertical frame. Tighten all the brackets and coupling screws. Fill the box with a rich, light soil mixture as described in chapter 8. Then tie four strings evenly spaced along the top pipe so they reach down to another string stretched and tied across the bottom of the vertical supports. The planter is now ready. For details on using it, see chapter 8.

A Portable Planter Box

A simple wood box can be built to grow plants on a patio or rooftop. It can also be elevated on sawhorses to allow wheelchair access to the garden. Make the box to the dimensions of a garden block—4 by 4 feet.

Buy two 8-foot-long, 1 by 6 boards, cut them in half, and nail them together to form the planter box. Staple or tack a piece of plastic to the bottom, or nail on a sheet of plywood if you want a more permanent structure or if you will need to move the planter when it is full of soil. A vertical frame can be clamped onto one side of the box if you wish.

For some ideas on using this planter for a patio, wheelchair, or rooftop garden, see chapter 17.

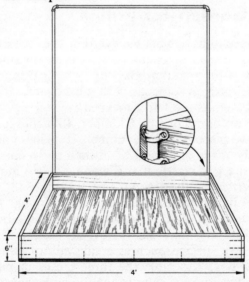

A 4-foot-high vertical frame is bracketed to one end of the patio garden.

Chapter 10
🌿 Starting Plants from Seed

Starting seeds is always one of the highlights of gardening. It's an activity that's full of high hopes and great expectations. You can almost picture those lush heads of lettuce and crisp, juicy cucumbers as each seed is planted. The details of when and what to plant, either indoors or out, how deep, how far apart, and all the other questions most gardeners have at this time, can be best answered by first learning a little about seeds, their requirements for sprouting, and what to expect from them. Once that's understood, all of the rest becomes almost self-answering, or at least easily understood.

One of the first questions often asked is "Should I buy seeds and start my own plants, or just buy transplants from the nursery at the right time?" Starting your own seeds naturally involves much more time-consuming work and trouble, but it is certainly more economical, and for a lot of people it is more fun and satisfying. If that appeals to you, and you have the time, then you should by all means start many of your own seeds. The choice of varieties of each vegetable is certainly much wider among seeds than among varieties available as plants in the nursery. Seeds are also much cheaper to buy than plants. But you will have to spend some money for basic seed-starting equipment and supplies, and you will have to plan ahead to order and start your seeds at the right time. You may want only

153

six pepper plants this year, but you have to buy a full packet of seeds. Of course, if you store these seeds properly, each packet will last you for several years without any further expense.

What to Grow from Seed

Which vegetables to start from seed depends a lot on your expertise as a gardener, your desires, and the time available. Some vegetables are difficult to start from seed or take a very long time to grow into plants that are large enough to set out. For those crops (particularly tomatoes, eggplant, and peppers) I would suggest buying plants at first, until you become a fairly experienced gardener (and also, of course, assuming you have the time and can supply the right kind of heat, light, and soil for growing these). Windowsill sprouting of those crops is not very satisfactory for the average gardener, although experienced gardeners are often successful, especially when they are able to supplement the natural light coming in the window with fluorescent light from a fixture directly above the plants. In addition, although seeds need warm temperatures to germinate, seedlings need more humidity and somewhat cooler temperatures than can be found in most of our homes in late winter. You really need a greenhouse, heated sun box or some other place with strong sunlight from above to start these crops.

The other summer crops that have large seeds, however, (squash, cucumbers, melons) are easy to start, and beginners can plant those seeds right in the garden. More advanced (and anxious) gardeners can start these same seeds indoors a few weeks ahead of time. Seeds for all the leafy and heading spring vegetables (lettuce, broccoli, cabbage, and cauliflower) can easily be started indoors or outdoors, but you must get them in early in the spring. If you're too late, then you have no other choice but to buy them as plants. The root vegetables are traditionally started in the ground, so plants are not available even if you wanted to buy them.

After you've decided which plants you want to grow from seed, you're faced with the task of deciding what kind of seed to buy and from whom to buy it. Is it better to buy through a mail-order catalog, or right in the store from the seed rack? It's mail order for me 10 to 1. The only time I select from a store rack is when I'm out of something and there isn't time to order it by mail. (The companies are often slow to fill orders during the busy season, and the mail service is getting slower every year.) Besides, who could pass up the sheer joy and delight of looking through several seed catalogs and making up a list of things to order? It's Christmas all over again! The catalog pictures are gorgeous and the descriptions make you want to grow everything. You have to remember, though, that these descriptions are quite often written by copywriters, whose job is to make everything sound the best, and to entice you into buying more and more. It's often necessary to set a limit of say, ten or fifteen dollars, and go back and cross out several packets on your shopping list before sending in your order; otherwise you'd have to double the size of your garden every year.

Remember, too, that by saving your partially used seed packets every year, you only have to buy new or different varieties for several years once your initial purchase is made.

Aside from the fun of ordering, and the excitement of having something garden-related to do in the middle of winter, the main reason that I select mail order is that the condition of storage is critical to the viability of seeds. The seed companies keep the seeds under excellent storage conditions, while the retail store might get very hot and humid before the seeds are sold, thus affecting the germination rate of those seeds. Of course, if your seeds are bought in the spring, chances are that hasn't happened, because every store receives fresh seeds every year. Summer purchases are more risky, and buying during the store's year-end sale at 50 percent off is always taking a chance.

Storing Seeds Properly

An understanding of what makes seeds sprout not only enables you to provide those conditions to get your garden off to a better start, but it also helps you understand how to store seeds. Two things are needed before a seed can break its dormancy—moisture and heat—and they must be provided together. If either or both are provided intermittently the viability of the seed is affected; in some cases the seed is killed. The first basic rule of seed storage, then, is to provide an environment that is cold and dry. Cold means as cold as 35°F—seeds will keep a long time at these temperatures. Dryness is important because without moisture the seeds can't swell and sprout. It is extremely important to keep them dry at *all* times—while using the seed packet indoors or outdoors, as well as while storing the seeds.

It's hard to find an ideal storage location around the house that provides both cold and dry conditions year-round. A shelf in the garage, basement, or laundry room is not a good storage spot; it gets too damp or hot there at some time during the year. One place that does offer an unchanging environment all year long is the refrigerator. If you keep your seed packets in a sealed glass jar in the refrigerator the seeds will remain viable as long as three to five years.

Seeds must be stored under proper conditions at all times, not just during the fall and winter. If you want to use your seeds year after year, you must get in the habit of not exposing them to any moisture or heat, even for a short time. This may sound extreme, but don't let seeds sit outdoors or in the garage any longer than you have to. Even while you're in the garden, don't lay the packets on the damp ground, or in the hot sun. Don't let the sprinkler or a rain shower get the packets wet. Each time one of these things happens the seeds lose just a little viability. If you don't want to buy all new seeds every year, open the refrigerator, remove the jar and take out only the packets you're going to plant that day. Then replace the sealed jar—don't let it sit out while you're gardening. You should even have your soil prepared and ready for planting before taking the seeds out to the garden. Remember to return those packets to the refrigerator as soon as you're finished planting. On very humid days you can leave the jar uncovered in the refrigerator for a few hours after replacing the seed packets. The dry, cool air inside the refrigerator will evaporate any moisture from the seed packets. Another good way to prevent moisture buildup is to place a desiccant powder in the jar with the seeds to absorb excess moisture. Put a tablespoon of powdered milk in a tissue, fold it up and lay it in the bottom of the jar. Replace the desiccant every six months, or approximately every third time the jar is opened.

Understanding Germination

Let's look a little closer at those two requirements for seed sprouting, heat and moisture, and the amount and duration of each that is necessary. To encourage germination, temperatures should be constant and warm—up to 70° or 80°F. Many studies have been done on the relationship between temperature and time to germination. In general, the time to germination doubles for each 10 degrees the temperature drops below the ideal level, (which is 70°F for many seeds). For example, at 70°F it takes only 2½ days for lettuce seeds to sprout, but at 60°F it takes 4 days (about twice as long). At 50°F, the germination time again nearly doubles and the seeds take 7 days to sprout. When the temperature is as low as 40°F, those lettuce seeds will take 15 days to sprout. Germination time of onion seeds goes from 4½ days at 70°F to 7 days at 60°F, then 13 days at 50°F and nearly 31 days at 40°F. Germination times for a number of other common vegetables are shown in the accompanying tables.

As you look over the tables, you'll be able to spot the summer or

GERMINATION TIMES AND TEMPERATURES

This chart shows the number of days required for vegetable seeds to sprout at different temperatures.

Crop	32°F	41°F	50°F	59°F	68°F	77°F	86°F	95°F
Beans	0.0	0.0	0.0	16.1	11.4	8.1	6.4	6.2
Beets	—	42.0	16.7	9.7	6.2	5.0	4.5	4.6
Cabbage	—	—	14.6	8.7	5.8	4.5	3.5	—
Carrots	0.0	50.6	17.3	10.1	6.9	6.2	6.0	8.6
Cauliflower	—	—	19.5	9.9	6.2	5.2	4.7	—
Corn	0.0	0.0	21.6	12.4	6.9	4.0	3.7	3.4
Cucumbers	0.0	0.0	0.0	13.0	6.2	4.0	3.1	3.0
Eggplant	—	—	—	—	13.1	8.1	5.3	—
Lettuce	49.0	14.9	7.0	3.9	2.6	2.2	2.6	0.0
Muskmelons	—	—	—	—	8.4	4.0	3.1	—
Onions	135.8	30.6	13.4	7.1	4.6	3.6	3.9	12.5
Parsley	—	—	29.0	17.0	14.0	13.0	12.3	—
Peas	—	36.0	13.5	9.4	7.5	6.2	5.9	—
Peppers	0.0	0.0	0.0	25.0	12.5	8.4	7.6	8.8
Radishes	0.0	29.0	11.2	6.3	4.2	3.5	3.0	—
Spinach	62.6	22.5	11.7	6.9	5.7	5.1	6.4	0.0
Tomatoes	0.0	0.0	42.9	13.6	8.2	5.9	5.9	9.2

Adapted from Harrington, J.F., Agricultural Extension Leaflet, 1954.

0.0 = Little or no germination

— = Not tested

hot-weather vegetables not only because they need a somewhat higher temperature to germinate quickly, but also because they won't sprout at all in lower temperatures. You can also see that although the spring or cool-weather vegetables such as lettuce and spinach can sprout at cooler temperatures, they take a long time to do so and actually do much better at the higher temperatures. Because we call them spring vegetables or cold-weather vegetables, we've been led to believe that these vegetable seeds actually *need* cooler temperatures to sprout. But that's not really true. Cool-weather crops need to mature in the cooler part of the year, but they prefer warm temperatures as they germinate and begin to grow. This is why a crop of cool-weather vegetables often grows better and produces more if planted in fall than in spring. The fall crop gets its start in the warm weather and matures in the cool weather of fall. But we Americans are geared to gardening in the spring, and not all of us plant a second "fall crop," even though it usually outproduces the traditional spring crop.

PERCENTAGE OF GERMINATION

This table indicates the percentage of normal vegetable seedlings produced at different temperatures.

Crops	32°F	41°F	50°F	59°F	68°F	77°F	86°F	95°F
Beans	0	0	1	97	90	97	47	39
Beets	—	114	156	189	193	209	192	75
Cabbage	0	27	78	93	—	99	—	—
Carrots	0	48	93	95	96	96	95	74
Corn	0	0	47	97	97	98	91	88
Cucumbers	0	0	0	95	99	99	99	99
Eggplant	—	—	—	—	21	53	60	—
Lettuce	98	98	98	99	99	99	12	0
Muskmelons	—	—	—	—	38	94	90	—
Onions	90	98	98	98	99	97	91	73
Parsley	—	—	63	—	69	64	50	—
Peas	—	89	94	93	93	94	86	0
Peppers	0	0	1	70	96	98	95	70
Radishes	0	42	76	97	95	97	95	—
Spinach	83	96	91	82	52	28	32	0
Tomatoes	0	0	82	98	98	97	83	46

Adapted from Harrington, J.F., Agricultural Extension Leaflet, 1954

— = Not tested

Testing for Germination

If you want to have a little scientific or educational fun, or you're just not sure some seeds are good anymore, you might want to try a germination test before you plant those seeds in the garden. It's very simple; you could ask the kids to help. It's also a good way to notice the differences in various seeds; their sizes, textures, shapes, and times to sprouting. Here's how to make the test. Place *exactly* ten seeds in a paper towel, roll it up, and wet it so it's moist but not dripping wet. After rolling it up, take a long plastic bag, the kind a loaf of bread comes in, label the plastic bag with the seed variety you're testing and the date, and then slip the towel into the bag, seal the end, and place it on top of the refrigerator, hot water tank or other warm place. Look up the number of days to sprouting for the type of seeds you're testing at the temperature you're going to provide, and note what day they should be sprouting. Open the plastic and check at least once beforehand just to make sure that everything is all right and no mold is growing. If some seeds have started to sprout, wait a few more

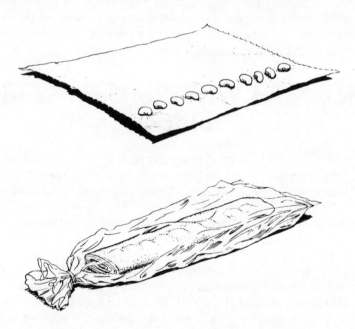

To test for germination, wrap ten seeds in a damp paper towel, enclose in a plastic bag, and put in a warm place. When the required time to germination has elapsed, count how many seeds have germinated. Multiply that number by ten to get the percentage rate of germination.

days to give all of those that are going to sprout a chance. Then open up the package and count the number of seeds that have sprouted to determine the percentage of germination. If seven out of the ten seeds you tested sprouted, that's a 70 percent germination rate and your seeds are still very good. If only four sprouted, that's 40 percent and I'd consider buying a new package of seeds or at least remember to plant three times the number you actually need when you're using those seeds. Some gardeners try to plant those sprouted seeds, but it's usually difficult because the roots have gotten long and are very easily broken.

Presoaking

Always try to presoak seeds that are big enough to handle comfortably. Soak them overnight in lukewarm water but don't let them dry out after you've wet them. This procedure will get the seeds off to a quick start, especially when planted outdoors. Remember that the first thing the seeds have to do is soak up water to start their sprouting process. If you plant dry seeds outdoors, it may take a fairly long time for them to soak up enough water from the soil to begin germinating. Soaking them beforehand can save several days in the sprouting process. And the quicker you can get that seed to sprout, the greater its chances for survival will be.

How and When to Plant Seeds Outdoors

Getting seeds off to a good start out in the garden is half the battle in gardening. The key is to plant the seeds at their correct final spacing (so no thinning will be necessary) in a loose, airy material such as vermiculite that drains quickly but holds moisture. (The moisture-holding ability of vermiculite is even more important to the seed in hot summer months when you're making additional plantings.) It's also important to provide a cover that keeps out the chilling winds, cold rains, and freezing snows, but traps all of the sun's warmth in the soil to speed germination. A plastic-covered cage (described in chapter 9) will perform these functions and will also keep out stray dogs, rabbits, and hungry birds, and will keep you and any interested visitors from stepping on the planted square.

This kind of careful planting will insure that you can start many plants from seed outdoors as successfully as you could in a greenhouse. These methods take some extra work and preparation, but they almost insure success and eliminate most of the later drudgery of thinning which is quite often the cause of many garden failures. It is much better to know that you have provided the ideal conditions for a seed to sprout and grow, and that the greater part of your work is over once the planting is finished.

Now let's put the techniques together and plant some typical squares of spinach, carrots, radishes, and lettuce. First, choose a 4-foot by 4-foot block in the highest, driest, sunniest part of your garden, and shovel off any snow or ice. Place a sheet of plastic over the block to be planted as early as you can in the spring, at least two to four weeks before it is time to plant. The sun will start warming and drying out the soil as the winter sogginess drains out, and the cover will keep any new rain and snow off the soil. This should allow you to prepare the bed for planting two weeks before your normal planting date.

I strongly recommend that beginning gardeners don't try to rush their planting date, but stick to the generally accepted dates for their area. The charts and maps in this book will help you calculate these dates, and you can also consult your local Cooperative Extension Agent for information. When you become more experienced you can experiment with earlier-than-normal planting using the same methods described in this chapter. They are not only good for early spring, or for giving an early start to summer vegetables, they are also effective for all plantings—spring, summer, and fall.

Remember the test for soil moisture described in chapter 5: a ball of soil squeezed in your hand should break up when poked with your finger. If it drips or oozes water, it's still too wet to work. If your finger just makes a hole or impression in the ball, it's also still too wet. If a ball won't even form, then the soil is too dry, but that isn't likely to happen in the spring. If the ball falls apart into smaller pieces when poked, the soil is just right for working and it's time to turn over the soil in your block. If you were unable to prepare your soil in fall, do it now, as described in chapter 5. Add lots of humus, peat moss, and a sprinkling of fertilizer rich in nitrogen, then carefully turn over the soil, remove any rocks and man-made debris, break up any clods, and then rake the surface level and smooth.

Using two straight sticks or string, divide the block in half each way, marking off four large areas, each 2 feet by 2 feet. Now divide one of those areas in half, again each way, making four squares, each 1 foot by 1 foot. Of the four vegetables we're planting, carrots take the longest to mature and grow the tallest, so locate them on the north side of the block so as not to shade any other plants. Spinach, radishes, and lettuce are all about equal in size and can go in any other square.

Plant the lettuce square first. Lettuce seeds should be planted 6 inches apart, so subdivide one small square in half both ways to create 4 plant spaces. The easiest way is just to take your finger and draw a line through

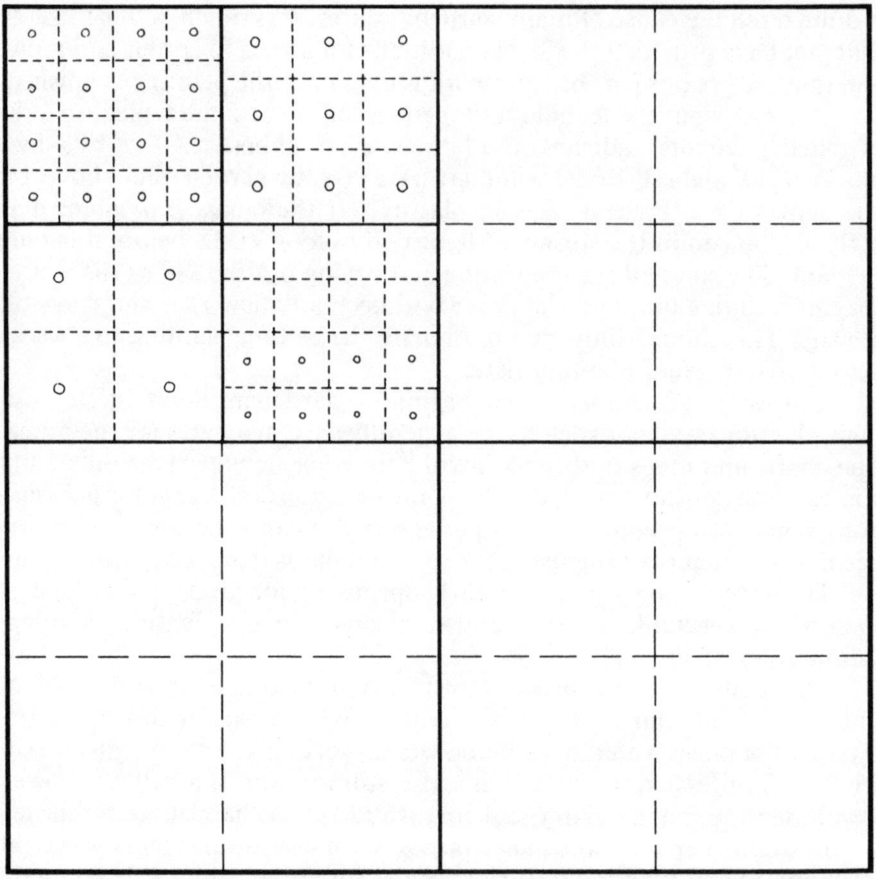

This diagram shows how to plant a square of (clockwise from upper left) carrots, spinach, radishes, and lettuce. Plant half the radishes at one time and the other half a week later to stagger the harvest.

the soil. Next, poke your finger about ½ inch deep in the center of each little plant space, half-fill the hole with vermiculite and place one seed in each hole. Then cover to the surface with more vermiculite. The next square will be for spinach. Since spinach requires a 4-inch space between plants, you subdivide this square into thirds both ways, creating 9 plant spaces. Again, plant the seeds ½ inch deep, using the same procedure as for the lettuce. Next, plant the radishes. They need a 3-inch spacing between plants. So subdivide the radish square into fourths both ways,

Left: The first step in planting seeds outdoors is to divide the squares into correct spacings. This photo shows four squares in varying stages of growth. The squares to be planted are marked off in 4-inch and 6-inch spacings, to hold bush beans and lettuce, respectively.

Right: When planting seeds, poke a hole with your finger in the center of each space, then fill the hole halfway with vermiculite. Next, place one seed in each hole, and cover with vermiculite.

creating 16 spaces. Since radishes mature quickly, and all at about the same time, plant only 8 spaces at this time. In another week or two the other 8 spaces can be planted, to produce a more staggered harvest. Use the same procedure as for spinach and lettuce but plant just a little deeper because radish seeds are larger. A hole about ¾ inch deep is fine. Half-fill each hole with vermiculite, drop one seed into it, and cover with more vermiculite to fill the hole. Last, it's time to plant the carrot square. Use the same spacing as for the radishes, 3 inches apart. Again, subdivide the square into fourths, marking off 16 plant spaces. Since carrot seeds are very tiny and they take a long time to germinate, we'll make a smaller hole, slightly less than ½ inch deep. Half-fill the hole with vermiculite, drop in one seed, and cover with vermiculite.

After the seeds are planted, the last step is to moisten the vermiculite and surrounding soil in all the squares with a fine–mist hand sprayer and place plastic-covered cages over the squares, covering all four newly planted vegetables. Nothing further need be done, except to keep a watch through the plastic, and on very hot, sunny days if the soil shows signs of drying, lift the cages and spray the squares thoroughly with water, still using your hand sprayer. Don't use a hose or you may wash away the vermiculite or seeds. Replace the covers after you've watered the plot. The radishes will sprout first, then the lettuce and spinach, and finally the

Place a plastic-covered cage over newly planted squares in spring to provide a warm, moist environment for germinating seeds and delicate young transplants.

carrots. There's no need to remove the cage when the radishes start to sprout—they will get plenty of light right through the plastic. As the weather gets warmer and the sun's rays more intense, you must watch closely to make sure the soil does not dry out. If there is any question in your mind that it's getting too hot under the plastic for already-sprouted plants, remove the cages.

Using this basic method you can gain two to four weeks for all crops and still get them off to a good start. The reason most authorities advise gardeners not to put out seeds or plants too early is because the soil is still too cold to sprout the seeds (but you have prewarmed yours), or that the weather may turn too cold, windy, or rainy (you enclosed your plants in a miniature greenhouse).

How Deep to Plant

The depth of seed planting is always a little confusing to new gardeners, especially if the seed is big and flat, or long and skinny. Most books suggest planting at a depth of two, three, or four times the diameter of the seed. But quite frankly, the diameter is sometimes hard to figure out with a small or oddly shaped seed, so I like to explain it this way. In vermiculite, which has lots of air spaces but still holds plenty of moisture, and which also offers little resistance to a sprout pushing up through it, the distance or depth of planting isn't critical, certainly not as important as when you're planting in soil, which is not as loose in texture. If a seed is placed too deep in the ground, the soil can crust over, forming a hard lid which the little sprout must push through. On the other hand, if you plant seeds too shallowly in soil, it can dry out quickly and kill the young seedling. You can see that correct planting depth is very critical in soil, but not as much in vermiculite.

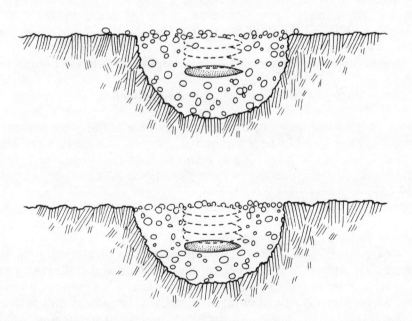

In cool weather, plant each seed deep enough so that three more of the same kind of seed could lie on top of it. In hot weather, plant the seed deep enough so that four more seeds of the same kind could lie on top of it.

Here are some good general guidelines to follow in determining how deep to plant seeds. In cool weather, plant any seed deep enough in vermiculite so that three more of the same seeds could lie on top of it. When planting in hot weather, place the seed deep enough so four more could lie on top. Seeds are planted deeper in hot weather to insure that they won't dry out in the soil. All seeds, no matter what their size or shape, can be laid in the hole horizontally. The hole you poke with your finger should be deep enough so that there's as much vermiculite under the seed as above it, half for the root to grow in and half for the sprout to come up through.

Troubleshooting

Knowing exactly how a seedling grows will help you to understand why so many seed plantings are doomed to failure. Once moisture has caused the seed to swell, it first sends down a root. After the root is secure and may even have started to branch, only then does the top start pushing its way up through the soil. I've seen so many gardeners look over their planted rows and decide that since nothing is showing yet, there's no need to water. Many times the root has already started down, but the weather dries out the soil and the plant, which had already sprouted below ground, dies from lack of moisture. There is a natural tendency to blame those cheap seeds or that blankety-blank seed company, but they are not usually at fault.

Sometimes just the opposite happens, particularly with carrots and parsley, both of which require a long time and constant moisture to sprout. A gardener gets impatient when he sees nothing happening, or sometimes even forgets where he planted that row of carrots, so he starts all over again thinking nothing is going to happen. Whenever I give a lecture and mention the above examples, I see many in the audience nodding their heads, indicating that it happens to a lot of us. If you follow my procedures for planting in a little pocket of vermiculite, the depth of the seed won't be so critical as before. You can afford to make a few mistakes and still get good results.

Covering the plot with a plastic-covered cage protects the planting from several other potential problems besides wind and cold. Heavy rain can really compact the soil surface. In addition, a heavy rainstorm can easily wash away any new planting, especially if the ground isn't perfectly flat and level. Covering the plot prevents these from happening.

For those who say this planting method is a lot of work, or entails too many special precautions, I say try it, and you'll be so pleased by your success that you'll never go back to conventional seed planting with all

Presprouting

This is a fairly new method that's gaining a lot of interest in Europe where spring weather is cold and damp. It's a very simple process in which you sprout your seeds indoors in controlled conditions, and then plant them outdoors as soon as the root sprout starts growing from each seed. The method makes sense, since some seeds take a very long time to sprout in the cool outdoor soil temperatures of springtime. The first step is to sprinkle five, ten, or however many seeds you want on a piece of filter paper or paper towel placed in a shallow dish. Moisten, and slip the entire dish into a plastic bag, then keep it in a warm, 70°F, location (on top of the refrigerator or hot water tank, or in a seed-starting incubator). You must watch the seeds daily, and when most have swelled and sprouted their first tiny root, plant them carefully in a garden square. Cover with sifted compost or vermiculite, water with a fine mist, and protect the planting with a plastic-covered cage. Your sprouted seeds should poke a shoot aboveground in a few days, compared with the few weeks required by conventional planting-out procedures.

Several companies sell kits with all the supplies and equipment needed, but these are geared toward planting hundreds of seeds. Because you are working with a smaller number of seeds, skip the fancy equipment and just take a small spoon and carefully lift the seeds out of the sprouting container. Or you could even cut or tear the paper into little pieces so that there's one seed in each piece and just lift the whole thing out carefully and place it in the soil. To be certain of the advantages in time, review the germination table showing seed-sprouting time at different temperatures, and compare the days required outdoors at whatever the soil temperature is then to the time required indoors at 70°F. Of course, the sooner you can get your seeds to sprout, the less chance there is that they will be killed by cold weather, or rot in the cold, wet soil. In addition, the quicker they sprout the faster they can grow. Presprouting is a new system that's worth experimenting with.

its pitfalls. And actually it doesn't take very long. For large seeds or ones that sprout fast and easily (radishes, beans, squash), you could omit the vermiculite if you have a loose, friable soil that doesn't cake or crust over. Dividing the square, poking the holes, and using the vermiculite all go very fast.

Starting Seeds Indoors

Seed starting indoors is usually a lot easier than out in the yard, but it also has its pitfalls. Here's my method. Knowing seeds like moisture and warmth, I still use vermiculite because I've found it to be the best material for seed starting. When watered from the bottom, the vermiculite acts as a wick to draw up water from a reservoir below the pot so that it's always uniformly moist, but not so saturated that all the air is driven out.

A lot has been written in gardening publications about recycling containers for seed starting, and I've tried them all. Some seem so ill suited that it's amazing they are still used and written about. For example, egg cartons and even eggshells are sometimes recommended, but they either don't drain well or hold so little soil that they can dry out very rapidly. My favorite containers after many years of trial and error are recycled margarine cups with drainage holes drilled in the bottom. I find the cups just the right height to allow the vermiculite to wick up moisture, and deep enough for young seedling roots to grow without entangling or forming a mat on the bottom and sides.

Here's how to start your seeds. Place the empty containers in the dishwasher to clean and sterilize them, then drill through a stack of them with the ¼-inch bit in your electric drill. (Don't try to punch or burn a hole; it makes an awful mess). Take each cup and mark the name and date of the variety you're planting with an indelible marker. Fill almost to the top with vermiculite, tap lightly to settle and even the surface, then sprinkle seeds evenly over the surface. Remember, don't sprinkle out 100 lettuce seeds if you just want six heads of lettuce (plant only 8 or 10 seeds). Then cover the seeds with a thin layer of vermiculite. Its depth will depend on the size of the seeds you just planted. Set the container(s) in a shallow pan filled with about 2 inches of warm water. When the surface of the vermiculite turns a darker color (in just a few seconds) you know it's fully wet. Remove the containers and allow the excess water to drain out. Then place them in a heated seed starter, or slip each one into a plastic bag and place on a tray on top of the refrigerator or hot water tank, or in another warm spot. If you don't have a thermostatically controlled seed starter, I highly recommend one if you're going to start many of your own seeds.

Start seeds in a margarine cup filled with vermiculite. To water the newly planted seeds, set the container in a shallow pan of water.

It makes it much easier to provide the gentle, even warmth the seeds need to get off to a good start.

You don't need light for sprouting; you don't have to have darkness either in most cases. Light doesn't become important until the seed sends a shoot aboveground, after the root has begun to grow. What does matter right from the start is constant moisture and heat. You must inspect your new plantings daily because there are a few other things that also grow where there's moisture and heat—disease-causing bacteria for example.

It is also important to check your newly planted seeds every day because just as soon as that first sprout appears (it is usually pale white, not green in color) you must move the container into strong light—direct sunlight wherever possible. Remove the plastic bag and place the cup on a tray with just a puddle of water, so the vermiculite can absorb just enough moisture to keep the roots moist. If your facilities don't include a greenhouse or heated sun box that provides overhead sunlight, you might want to provide artificial light for your new seedlings. A 36- or 48-inch double-tube fluorescent fixture will usually provide enough light. Turn on the lights in the early morning and again in the afternoon and evening to provide 12 to 16 hours of light (from the sun plus the lamp) for your plants. The fluorescent fixtures work well because they don't give off a lot of heat and won't burn your plants like incandescent lights can.

⌘ Chapter 11
Transplanting

A "transplant" is nothing more than a young plant that is started from seed in one place (usually in a container indoors) and moved or transplanted to its permanent location in the garden when it has reached a certain size. There are two main reasons for using transplants rather than sowing seeds directly in the garden: to give plants more time to grow, and to save space. Time is for most people the most important reason to use transplants because seeds can be planted indoors and seedlings raised to transplant size before the soil or weather conditions in the spring garden are suitable for planting seeds outdoors. You can raise your own plants, or buy young ones at a nursery. It all depends on the time and facilities you have available, as well as your talents and inclinations. The other reason for working with transplants is to save space in the garden by using it only for the final maturation of crops, rather than as a nursery for little seedlings. In this way your garden space is kept at a constantly high level of productivity.

Seeds can be planted fairly close together in a seed flat or cup, and the seedlings later transplanted to containers, where they can still grow in less space than they will need to mature fully. Only after the young plants grow and begin to crowd each other is it necessary to provide more space. Actually, you can start seeds in just 1 percent of the space required by the mature plant, then your seedlings can be grown in 10 percent of the same area required for the ultimate plant. In addition, you can usually provide better growing conditions in a small, confined space than you can out in the garden.

It is easy to see how you can keep a garden of limited size productive to its maximum capacity by growing young plants alongside the garden in containers until there's room in the main garden to move them in for the final step of growing to maturity. Of course, this takes a toll in time, effort, and planning. In addition, each plant is slightly shocked by each move and receives a setback of from several days to up to two weeks; the larger the plant, the longer it takes to recover from the shock. So it takes somewhat longer than normal for plants to reach maturity, and sometimes productivity may also be affected somewhat.

But I believe those disadvantages are outweighed by the many advantages of starting plants out of the garden. Working with transplants enables you to gain a great deal of time and productivity in your available garden space. If you were to start growing everything from seed right in the garden, you would have an almost-empty garden most of the growing season (assuming you kept the weeds in check). Most of the summer vegetable seeds couldn't be planted until all danger of frost was past— which is not until May in most parts of the country. And you'd have to wait a long time for crops like tomatoes that require from 120 to 150 days to grow from seed to the first harvest. If you started your tomatoes from seed outdoors, harvest would not begin until late August or even early September. Since this leaves such a short time for reaping the "fruits of the vine," most gardeners rely on transplants grown in commercial greenhouses, or start their own indoors six to eight weeks before the last frost. Gardeners using transplants can expect the tomato harvest to start in mid-July in many parts of the country—that's an extra six weeks of harvest.

The same is true of any summer vegetables that require a long time to sprout and grow to transplantable size (peppers and eggplant, for example). However, other summer vegetables such as beans, squash, and cucumbers sprout and grow very rapidly. Notice that the size of the seeds usually determines how fast a plant sprouts and grows—large seeds generally sprout faster and grow quicker. These large-seeded, fast-growing crops are usually sown directly in the garden at the proper time—after all danger of frost is past. You can start them indoors about two weeks ahead of time, but it's not always worth the effort because of the transplanting shock that can occur.

Some of the spring or cool-weather vegetables can also be started earlier. Onions, lettuce, and all members of the cabbage family can be brought to a much earlier harvest by starting them indoors during the winter. Other cool-weather crops (like peas) are usually direct-seeded outdoors in the garden at their appropriate time.

One word of caution here: although transplants are a great help in the garden, it's important to remember that not all crops take well to transplanting. There are some vegetables, root crops in particular, that do not transplant very well, no matter how careful you are. They should always be direct-seeded in the garden. The chart on Best Starting Methods for Crops lists those vegetables which sprout quickly and thus offer little advantage in transplanting.

Knowing that a plant goes into shock each time it's moved or transplanted, a wise gardener learns how to handle a plant and its roots gently. Taking certain precautions can prevent an undue shock and speed recovery so the plant starts growing again rapidly. Chapter 10 covered the seed-starting techniques I recommend for both indoors and outdoors. Now I'll explain the methods of transplanting that will provide good results in your garden.

When to Transplant Seedlings

How long to leave the seedlings in the seed cup before transplanting either indoors or outdoors is always a difficult question to answer. Most

BEST STARTING METHODS FOR CROPS

Direct-Seed Only	Direct-Seed or Transplant	Transplant only
Beans	Swiss chard	Broccoli
Beets	*Cucumbers	Cabbage
Carrots	Lettuce	Cauliflower
Corn	*Muskmelons	*Eggplant
Onions from sets	*Summer squash	Onions from seed
Peas		Parsley
Radishes		*Peppers
Spinach		Tomatoes
Winter squash		

*Transplant with care

books recommend waiting until the second set of true leaves appears, but I've found that for most gardeners that's too long. Under the ideal growing conditions that can be provided by plantsmen and nurseries, that advice is fine. But few home gardeners can duplicate those ideal conditions, and without them the plant's roots keep growing, getting rather long and leggy, while the top elongates even before the second set of leaves appears. Also there is a tendency for the gardener to wait until the second leaves are large enough to identify. By then it's usually too late to transplant, because the seed cup is full of a mass of tangled, interwoven roots.

Instead of waiting for the second set of true leaves, transplant your seedlings when the first set of true leaves appears, or as soon as you can handle the tiny plants without breaking them. The smaller a plant is, the

Tiny seedlings are ready to transplant indoors or outdoors when they have developed their second set of leaves (the first set of true leaves).

less shock it will undergo from being transplanted. It has also been found that the less a seedling is handled and replanted the better it will grow. (The one exception is tomato plants, which seem to thrive and grow better when replanted, each time deeper and deeper.) It's best to transplant the seedlings directly into the garden if soil and weather conditions are suitable. If it's still too early in the season to set out the young plants, they can be transplanted indoors into other containers.

The timing is important because the older the seedling becomes, the more shock it will sustain when transplanted. On the other hand, it's very difficult to handle a young seedling when it's so tiny, and sometimes you can cause more damage than if you had let it grow for just a little longer. It depends a lot on how gentle you are with the plants, and how easy it is for you to do this delicate work. On a practical level, of course, what usually determines when you transplant is when you have the time in your busy schedule.

Since you will probably have only a few hours to devote to transplanting during any one week in the busy spring, I recommend that you try planting only ten seeds of every crop that you want and no more, not even an extra one or two for good measure. If you are especially fond of a particular vegetable or a certain variety, the next week you can plant ten more seeds of that same variety, but never more. Limiting the amount of seeds will make it easy to transplant just the ten seedlings (or whatever percentage sprouted from those ten seeds) of each variety. If you have a particularly poor sprouting experience you can always replant another ten seeds—you've only lost a week or so. And realistically, can you think of any vegetable (grown from transplants) of which you're going to want to harvest more than ten? Even allowing for the few seeds that don't sprout, and the few plants that succumb to disease, pests, and transplanting shock, you'll still have a lot to harvest.

If by chance you did overplant seeds and you won't be able to use those extra bunches of Oak Leaf lettuce or heads of Jersey cabbage, now is the time to take corrective action. Transplant only the number of seedlings that you want to mature, and then place all those remaining in the compost pile or turn them under in the garden. Do it right away before you change your mind and decide that "maybe I ought to save these just in case." The "just in case" hardly ever happens.

If you'll try using this system of controlled planting you'll have more time to transplant each crop at the proper time when the seedlings are still young and small. The end result will be a better harvest, because the seedlings will recover quickly and resume growing at a steady, rapid pace.

Getting Ready to Transplant

Before starting the transplanting procedure it is important to consider the soil, the containers, and the techniques for transplanting.

Soil

The soil for transplants should be your very best—the richest in organic matter and loosest you have. I think the best transplanting media are the prepared mixes sold at garden supply centers. They are sterile, uniform in texture, lightweight, easily handled, and relatively inexpensive considering you don't need a lot. But many gardeners prefer to make their own planting mixes. If you'd prefer to make your own mix, try this formula: mix equal parts (for example, one pail full) of coarse vermiculite, screened peat moss, coarse sand, decomposed leaf mold (screened through a ¼-inch mesh), and good garden soil (also screened through a ¼-inch mesh). Add 2 cups of fertilizer, as described in chapter 5. In addition, add a cup of lime, and a half-pail of screened wood stove or fireplace charcoal. A strong plastic garbage bag makes a convenient container for mixing and storing your transplanting medium. Line a large plastic or metal garbage can with the plastic bag, dump in the measured ingredients, then close and tie the bag. Turning the can on its side, carefully roll it around on the ground. Everything will mix well without spilling or creating a lot of dust. Then open the bag and add two equal parts of water (for example, two pails of water for the above quantities), close the bag and let stand overnight. The next day the mix will be uniformly moist throughout, but not soggy. It will also be well mixed and ready to use and any leftover mix can be stored until you need it.

Containers

If you will be transplanting some plants indoors before setting them out in the garden later on, you'll need to give some thought to the type of containers into which you want to transplant your young seedlings. There must be hundreds of kinds of containers for seedlings on the market. The most common type is made of plastic, and is divided into 6, 8, or 12 sections. The 6-section trays, which are sometimes referred to as six-packs, seem to be the most common. Some trays have no separations for the individual plants. Don't use these even though they are less expensive; they allow the plants' roots to grow together, and the roots then require cutting when transplanting. Other trays have individual sections for each plant, and they come in all sizes, shapes, and colors. Don't select a container that is divided into lots of small sections in the name of economy (getting more plants per tray). The plants will quickly outgrow this type of container; the roots just wind around the bottom, and the plant becomes rootbound, to its detriment.

A fairly new product on the market is a Styrofoam tray in which the sections are shaped like inverted pyramids. Such trays, called Speedling or Todd trays, are reported to ease transplanting shock because of the way the roots grow. There is a hole in the bottom of each section of the tray,

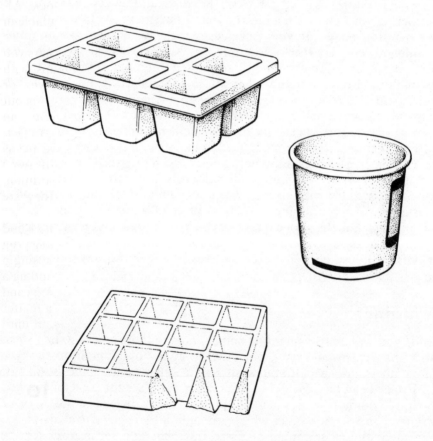

If it's too early to transplant into the garden, seedlings can be transplanted into plastic trays (top), yogurt cups (center), Speedling trays (bottom), or other containers.

and the trays are elevated on blocks or screens to allow light and air underneath them. The roots grow downward, then stop because they are exposed to air and light. Instead of continuing to grow and curling around the inside of the container as they do in most pots, the roots produce many branches. This is called air pruning. When the seedlings are transplanted, they have lots of these tiny "feeder roots" instead of just a long taproot, so they are able to draw moisture and nutrients from the soil more readily. Speedling trays are presently used mostly by commercial farmers rather than home growers. I've had mixed results with these trays. They are hard to keep watered, and they're too big and bulky unless you cut them in half (which is easily done with a hand saw). But they have produced a good, stocky plant that transplants easily without a great deal of shock. Although expensive, they are reusable year after year. They are available in garden supply centers or through mail-order catalogs.

Of course, there are also many homemade or recycled containers you can use for seedlings. My favorite are waxed cardboard yogurt cups, with drainage holes punched in the bottom with a pencil, screwdriver, or ballpoint pen. You can plant cup and all in the garden by just tearing out the bottom when it's time to plant; the sides and rim even become an automatic cutworm collar. I like them much better than peat pots. In fact, I find peat pots to be a distinct disadvantage, unless the entire pot is removed for planting. The top rim of the peat forms a wick and draws a lot of moisture out of the ground and away from the roots. In addition, I find that roots do not readily grow through these pots as they are assumed to.

Of all the other sorts of recycled containers you read about, I find several disadvantages with most; cottage cheese cups are too big, egg cartons are too small, milk cartons flex and bend too easily, causing a disturbance of the roots each time they are handled or moved. Finding a reasonably sized strong container that suits most growing conditions and plants, and is still inexpensive or readily available, is quite often a matter of personal choice. So try all the suggestions you hear or read about until you find those that suit you best.

Transplanting from Seed Cups to Trays or Pots

Now for the actual techniques of transplanting. Make sure your soil is moistened the night before. You can't work properly with dry or soggy soil. Then fill your container, but don't pack the soil down tightly. I found that an easy way to settle the soil once the container is filled is to drop or bang the tray on a table or workbench; that's usually all it takes. Then with a pencil drill a hole in the soil in the center of each compartment to put the plant in. It's a good idea to make sure your cups of little seedlings are watered the night before transplanting. Then be sure they are set out to drain. The watering will insure that the plants are turgid and firm, and proper drainage guarantees that the vermiculite won't be soggy and cause the seedlings to be hard to separate. Working in the shade (never let the sun or wind strike the roots of a plant, even for a moment; they will start to die immediately), you can use a pencil to loosen up the plants and vermiculite in the seedling cup very easily. Then, working with the pencil, you push up or separate each seedling from the rest. The more vermiculite you can keep clinging to the roots, the better off your plant will be. Holding the plant by just the seed-leaf or leaves, and with a pencil underneath the roots, lift the little plant into the new tray or container and deposit it in one of the holes you made. Make sure it sits comfortably down in the hole, at least as deep as it was growing before or even slightly deeper (up to the seed-leaf). Then gently tuck in soil all around the plant with the point of the pencil. Some soil may need a little extra push with the

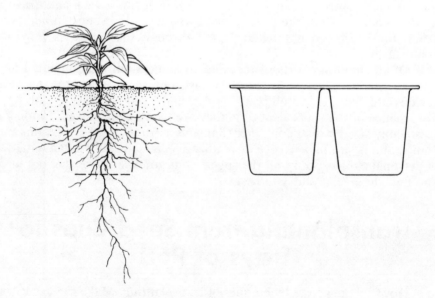

If the seedling's roots are too big for the container, carefully trim them to fit. It's better to prune the roots than to crowd them into the container.

fingers to firm it up just enough to make good contact with the plant roots, and to provide support.

Experience will guide you throughout this operation. Sometimes the seedlings have grown too large and the roots are tangled or long and matted. Rather than stuff the long roots into the new hole, it's better to take the scissors and cut off the extra length. Trim just enough to allow the roots to fit comfortably in the hole. As a general rule, the root should be about twice as long as the stem. This kind of root pruning won't hurt the plant; in fact, it will force the plant to send out tiny new feeder roots, and it will do much better than it would if it tried to continue growing with its taproot all bent and twisted into a hole. After you have finished transplanting your seedlings, mark the name on the containers with a permanent marker, and the date if you want to keep that information. (Be

Transplants can be watered from below, by floating the container in a pan of water to permit gentle, even absorption of moisture into the soil.

sure you get pens with indelible, not water-soluble, ink so your labels won't "run" if they get wet.) Then place the containers into a shallow pan of warm water, about 2 inches deep. Some gardeners like to add a little manure tea, fish emulsion, or other soluble fertilizer to the water, and I agree with that.

When the soil has absorbed all the water it can, in about 10 to 15 minutes, remove the containers and set them down in the shade to drain. Keep them in the shade for a day or two to lessen the transplanting shock. If it's hot and sunny don't rush the seedlings out of the shade, but move them if possible from full shade to bright indirect light, then to direct sunlight the third day. If any wilting is observed, move them quickly back into the shade.

The used vermiculite from the seed cup should not be reused for seed starting, since it might have picked up some harmful bacteria or disease-causing organisms that would hurt young seedlings. Add any leftover to your garden soil, and start every batch of seeds in fresh, sterile vermiculite right out of the bag. Clean the seed cup, cross out the name and date or rub it off with steel wool and the cup can be reused. Some people like to put their seed cups through the dishwasher to sterilize them.

Transplanting into the Garden

If you're moving young seedlings directly into a garden space, you use just about the same procedure as indoors. Prepare your soil in each square to be planted, then mark off the individual plant spaces with a stick or your finger. Divide a small square in half for every 6-inch spacing, in thirds for the 4-inch spacing, and in fourths for 3-inch spacing. Use your sharpened pencil for digging out and planting the young plants, just like you did indoors. The only difference you'll notice is that the soil might be a little coarser or rougher than your indoor potting soil. If your garden soil is rather stony or very rough, you might take a bucket of good potting soil along, and use it to replace one trowel full of your garden soil at each plant hole.

When you're in the garden, remember to work so the young plants are in the shade (you can if necessary move your body so you're working in your own shadow, or even erect a simple sun shade). Never transplant during the hottest part of the day; late afternoon is best but not always convenient. The worst time to transplant is early morning, particularly if you have to be away that day. It may be nice and cool at that time, but then while you're away at work the new transplants must withstand the hottest and sunniest part of the day without the benefit of any extra water.

Left: When you're ready to transplant young plants into the garden, begin by dividing the squares into the proper plant spacings.
Right: Dig a hole and carefully set in the plant. When handling the transplants, always support them on the bottom to avoid damaging the stems and leaves.

They may be wilted and dead by the time you come home. It's better to do other garden chores in the early hours (weeding, watering, harvesting, planting seeds) and leave all your transplanting until afternoon or evening.

When the transplants are in the ground it is imperative to put up a sun shade—always. If you use a wire cage covered with shade film (as described in chapter 9) it will have the added advantage of shielding the plant from winds and heavy rains, as well as hungry rabbits. The other necessity for new transplants is a drink right after they are planted. Have a bucket of sun-warmed water handy and water each plant in a square as soon as you're finished. Don't go on to planting other squares thinking you'll water the entire garden later. Do it as each square is completed.

If you're moving grown-up transplants rather than seedlings into the garden, it is much easier and quicker even though you follow all the same procedures. All the same guidelines apply: prepare the soil as explained previously, work in the shade (in late afternoon if possible), water each plant when finished, and provide shade for a few days.

When to Transplant Out

Deciding when to make the move usually depends on the time of year, the weather, and when a square is available in the garden. In most cases the sooner you set out a plant the better, since the plant will sustain some shock during the move. It's tempting to leave the plant inside where it will probably grow faster, because of the warmer growing conditions and the better protection from the elements. But then the larger plant will suffer a more serious shock when you finally do plant it outdoors. Transplanting time is also to an extent determined by what kind of container the seedling is in, and how rootbound the plant becomes.

A little experimenting each season will help you decide just what's best for you and your particular garden conditions. Of course, if your garden space is at an absolute premium, then it does pay to keep it filled with larger plants while the medium- and smaller-size transplants are off to the side growing in pots or trays. Usually, however, you will move plants from the seedling cup to the transplant container, to the final garden location in stages. This means that all spaces in the garden contain plants that almost fill the space. It takes a lot more planning and work to transplant several times, but it will provide a larger harvest from the same space.

Remember in all cases to water the transplants the night before you plan to move them, as well as the garden square you're going to move them into. You don't want to work in just-watered, mucky soil because it will pack down too tight from just normal handling and working. It's also not a good idea to work in dry soil, even if you promptly water it after planting. Those tender roots will start drying out and dying as soon as they are handled and moved.

So what do you do if you forgot to water, didn't have time, or just suddenly decided now to do some transplanting? You can either go ahead and break the rules, or water now and wait as long as possible to transplant. We've all done both at times; a lot will depend on the circumstances at the moment. But if it comes to a choice between working in too-wet or too-dry soil, I'd opt for the latter if at all possible. It is imperative to avoid compacting the soil, which can easily happen when it is too wet. If you plant in dry soil, just water as soon as the planting is completed.

How To Transplant

Since a lot of time and effort went into growing those transplants, don't spoil it all by using a heavy hand when removing the plant from the container and transplanting it. Any stem or leaf that is broken or even bruised will hurt the chances of a fast recovery in the plant's new home. Keeping the plant roots moist and out of the wind and sun is a must, but gentle handling is also a good habit in gardening. Practice until you've developed a sure, smooth method of removing each plant from its container. Never pull up on the main stem to remove a plant or even just to hold it. Always support it from underneath, and when removing the plant turn the pot upside down so gravity helps. Push on the bottom or rap the edge against a hard surface. You should treat a young plant just like you would a small baby; hold it with one hand while supporting it underneath with the palm of the other hand. Very often for small containers you can shake the plant loose with a swift, short, downward jerk while supporting the upside-down plant root with one hand, stem between two fingers.

The last step, but a very important one, is to always plant in a saucer-shaped depression. This is to facilitate watering throughout the rest of the plant's life. It is important in a flat garden but critical to gardens planted on sloping land. When you read chapter 12, you'll see that my method of watering is quick and easy but very personalized. You give a cup of sun-warmed water to each plant; no overhead watering is necessary. The depression around each plant insures that the water doesn't run

Always support a plant from the bottom when removing it from a container. Grasping a young plant by the stem or leaves could damage it.

all over the garden, but stays to benefit each particular plant. The water will all sink right down to the plant roots, with the result that plants will develop a smaller, more compact root system that allows you to plant close together without lowering yields. The saucer will also make it very easy to fertilize the plants later on. Any fertilizer placed in the saucer will all be carried by subsequent waterings to the plant's root system. For gardeners who like to feed plants with manure tea at every other watering, this method is ideal. The larger the plant, the larger the saucer should be.

When you're planting, picture the shape and size of the mature plant and make a shallow saucer equal in diameter to the plant's final size. If you can't picture the mature plant, just make sure the saucer extends to the boundaries of the space allowed for that plant. That is, if you're putting four lettuce plants in a square, the four depressions will almost touch each other and fill most of the square. The saucer doesn't have to be deep; in fact it's better shallow, so it can hold about 1 inch of water. If you make a small saucer now and try to enlarge it later when the plant grows bigger, you may disturb and damage some of the roots, particularly those of shallow-rooted vegetables such as lettuce. Another advantage of this planting method is that when you water, you won't be wetting the soil in between the plant saucers, so you won't be encouraging weeds to sprout and grow. Less weeding means more time for tending your plants. If you live in a place where water is dear or short of supply, you'll find this method uses less than 10 percent of the amount of water usually required for overhead watering in a row garden, yet more than satisfies all of your plant needs.

How long to leave the shade cage in place over the new transplants

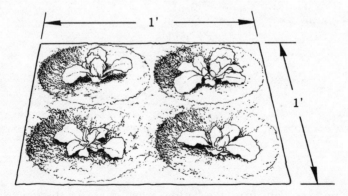

To conserve water, plant each plant in a shallow, saucer-shaped depression.

depends a lot on the season, sun, temperature, recent rainfall, and wind. In addition, plant size and condition must also be considered. As a general rule, give the transplants shade until they can stand on their own without wilting during the day. That's usually a period of two or three days, but it could be up to a week under the worst conditions. I used to always use a wood shingle for shade, and still do sometimes for large individual plants. It's quick and easy and has the advantage of shading only during the very hot part of the day, thus allowing the plant to start growing with more light. Although one shingle doesn't provide too much wind protection, you could add two or three more. Just position the shingle so as to shade the plant from the noonday sun. The plant will get plenty of light, and some early and late sun, which might be all it needs the first few days.

There are many devices you can make at home for shading, wind protection, and hardening-off of seedlings, as well as a few new commercial products. My advice is to try several kinds of protective devices just like you did the transplanting containers to find your favorite, but do use *something*. Make it a habit to protect all your transplants. In the square foot garden it's easy to shield an entire square, and certainly easier than covering a long single row.

Hardening-Off

The other consideration involved in transplanting is this business of hardening-off. So much is written about it, and although it's a necessary step when using transplants, I find it's frankly a pain in the neck. If more gardeners fully understood ahead of time the work and nuisance involved in the hardening-off process, they wouldn't be in such a hurry to start their seeds extra early each year. Every plant variety has a normal growing season, as we've learned. Obviously spring or cool-weather vegetables can sprout and grow in much colder temperatures than summer or warm-weather vegetables. The same is true in regard to frost.

Left to its own devices, nature will automatically start each type of seed when its time comes and not usually before, but we gardeners find this growing season too short, so we try to improve on things and speed up the natural course of events to suit our needs. That means planting seeds early indoors and moving transplants outdoors as soon as they can safely withstand the temperature and weather. Obviously we gain time this way, because instead of the seed just starting to sprout in its accustomed time outdoors, there we are with a large-size plant already growing. Even taking into account the shock and setback undergone by a transplant, it is usually much further ahead than the same kind of plant grown from seed sown directly in the garden. The problem comes in the fact that the transplant has been grown under protected, almost ideal conditions. In the greenhouse or indoor garden there's lots of sunlight, warm air, protection at night from freezing, plenty of water, perfect soil, lots of nutrients, few pests, no wind, no pelting rain, hail, or snow—sounds pretty nice, doesn't it? Now try to move that plant out into the hostile garden world where environmental conditions are just the opposite and it will probably succumb in a short time. So before a plant can be permanently moved outdoors it must be *gradually* acclimated to the new, harsher conditions of the garden. In other words, it is hardened-off by gradually moving it between the two locations. At first it spends just a few hours outdoors and is then brought back indoors. Each day the plant can spend a few more hours outdoors, until it can be left out overnight (but covered). At this point the seedling is said to be hardened and ready for a permanent move into the garden.

Now, all of this takes a lot of work, either physically carrying trays back and forth, or opening the sun box top wider and wider each day but remembering to close it at night. If you do everything the way it is supposed to be done you have to ask eventually "Is it all worthwhile?" Of course, if you're not too far out of season it's not as critical. Then it's possible to transplant into the garden and just provide some protection for the plants with a plastic-covered cage, or some of the commercial hot caps. That becomes a much easier process and does seem to make a lot more sense. One thing that will help a lot is to place a plastic-covered cage over the square a few weeks beforehand in order to preheat the soil and warm it up. The cage will also keep off the spring rains and snow. More about that in chapter 15.

Chapter 12
☙ Watering

Too much or too little water has probably caused more failures in the home vegetable garden than any other growing condition. What's worse, the reason for these failures is usually unknown or unrecognized by most gardeners. For the beginner, how to water properly is usually one of the most difficult aspects of gardening to learn, much less truly understand. Rules and advice on proper watering techniques are often contradictory. How often? How much? When and how? Not only do various authors and garden experts have their own favorite watering methods, but so much depends on the soil, the part of the country in which you live, the time of the year, the weather, and the crops themselves.

Without the proper amount of water at the right time, lettuce can get bitter and bolt to seed, cabbage heads split, tomato blossoms drop or the fruit develops blossom end rot, radishes get pithy, and on and on. When new gardeners do notice yellowing leaves or dropping blossoms and go to their favorite book to find the cause of the problem, quite often the answer they get is "either too little or too much water." How is a poor beginner to know which type of water problem he has and what to do about it?

The most important part of the answer lies in understanding the structure of your soil—for that's the first key to understanding proper watering techniques. The type of soil helps determine how much water is

187

made available to plants, and how quickly the water in the soil will drain away after each rain or a watering. As we saw in chapter 5, soil is often classified as sandy, loamy, or clayey, and each type requires different watering techniques. It's also important to know how plants take up water, and what conditions the roots need for proper growth.

Roots are the foundation of the plant. If the roots are healthy, the top of the plant will be healthy and vigorous, too. Roots must have air movement through the soil to remove carbon dioxide they expire (give off), and to bring in fresh oxygen for new growth. The roots must also have a constant supply of moisture available for rapid growth. Soil structure and composition determine how well the plant roots can be supplied with both air and moisture at the same time.

It helps to realize that plant roots do not actually grow *in* soil. They grow in the air spaces between soil particles. Sandy, loamy, and clayey soils are composed of different sized and shaped particles. Sandy soil has lots of air spaces between its large particles, while dense, clayey soil with its tiny particles doesn't have very many air spaces for the roots.

When you water your soil, the water fills all the air spaces and drives out the air. As the water drains down through the soil the air follows it, and replenishes the plant with oxygen. But the plant roots stop growing while they are submerged. (These are a different kind of roots than those that would grow in water, as when you grow hydroponically, or root a house plant cutting in water.) If the soil remains waterlogged very long, plant growth will suffer.

When a plant has too little water, several things happen to the plant, including a condition known as water stress. Growth is interrupted again, but for the opposite reason—too little moisture. This shock tells the plant that it doesn't have long to live, so it begins flower and seed development to accomplish its role in life: reproduction. That's why the edible part of the plant changes in taste to us, as the plant hastens the seed-ripening process. Leaf growth stops, and all the plant's energy goes into this final act. If lack of moisture continues, the plant will wilt and die. If the plant is replenished with moisture, it will start growing normally again. But its growth was interrupted and that will have an effect on the final harvest. If growth is intermittent throughout the season due to uneven moisture, as so often happens, the gardener will not be aware of any problems until he or she actually eats the harvest. At that point it's very difficult to connect the bitter flavor of the lettuce with the few dry periods that occurred several weeks previously. That's one way in which improper watering goes unrecognized by most gardeners as a cause of crop damage.

Knowing what plants require of an ideal soil—lots of open pore spaces and lots of spongy organic matter to hold water—you can also see

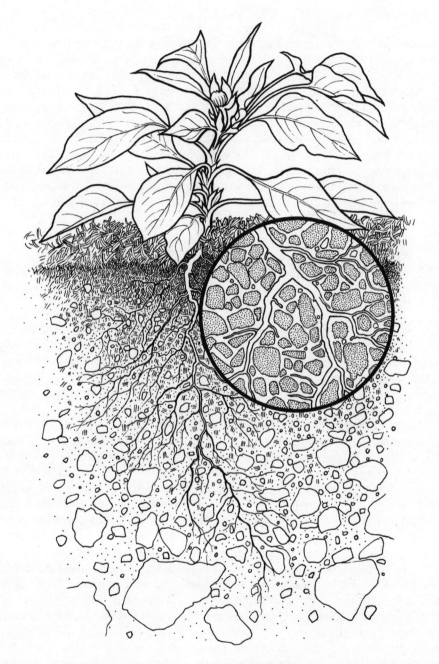

Plant roots do not actually grow *in* soil; they grow in the spaces between soil particles.

why loose, friable, easily worked soil is so important from a watering standpoint. Compaction has a great deal to do with the water absorption and holding capacity of any soil, regardless of its composition. The more you walk over and ride over your growing soil, the denser and more compact it gets, especially the surface layer, making it extremely difficult for water and air to penetrate to the roots. This effect is even more pronounced when the soil is wet. Like a child making mud pies, when you work in wet soil the air spaces between particles collapse and do not re-form when the soil dries. That's why you read so often not to turn over or work your soil in the early spring when the soil is still too wet. Because the square foot garden contains walking paths, you won't walk on your soil and compact it during the growing season, either. Your soil will stay loose and crumbly all year.

How Much and How Often to Water

An understanding of the varying drainage capabilities of different kinds of soils, and the important ability of organic matter to absorb and store moisture, is the first step in learning how often and how much to water. Water moves through the three primary types of soil in different ways. Since clayey soil has a very fine, tightly bound structure, water drains through it very slowly, and watering is fairly inefficient. You have to apply a lot of water before the moisture will sink to any usable depth, and you have to water slowly, or it will just run off on the surface. Plants growing in clayey soil need to have water applied at a slow rate for a long time to do any good. Of course, a clayey soil dries out very slowly, too, so you don't have to water as frequently. Sandy soil is just the opposite. It drains so fast that you have to water fairly frequently. But when you do water, you don't have to apply as much or for as long a period of time. Therefore, you can add whatever water is required very quickly. Loamy soil is the happy medium between the other two types.

As you can see in the accompanying chart, there is a great deal of difference in the frequency and quantities with which plants growing in the three types of soils need to be watered. Thus, it is impossible to give very accurate watering instructions in a book that will be used by gardeners throughout the country. You must become familiar with the structure and composition of the soil in your garden in order to give your crops the right amount of water. As you will see, weather conditions and the age and type of the plant also affect how much and how often you should

QUANTITY AND FREQUENCY OF WATERING

Since sandy soil drains so quickly, you have to water more often, but not as much; clayey soil, on the other hand, needs twice as much water but only half as often. The watering quantities suggested for individual crops in chapter 18 are based on average conditions; adjust them accordingly for your soil and weather conditions.

To wet the soil in one square (12″ by 12″) to the following depths, you need to apply the following:

Soil Type	6″ deep	12″ deep	18″ deep
Sandy	2 cups every 2 days	4 cups every 3½ days	6 cups every 5 days
Loamy	4 cups every 3½ days	6 cups every 5 days	10 cups every 9 days
Clayey	6 cups every 5 days	10 cups every 9 days	16 cups every 13 days

water. The best approach is to make sure your soil contains plenty of organic matter, and to observe your garden carefully and water when your plants need it, not just when this book or any other one tells you to.

Other Guides to Proper Watering

In addition to soil structure, watering techniques must, of course, also be geared to the requirements of the plants themselves. Some crops grow best with a constant, even supply of moisture. These include all of the root, leaf, and head crops (carrots, beets, radishes, lettuce, Swiss chard, spinach, cabbage, and broccoli). Such plants develop fairly shallow roots which depend heavily on constant soil moisture close to the surface. If the top 6 to 12 inches of soil dry out, the plant will go into shock because of water stress and the final harvest will suffer.

In contrast, fruit or seed crops (such as tomatoes, cucumbers, eggplant, peppers, corn, beans, squash, and melons), like to send roots deeper into the ground and grow best with deep but infrequent waterings. When these plants receive too much water, too often, they refuse to produce a good fruit crop, but instead grow lots of leaves and bushy tops. Remember that when there is a shortage of moisture plants tend to flower and go to seed. You can see why you want the root and leaf crops to receive an uninterrupted moisture supply, but you do want the seed and fruit crops to go through the wet and dry cycles. As long as they have deep roots, plants won't lack for some moisture, and won't wilt and die.

Another consideration for the amount and frequency of watering is the age of the plant. Newly planted seeds require constant moisture right at the soil surface in order to germinate, so it's necessary to sprinkle them daily, sometimes twice a day if the weather is very hot and sunny. Additional tips for insuring constant moisture can be found in chapter 10. When the seeds sprout, they must have moisture at their root level, which is still very shallow, and as the stems poke above the surface they will still need constant moisture, but deeper now as the roots grow downward.

Young transplants also need a constant supply of moisture because they are undergoing a transplanting shock when moved, but you must be careful not to give them too much, particularly if your soil is composed of heavy, water-retaining clay or lacks adequate organic matter. The combination of just the right amount of moisture and the ideal growing conditions leads to a well-established transplant. Shading is important, too for a young transplant, particularly in the warmer weather and on hot, sunny days when moisture evaporates from the leaves quickly.

Another factor that enters into watering is the wind. If your garden is on a windy site, or you're going through a spell of windy weather, you'll find plant leaves and surface soil dry out much quicker, so plants will need more frequent watering.

I hope the guidelines for watering are coming together now—the ability and capacity of various types of soils for absorbing and holding moisture and air, the importance of organic matter in the soil, the special needs of various crops for either a constant or interrupted supply of water.

Now you see why it's such a complicated and confusing subject, this business of watering, and why it's difficult to make general rules. The "inch of water a week" so often recommended loses most of its meaning when all the variables are considered. By knowing *your* soil and *your* crops you should be able to provide the conditions that each plant likes best. The result, of course, will be a better and quicker harvest, and much less frustration for you, the gardener.

Watering Methods

Now let's look at some methods of watering. Is it better to water from above or at ground level? What type of equipment is best to use? Each way of watering has its place, and you must decide what's best for you and your garden. Here are some considerations to bear in mind.

Although it is the most widely used method, overhead watering is probably the poorest way to water crops. It wastes a lot of water and wets the foliage, which can lead to disease and attract undesirable insects. But it is the easiest method for large gardens and is commonly practiced.

Ground level watering is a very efficient, water-saving method because it puts the water closest to the root level. But it is difficult and time-consuming except in a small garden.

Overhead sprinklers, whether they are rotary, oscillating, or fan type, are not needed in the square foot garden. A good, sturdy bucket and cup is all the watering equipment you need. Buy a strong bucket, but one that's not so big that you can't carry it when it's filled with water. If you already have a garden hose, a long-handled hose extender with a mister, a bubbler, and a shut-off valve will make it more useful to you.

Watering the Square Foot Garden

Since your garden is one fifth (or 20 percent) the size of a conventional garden, you've automatically eliminated 80 percent of your watering and space requirements. The 20 percent that's left can be taken care of with a time-tested method that is easy, quick, and compatible with good plant growth—hand dipping from the water pail!

If you planted every plant in a slight saucer depression, as described in chapter 11, and if you've gotten to know your soil and the requirements of your plants, you can now dip a cup or two of water into each plant "saucer" as the need arises. For example, in my garden on Long Island the soil is very sandy and I need to water twice a week for all leaf and root crops, once a week for all seed and fruit crops, and sometimes daily for young transplants. It doesn't take long. It takes under 5 minutes to water all the plants in the average block (4 feet by 4 feet) by hand. How do you remember when to water which type of crop? Just set up a regular schedule, say every Saturday for all plants, and every Wednesday for leaf and root crops only (weather permitting, of course). If you have as many as six blocks in your garden, that's only 25 to 30 minutes a week—not much for a well-watered garden.

If you live in the southwest, or another dry climate area where irrigation is usually required to provide enough water for plants, you can connect the saucers around the plants with a slight trough. As you water each plant, any runover will be carried directly to the next plant, without wetting the entire surface of the garden.

I always recommend watering from a bucket instead of a hose so that you can let the water warm in the sun before you use it. Plants

Water each plant with a cup. The saucer-shaped depression around each plant helps to hold the water until it can soak down through the soil to the roots.

are a lot like us—they like warm water, not cold. Cold water causes plants to go into slight shock, and when you water from the hose or the cold water tap, your plants will stop growing momentarily. Why not treat them to water warmed all day in the sun? Just get in the habit of filling your buckets after each watering and letting them sit in the sun, so the water will be warm when you're next ready to use it. In addition, most city water contains chlorine and other chemicals that evaporate or settle out if the water is allowed to stand in a bucket for 24 hours before you use it.

By using the bucket and cup method you'll also be practicing conservation and placing all the water right where it's needed, at the plant's roots. When you keep the surrounding area dry on the surface you lessen the chance of weed seeds sprouting, another big advantage to directed watering.

The other advantage of dipping a cup of water to each plant once or twice a week is that it gives you the opportunity (actually trains you) to look closely at each plant. Now you'll be able to spot trouble in the form of insects or diseases when it first strikes and take some early action. You'll also find that you enjoy your plants and your entire garden much more when you're this close to them. They truly become just like children as you care for them while they grow to maturity.

Mulching to Conserve Moisture

I'm a great believer in mulching and have practiced it for many years. In my experience, mulching really does keep the soil moist and friable, easy to work, and more even in temperature. Mulches also help keep ground moisture from evaporating and keep rainwater from splattering mud on your plants. I've mulched with just about every material known to man, even a few new ones I've never read about. One fall at our community garden I wanted to test and demonstrate mulching. So we set up a demonstration garden with 4-foot by 4-foot blocks, planting the same fall crops in each square, but using a different mulch material in each block. We used everything from newspapers (too messy looking), to tar paper (too stiff and unyielding), burlap (weeds grow right through it), hay and grass clippings (works well if thick enough), and old carpet (the best material we found). We even tried the dust mulch method, but found it was too much work and made it hard to tell when the garden needed watering. We tried many other materials with mixed results.

But mulching in general is well worthwhile. Although it does not produce as pretty a garden as a well-weeded, manicured plot, it sure looks better than a weedy, forlorn-looking garden.

Various intensive gardening methods that have become popular in recent years make use of what is called a living mulch. This is achieved by spacing wanted plants close enough together so that when mature they cover all of the growing soil, thereby leaving no room for weeds. Of course, when the plants are young the living "mulch" isn't effective, and if you're just planting seeds they will be in direct competition with weeds. In various stages of planting there are many weeds, and they must be dealt with. Once the vegetables are half grown they do shade most of the ground, and do crowd out weeds. But if you put down a layer of conventional mulch you won't have to worry about all those weeds in the early stages. Planting in the mulch is practical in gardens where seeds or plants are precisely located, but is not practical in other gardens where seeds are scattered in wide rows.

In the square foot garden you can mulch if you like with any material. Put it on after you have prepared your soil in that square, then just poke a hole through the material at each premeasured space for your seeds or transplants. Since you're planting in small spaces that are fairly close together, I'd suggest mulching with a fairly fine material that is easily moved. For example, partially decomposed hay would be better than coarse, freshly baled hay; or you could use dried grass clippings or small squares of newspaper, cardboard, or carpet with holes cut in at the proper distance. You can even cut a stack of cardboard or carpets in 12-inch by 12-inch squares and then drill properly spaced holes right through the entire stack at once.

Conserving Water with the Hill and Furrow System

For summer plantings of closely spaced vegetables like carrots, onions, and radishes, I shape the soil in each square into what I call the hill and furrow system. It simply means creating a furrow every 3 inches for carrots, and planting seeds at the bottom of the furrows (still with the recommended square foot spacing). This way, any and all water runs down the hill and into the furrows, so you capture most of the water that's available. It's very quick and easy to shape the soil, and it somewhat

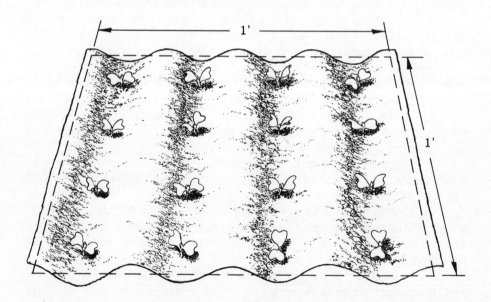

Another way to conserve water is to form the soil in each square into hills and furrows. Plants are planted in the furrows, at the usual square foot spacing.

resembles a piece of corrugated fiberglass when you're through. This really works great whether you water by the cup and bucket method, or from overhead, or simply whenever it rains.

For even better water conservation, you can cover the connecting ridges or hills with a mulch such as long folded newspapers, tar paper, or pieces of carpet. I've even tried various kinds of plastic and fiberglass with surprisingly good results. The mulch eliminates all weeds and directs any water right to the plants. Don't try the hill and furrow method in the rainy wet weather of early spring, or if you have a poorly drained soil. The soil would then become waterlogged and plants would be left standing with "wet feet."

Some Watering Tips to Remember

- Don't water from overhead.
- Keep a bucket or two full of water in a sunny spot in the garden to have warm water always ready for plants.
- Mist newly planted seeds daily, or twice a day if necessary to keep the soil moist.
- Plant each plant in a shallow depression to conserve water and prevent run-off.
- Water immediately after transplanting.
- Find a favorite watering cup that is comfortable and easy to grasp. I like short cottage cheese containers best.
- With the cup and bucket method, the time of day when plants are watered is not as critical as with overhead watering. However, if you have a choice, water in the morning.
- If you water with a trickler hose or bubbler attachment on the end of a regular hose, obtain warm water by placing several coils of hose in the sun. At a slow trickle the water will be warmed as it passes through the warm hose.
- Mulch your garden to keep ground water from evaporating.

Chapter 13
▣ Controlling Weeds, Pests, and Diseases

What's a gardener's worst enemy? Would you say it's weeds, pests, weather, or lack of maintenance? All are common problems, no doubt about it, but for most people weeds are the biggest problem. In fact, recent studies at Cornell University have shown that carrots grown in a weeded test plot produced ten times as much as their neighbors in a similar unweeded plot. That is a remarkable difference and in itself should be enough to make it clear that weeding is a necessary garden chore. Why is there such a dramatic difference between the production of weeded and unweeded gardens? Well, if you look at any weed you'll see an aggressive, fast-growing plant that needs just as much sun, moisture, and soil nutrients as any vegetable plant. The soil can supply just so much, and the aggressive plants are going to get the most. Unfortunately for gardeners, most weeds are simply tougher and more aggressive than most of our vegetable plants. Needless to say, when you allow weeds to take over your garden, your harvest of vegetables is going to suffer drastically. In addition, the sight of a weedy, unkempt garden is depressing and quite often results in the gardener losing interest and giving up for the year. This is a common occurrence—I've seen it happen over and over again.

Weeding the Square Foot Garden

When I first started developing the square foot method I was determined to find a simple gardening procedure that would eliminate or at least greatly reduce the weeding problem. Most people hate to weed and put it off until the last possible moment or never get to it at all. Interestingly enough, though, once tackled, there is a great deal of satisfaction to be derived from weeding and cleaning up the garden. When the results start to become visible, the gardener is encouraged to continue. But there's just so much time in any given day or week that can be allocated to weeding.

The solution to the problem seems obvious: prevent the weeds from starting, or at least pull them before they get too large. But how? Well, as soon as I could see that a large garden could become quite small and still produce a reasonable harvest, it became apparent that simply reducing the area to be weeded by 80 percent was certainly part of the answer. The remaining part of the solution was splitting up the small area into manageable squares. Now the chore was confined to a clearly defined area that could be easily identified and managed. If gardening chores could be concentrated into just one little 12-inch by 12-inch square at a time, the work became easy to manage.

Of course, the effort involved in weeding one square was very easy, and I found it a snap to then go on to the next square, and then the next until in just a few minutes definite progress had been made toward a totally weeded garden. The result was a perfectly kept, weed-free garden that was a delight to see and took very little time to maintain in good condition all season.

Obviously, other factors besides that of time will be influenced by the weed-free condition of your garden. For one thing, without weeds to soak up the soil moisture, your watering chores will be reduced considerably. As you've seen in chapter 12, constantly available moisture in the soil is important to healthy plant growth. Because weeds will not be competing with your garden crops for nutrients, you won't have to fertilize as much as you would otherwise. Without tall-growing weeds to shade out your young and weaker vegetable plants, more sunlight will be available to crops, resulting in faster and better growth with earlier, larger, and longer harvests. Further, since you have time now to control weeds by weekly hand picking, you won't need any expensive tools or gadgets. This will save you money and it will also save wear and tear on your body—you'll no longer have to tackle that back-breaking job of hoeing weeds in the hot noonday sun.

The best time to weed is every time you pass your garden, but not less than once a week. If you make your goal to weed only one square at a time, every time you walk past your garden, it becomes a very easy chore. Or, depending on your habits and temperament, you might choose to weed an entire block all at once, one morning a week. One of the advantages of doing at least one square a day is that it gets you out to the garden every day to keep a constant check on its progress. If you can get into the habit of being able to look at just one square at a time and see everything in that square, nothing else, you will begin to see the tiny weeds just after they sprout. You'll also notice whether the garden needs watering, if pests are present, and what's ready to harvest.

Many gardeners find as I did that once they get started it's so satisfying to clean up one square that they can easily go on to the adjoining one, then one more, then just one more. In just a few moments you have four small squares weeded and looking great. You can even do it in your good clothes, any time of the day. Other gardeners like to combine weeding with all the other gardening chores, and do everything in one session. Do your weeding whichever way is most comfortable for you; just be sure to do it. A six-block garden (10 feet by 15 feet) can be maintained in less than one hour per week. That includes both watering and weeding. Of course, if you don't pull your weeds every week, they will be bigger and more numerous, and the maintenance time will obviously be longer.

The secret to a weed-free garden lies both in keeping up with the weeding and having a small area to take care of. Another factor that discourages weeds in the square foot garden is that the close plant spacing gradually creates a living mulch. As the plants grow, their leaves tend to throw more shade on the adjoining ground until the planted vegetables cover the entire area. At that time very few weed seeds will sprout, and those that do grow will be weak and spindly and very easy to pull out of the loose, crumbly soil.

My method of weeding is simple: just grasp the weed as close to the soil line as you can between your thumb and index finger and pull up. Try to get the root as well as the stem and leaves. It's much easier when the soil is wet or at least slightly moist; the roots then pull out completely and there is less chance that the weed will resprout. Distinguishing the weeds from the newly sprouted vegetable or flower plants is also very easy. Since you've followed the spacing guide and planted seeds only in regular spots, everything else that has sprouted must be a weed (unless you spilled a few seeds, but you wouldn't want them to grow anyhow). Pull everything except what's growing in the measured spaces where you planted. If there are weeds in those areas right next to the vegetable seedlings and you're not sure which is which, wait until both are big enough so that you can clearly identify them. Don't wait too long, though, because that weed is stealing moisture and nutrients from the plants you are trying to grow.

As you can see, weeding is so simple and easy there's not much to say or learn about it. Get them out when they're young, at least once a week, and you'll have no troubles.

Pest Control

Keeping pests under control requires constant vigilance from every gardener. You could control bugs by spraying once a week with a multi-purpose chemical spray that kills almost everything in sight. But synthetic pesticides are expensive (they're petroleum based), and there is a great deal of concern about their long-range harmful effects. Better than using poisons and much easier, safer, and cheaper is to try the simple pest control methods described here. Again, the methods work so well partly because your garden is very small. As you work, you're close to each plant, and have the opportunity to constantly see what's going on. When all your plants are 2 to 4 feet in front of your nose you can't help but see trouble when it flies (or crawls) by.

If you have cabbage worms, for example, you will notice the partially eaten leaves right away, probably in the first few days after the worms start doing their damage. With your attention drawn to the plant under attack, you'll soon discover telltale worm droppings collected at the bottom of the leaf, and then you'll spot the critter lying along the stem of a large leaf and almost identical to it in color. Using the same two fingers that you used to pull up all the weeds, pick off the worm and step on it for the most foolproof, guaranteed organic control method known to mankind. After finding one worm, you'll probably remember all those pretty little white butterflies you saw fluttering about the yard last week. Now you know what they were doing—laying eggs on your cabbage plants! Knowing there's one worm, you're sure to find more. A careful inspection of each cabbage plant (and all the other cabbage family members: broccoli, cauliflower, and brussels sprouts), will reveal any other partially eaten leaves, droppings, and little fat worms.

Now here's how you make all that work pay off. It's my method of keeping a watch out for any more relatives of those squashed worms. After you're finished with your full inspection, cut out any damaged portions of the leaves (it won't hurt the plant) and wash away the droppings with a gentle spray of water. In other words, destroy not only the worm itself, but all traces of its presence. There are a couple of reasons why this is a good idea. First, because it looks better; but more important, if you missed a worm (and it's not hard to do, they are so small and camouflaged) it will continue to eat and leave droppings, but you won't know it if you haven't picked off all the damaged leaves. On later inspections you'd think the nibbled leaves were probably the damage you found on that initial inspection. But that missed worm would go on eating and doing more damage to the plants without your knowledge for several days. If you carefully clean away all traces of worms as you destroy them, you will always be able to spot new damage and can catch the culprit before too much harm is done to the plants.

The same procedure will apply to any and all damage or evidence of other pests—remove it as soon as you see it and destroy the bugs. Besides, it's much nicer to look at a clean, healthy garden, and not one that's all chewed up and partially destroyed. Within reason and certain limitations, most plants will not suffer when you remove damaged leaves or portions of them, but will soon grow new ones. It's not necessary to remove an entire leaf if only part of it is damaged. Take a scissors and cut off the damaged portion, leaving a neat, smooth edge. If you are squeamish about picking up any kind of bug in your bare hands, keep a pair of inexpensive gloves handy for the job, or use an old pair of tweezers.

Cutworms

Hand picking and destroying insects is a very safe, simple procedure that works very well in the small squares of your garden. The quicker you

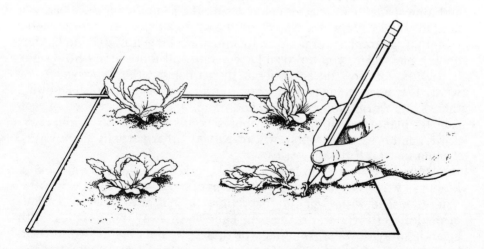

When you find a plant cut down by a cutworm, scratch around in the soil next to the plant until you find the worm, then destroy it.

can spot the trouble, the easier it is to control it. Many harmful insects can reproduce in astonishingly short periods of time (some in just a matter of days), and in astronomical proportions, too. If you wait too long you'll be fighting a losing battle. For example, consider the case of cutworms— a terrible nuisance in early spring. They hide in the soil all day and come out at night to cut down your young plants, one each night. The plant looks like it was toppled by a miniature chain saw—you'll find the cleanly severed top lying intact on the ground. The cutworm is a fiendish devil because it totally destroys an entire plant in just one night. The plant cannot recover or resprout, as it can when the leaves are nibbled by a rabbit or a slug. Luckily the cutworm eats through only one plant a night. It must get very sleepy after its big meal, because it will always burrow into the soil right next to the toppled plant and sleep until the next night. Then it comes back up to the surface, crawls to the next plant and does its job again. It's hard to imagine how the worms can live on just one stem per night. They get quite large, too, about half the size of your little finger. Of course, you can put cutworm collars around all your plants, but it's easy to forget to do that, and besides, you'd have to put a collar around almost every plant in the garden because they eat almost anything. Inspecting your garden daily is vital if you want to get rid of cutworms. If you don't get out to see your garden but once a week, one little cutworm can destroy seven plants before you notice it. But now with a small garden you'll be able to spot it the very next morning.

To catch him, take a sharpened pencil and dig carefully in the soil around the toppled plant. You will only have to dig about ½ inch deep. If you don't find the worm right away, keep digging in concentric circles, and just a little deeper until you spot it. It will be there, I can almost guarantee it. If you notice the cut-down plant the very next day, the worm will not have gone far. However, if it's been several days, it could be anywhere in the garden. When you do find it, step on it right away, don't put it down to look at later. (Cutworms wake up surprisingly fast and can make disappearing tracks almost while you're looking the other way.) Then remove the destroyed plant (both top and roots) and replant the space. If you have a lot of plants cut down, you might have a heavy infestation and it would be worthwhile to place collars around the remaining plants.

Slugs and Snails

Slugs and snails are other very common garden pests. They will eat just about anything in their path, and they seem to lurk in every garden. They are particularly fond of young vegetables and soft leaves, so all of your leaf vegetables as well as newly sprouted or transplanted plants are likely targets. Slugs and snails can be detected by the silvery, slimy trails they leave behind, as well as the holes they eat in the leaves. They eat by night and rest by day in dark, damp places. They can be found under boards, mulch, or any other cool resting spot.

One simple way to control them is to come out either at dusk or dawn with a flashlight, and after putting on some gloves, hand pick them off the plants. They can be dropped into a cup filled with salt water, which will kill them. Another way is to set traps for them. Wood walking planks set between your garden blocks are ideal traps because they are right next to the plants. The slugs are quite likely to crawl under the planks during the day, so if you have an infestation or see signs of damage, lift your walking planks and you may be surprised at what you find underneath. Again, hand picking and drowning in salt water is a quick way to get rid of these pests.

Four-Legged Invaders

Another source of trouble for all plants in all gardens at any stage of growth is rabbits, woodchucks, and deer. Any one of these animals can devour an enormous number of plants in just one night. Although you may occasionally find them in the garden in the daytime, they do most of their damage when the gardener is not around. The only sure way to keep them out is by surrounding the garden with metal fencing. An 18-inch-high fence made of chicken wire with 1-inch openings is tall enough to keep out rabbits. Woodchucks require a somewhat taller fence, but also some added protection at the bottom, as they are diggers. And the deer can only be kept out with an extremely tall fence (some say at least 12 feet tall) or a 4-foot-high fence with an electrified wire running above it about 6 feet high.

For any of these animals, but especially for woodchucks, bend the bottom of the fence outward as a kind of skirt that lies flat on the ground. A 6-inch-wide skirt will keep rabbits out of the garden, but you'll need an 18-inch skirt to keep the woodchucks from tunneling underneath it.

Be sure any fence you put up is tight at all the corners or gates. These critters are ingenious at finding the slightest little opening and taking advantage of it.

Other Pest Control Strategies

Pest damage can become very discouraging and sometimes even overwhelming for the beginner, as well as for the advanced or expert gardener. But keep in mind that you're always going to have some pests around the garden—birds from the sky, rabbits and deer from the woods, bugs from everywhere. These creatures far outnumber us, and I'm sure they do think that we plant our nice gardens for them. So try to keep a step ahead and protect your plants whenever you can, especially if you know they are at a vulnerable stage of growth or if there are signs of pest problems in the area.

Keep in mind also that a few pests aren't the end of the world, and a little damage isn't always the end of the plant. For example, flea beetles eat little round holes in leaves of peppers and tomatoes, but they don't seriously damage plants and I wouldn't cut off a leaf because it had a few little holes. Get in the habit of really knowing your plants. See what they are really like, their color, texture, leaf shape, and structure, so you will be readily able to notice any differences. In addition to knowing the plant itself, learn to observe and identify evidence of pest problems, such as chewed leaves, discoloration, droppings, and other signs.

There has been so much written about companion planting, natural pest controls, and homemade remedies that I will not go into much detail on specific pest control measures here. Some of these controls work and some of them don't, and it seems a new one is discovered every day. My advice is to read whatever you can, but don't get too excited by each new "breakthrough." Try it if you like, but don't expect it to work miracles. My personal feeling about all pest control is that a given method will work some of the time for some people for some plants.

The trouble with most homemade remedies is that they are not tested with any scientific methods or compared against an unprotected or controlled group. The factor that did eliminate the pests is not always as obvious as it may seem. Sometimes pests may be destroyed just by the weather, circumstances, or time. I've talked to gardeners who said that after they put down a thick hay mulch on the garden it was overrun by slugs, so they would never use it again. I've also talked to other gardeners who swore by mulch because after they started to use it they had no more slug problems that year. What wasn't tested or defined was the possibility that the slugs were just in a particularly heavy or light concentration that year. I've tested thick mulch in my garden by leaving one plot bare and mulching an adjacent plot, year after year, and I've never seen any real difference in the number of slugs in the two plots. If they were heavy one year, they were heavy in both gardens; if the infestation was light, it was light in both.

Introducing biological controls and insect-repellent plants into your garden are other pest control measures you might want to investigate. Such methods work well in a small garden. Biological controls include practices like attracting to your garden birds that eat undesirable insects, and introducing insect predators like ladybugs and praying mantises. These "good" insects eat "bad" insects and do not harm plants. Many plants, herbs, flowers, and vegetables are said to attract or repel certain insects. The array of information that has been published on the subject is mind boggling and beyond the scope of this book. If these ideas appeal to you, get one of the many books on the subject and try them out. In my mind, the real secret of pest control is learning to identify the presence of pests and eliminating them immediately.

Plant Diseases

One day your garden looks great and suddenly, within just a few days, your cucumber vines might be all wilted and turning brown. The cause was probably a bacterial wilt disease spread by the cucumber beetle. Many diseases are difficult to identify and in fact, by the time the symptoms are prominent enough to notice, it's usually too late to do anything. The only recourse at that stage is to pull out all the infected plants and discard them (wrap them up and put them out with the trash—don't add them to the mulch pile).

Preventive measures can do more than anything else to insure a disease-free garden. Start with a well-prepared, balanced soil and healthy plants. Don't wet the leaves when watering, rotate crops every year, and just hope for the best. If disease strikes, just pull out the plants and accept the loss.

In summary, then, here are the measures I recommend for controlling problems in the garden, and the order in which you should practice them:

1. Buy only disease-resistant varieties of vegetables.
2. Keep a neat, clean, weedless garden.
3. Grow healthy plants in good soil.
4. Mulch heavily and water properly.
5. Inspect the garden daily to spot trouble early.
6. Hand pick and destroy pests.
7. Use homemade natural remedies wherever possible. Simple, effective controls include spraying green worms with salt water; washing aphids from plants with a clear water spray; making cardboard collars for seedlings to foil cutworms; and trapping slugs under a shingle or piece of raw potato at night and crushing them in the morning after they have collected under the trap.
8. If an infestation of a particular insect gets out of hand, try one of the botanical insecticides, such as pyrethrum or rotenone. These plant-derived

substances are powerful insecticides, but they break down quickly and thus will not harm humans or animals.

9. If none of these measures works, pull out the crop and destroy it. It's not worth the use of stronger chemicals to save it.

For more details on control measures for specific pests, I urge you to read one of the many excellent books available on pest control in the garden.

Chapter 14
▧ Enjoying the Harvest

The square foot method certainly allows you to garden with a minimum of time, space, and effort, but probably one of the greatest rewards is the continuous but manageable harvest. Many gardeners I've talked to admit that sometimes, particularly in the middle of the season, the huge surplus of harvest actually becomes depressing because of the work involved in cleaning, cooking, and preparing. The conventional, single-row garden seems to produce a feast-or-famine type of harvest. Since so much is planted at once (usually a long row of each vegetable) it tends to provide a huge harvest all at once. Harvesting your square foot garden can and should be quite different from the kind of hectic harvest season to which you are probably accustomed. The harvest can now be spread out into a continual flow of usable produce. Because your planting was done a little at a time—square by square with a new crop planted every week or two —you'll enjoy a harvest the same way. Vegetables can be picked a few at a time, and continuously over a much longer period of time. If you try some of the "out-of-season" growing methods described in chapter 15, you'll be able to extend the harvest season still further.

From late spring on, your square foot garden will be full of quite a variety of vegetables all in different stages of growth. There will always be something ready for harvest, but you won't have overwhelming amounts of food to pick, clean, and cook or preserve. This calls for a different method of harvesting to fully appreciate the value of your controlled and staggered plantings in each square.

Rather than trudge out to the garden once or twice a week to make a gigantic picking, try harvesting every day for a small salad and every two or three days to get vegetables for side dishes and main courses.

The method of picking for a salad, for example, is really fun. Every day, go to the garden and look around at what's growing and ready for harvest. Pick anything and everything that can be used in a fresh salad. Sometimes you'll pluck only a few lettuce leaves, and a few leaves of Swiss chard, beet, and spinach along with perhaps a single radish, one onion, and a baby yellow squash. This might not sound like much, but when these vegetables are all washed and cut up, you'll have a wonderful fresh salad for one person.

The next day you might find a few string beans or sugar snap peas, a green pepper, and a nice mixture of several varieties of lettuce leaves. These will give you another, very different, salad. Then the following day, you might dine on just one small head of lettuce spread open and topped with some cottage cheese mixed with fresh chives, chopped radish, or parsley. Another time you might have some leaf lettuce (you should have about six varieties of lettuce always growing) topped with marinated beets, beans, peppers, or onions. You can see that the object here is to just go forth daily and pick whatever strikes your fancy. It's just like going to a fresh vegetable market and selecting whatever looks good that day. But you must visit your garden every day to maximize the effect.

It's interesting to note that whenever you go out to eat in a restaurant, a salad is almost always served (and eaten with relish), but often at home we neglect to mix and serve a salad at every daily meal. I think that's a shame, especially since vegetables fresh picked from the garden are lots more nutritious than the limp lettuce and soggy tomatoes that have undergone shipping and storage before finding their way onto that restaurant plate. I hope the small and varied harvests produced by your square foot garden will inspire you to eat more delicious fresh salads.

Once you get in the habit of selecting a mixture of different vegetables for your salad you'll see how much fun it is to create a new combination each night. Occasionally, other members of the family might like to join in to pick their own, and you'll be treated to a fresh-picked version of the salad bars that are so popular now at many restaurants. It is also fun sometimes to harvest the vegetables and set them out on the table in separate bowls so everyone can create their own variations. A little imagination in serving and selecting can make a fresh salad become a major part of every meal at home. The flavor of freshly picked vegetables is beyond compare—far better than the vegetables available in supermarkets, that are picked immature, stored, and shipped from out of state. Aside from the savings in dollars, think of the pride and feeling of accomplishment that can grow with the knowledge that your family is eating the freshest possible food, and that you grew it all yourself.

Harvesting and Using Spring or Fall Vegetables

When harvesting any of the spring crop, remember to pick often and, most important, to eat the produce as soon after picking as possible. The flavor and quality of vegetables such as peas starts to deteriorate as soon as they're off the vine, so pick and clean them just before dinnertime.

Don't let any of your spring vegetables get too large, as they tend to grow tough, stringy, or pithy when they reach full size. As a general rule of thumb, if you harvest most spring vegetables when they are about half grown, you can't go wrong. If you let your vegetables grow too large or sit too long after harvesting you will be missing one of the true joys of gardening.

Some vegetables (peas, for example) will continue blossoming and

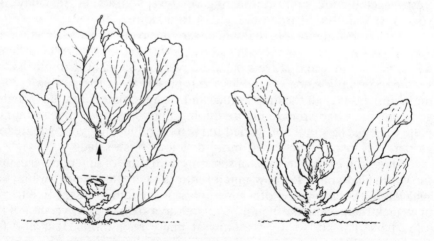

If you cut off a lettuce plant above the ground a new crown of leaves will form to produce a second harvest. The other way to harvest leaf crops is to pick individual leaves as they grow large enough.

producing new fruit if you pick what has already formed, while others, such as lettuce and spinach, keep growing new leaves from the center as the outer leaves are cut. Broccoli will produce lots of side-shoots after the large central head has been cut. As long as the weather doesn't get too hot most of these vegetables will produce a continuous or second crop for you.

If you would prefer to harvest the whole plant at once, you can do so when the outer leaves are mature. Cut off the entire plant slightly above the center core with a large pair of scissors or grass clippers and the plant will sprout new leaves.

It's always a special thrill when you pull up the root crops and find such colorful surprises as bright red radishes, round white turnips, and long, golden carrots, since you haven't been able to watch them grow and develop. Root crops can be harvested at any stage of growth from the time they are the size of a marble or your finger until they are fully mature. Don't wait until all are full grown before you pull them—young beets and carrots and other root vegetables are very sweet and tender.

One way to tell when root crops are big enough to harvest is to use your finger to dig away a little soil from around the stems every week or so to see how big the roots are getting. When it's time to harvest, just pull up those with the largest tops, leaving the others to grow a little larger.

All of the spring crops, lettuce and spinach greens, peas, root crops like radishes, beets, carrots, green onions, and turnips, can be served raw as appetizers or in salads. With the addition of some hard-boiled eggs, diced cheese, or meat you have a super chef's salad, and you're not only the chef but the farmer as well.

Harvesting the Summer Crop

Here are some pointers on harvesting and using your summer crop. First, as with the spring vegetables, always remember that bigger is not necessarily better. If you want bigness, they sell it by the pound at the supermarket. But only the finest restaurants serve small, young vegetables, and there you pay plenty for them. However, if you pay attention to your backyard harvest, you can have the same succulent, young produce at home without the expense.

The same rule of thumb that is used to gauge the right time to pick spring crops can apply to most of the summer vegetables, too. Beans, cucumbers, eggplant, yellow squash, and zucchini can all be harvested when they're about half the size they'll eventually reach. When you let these vegetables become large and mature, they become tough and woody,

Coping with Zucchini

"Zucchini surprise"—that's exactly what you get every morning when you peek under the leaves of your huge zucchini plant. Yesterday you thought you picked every squash that was of an edible size, yet today there are more. It's incredible. You almost suspect that someone came in the middle of the night and stuck some on.

How to keep ahead of this plant is one of the great summer challenges. When the neighbors say "We still have the ones you gave us last week," and the kids moan, "Oh, not squash again!" you begin to regret planting so many seeds back in May and vow never to do it again. (At least not until next year.)

It's only when the squash borer gets into the plants and kills them all in early August, leaving you without any squash for the rest of the summer, that you begin to take back all those terrible things you said about that marvelous plant. So let's enjoy them while we can, and that means using them in new and different ways.

Everyone has had zucchini cooked as a vegetable dish. You can stir-fry, steam, boil, bake, or stew it with a variety of seasonings or other vegetable combinations. Unfortunately, those usual dishes get tiresome and monotonous for most families. The secret of success, then, is to find new recipes that not only give a different taste but, most important, use a lot of squash in each recipe.

If you have never had zucchini fresh and raw, you should try it. Pick them extra small and young (4 to 6 inches) and just before serving cut in slices, strips, or chunks, with the skin on, and serve raw as an appetizer with a dip, in salads, or just seasoned with your favorite dressing. Try sour cream or yogurt dressings, which are particularly good with raw squash.

In order to use plenty of squash but with a new taste, my family has tried many different recipes and I'd like to share one of them with you. It uses a lot of squash and can be a main dish with or without the addition of a cup of cooked hamburger or other meat. It also tastes as good the next day, either cold or heated up.

STUFFED ZUCCHINI

6 medium, whole zucchini, scrubbed and trimmed
2 cups peeled, chopped, fresh tomatoes
1 cup bread cubes, cooked in butter until crisp
salt and pepper to taste, optional
grated Parmesan cheese

Simmer the zucchini in a little water until barely tender (8 to 10 minutes). Drain, and when cool, cut in half lengthwise. Scoop out the seeds from each half and invert the halves on paper towels to drain. Arrange the zucchini, cut side up, in a baking dish and fill the cavities with the chopped tomatoes and croutons (which have been mixed together). Sprinkle with salt, pepper, and cheese if desired. Bake at 400°F about 30 minutes or until tender and lightly browned. Serve piping hot. Serves 6.

the seeds inside become fully developed and the plants stop producing, their mission in life (to reproduce themselves) fulfilled. When you pick the vegetables young, not only will you get better-quality vegetables, but also the plants will keep on producing new fruits as long as the growing season lasts.

Keeping up with the harvest is so important that I recommend that you pick daily for a salad and at least two or three times a week for everything else growing. Eat or preserve what you need, give what you can't consume to your friends and neighbors, and return any leftovers to your compost or mulch pile. Do not leave them on the plants to mature. You can also set up a regular picking schedule, say Monday, Wednesday, and Friday, and harvest your entire garden. That way the zucchini won't go unnoticed until they're the size of small baseball bats.

Using the Harvest

There are many advantages of serving vegetables raw. For one thing, you won't have to heat up the stove or oven when the weather is hot, and you won't have to wash a lot of pots and pans. But more important, raw vegetables are more nutritious than cooked ones, and are a good source of the dietary fiber, or roughage, that doctors tell us is badly lacking in the diets of most Americans. Pick your vegetables extra small if you plan to serve them raw. Wash but do not skin them (most of the vitamins lie just below the skin), and slice or cut them into sticks. Raw vegetables (called crudités by gourmets) can be served with a dip as an appetizer or snack. Or serve them with your favorite salad dressing. Most people have never tasted raw sugar snap peas or zucchini, but served in these ways they are a delicious change from the ordinary.

Greens should be picked in the early morning or late in the evening when the plants are fresh and perky. Wash the leaves in cold water and spin or pat dry. Refrigerate until you're ready to use them; greens deteriorate quickly and lose vitamins if they are not stored in the refrigerator.

Mention salads in the spring and early summer and everyone can think of many great combinations of lettuce, radishes, scallions, and other cool-weather vegetables. But as soon as the hot weather ruins the lettuce our thoughts turn back to the supermarket for the basic ingredients. This is not necessary if we adapt our thinking and imagination to different vegetables and different methods of serving. If you forget the standard lettuce wedge or tossed green salad during the hot summer months you can enjoy many different salads fresh from your garden.

Aside from the obvious sliced tomatoes and cucumbers, there are several other ways to serve vegetable salads.

Most of the common summer vegetables, as well as corn, beets, and Swiss chard stalks, can be cooked ahead of time and chilled before serving.

DIP FOR RAW VEGETABLES

Beans, peas, carrots, beets, radishes, cucumbers, peppers, squash and cherry tomatoes can all be served raw with this dip as a snack or appetizer. Remember, you've picked your vegetables while they were young and still small, so they'll be tender and sweet. If you've never eaten many raw vegetables, don't turn up your nose until you've tried them this way!

8 ounces plain yogurt or sour cream
1 clove garlic, crushed
1 teaspoon grated onion
2 teaspoons chopped fresh chives and other herbs
(dill, parsley, or whatever you like)

Mix thoroughly and chill before serving.

HOMEMADE SALAD DRESSING

A salad is, of course, the traditional way to serve raw vegetables. Try adding grated raw or cooked beets for interesting color and flavor. Scallions are a good, mild substitute for onions in a salad. Serve cherry tomatoes whole, cut up into wedges, or even sliced into tiny circles. And try adding some nasturtiums (blossoms, leaves, and stems are all edible) for an unusual taste treat. Be adventurous!

A tasty salad dressing can be made from:

8 ounces plain yogurt or sour cream
1 tablespoon ketchup
1 teaspoon mustard
2 tablespoons mayonnaise
1 tablespoon honey

Stir very thoroughly to blend the honey. Chill before serving.

For this method the young and small sizes are most tender, but you can use larger sizes since you will be cooking them. Use any combination of dressings and herbs. You might try mixing your own dressing starting with sour cream, yogurt, or mayonnaise as a base. Experiment with different seasonings.

A marinated vegetable salad offers a new and distinctive taste as well as being an excellent way to use leftovers. Start with raw, sliced, or diced tomatoes (red or green), cucumber, yellow or green squash, or any of the cooked vegetables already mentioned. Just cover them with vinegar, season to taste, and chill at least six hours before serving. You can serve marinated vegetables separately or mixed in any combination as a side dish, or on a bed of Swiss chard or beet leaves with or without meat, eggs, or cheese as a main dish. And don't forget seafood! Marinated vegetables mixed or topped with fresh raw or cooked oysters, clams, mussels, shrimp, or fish are a real summer gourmet treat.

Many greens do not grow well in hot weather. Lettuce bolts to seed and becomes bitter and spinach just won't grow during hot months. But there are some less common leafy vegetables that do hold up in hot weather, and they can be used as salad greens. Swiss chard and New Zealand spinach are two leaf crops that grow well all summer long and produce excellent greens. A different way of serving them is to tear the greens into bite-size pieces and pour over them a hot, cooked dressing of vinegar and honey with bits of sautéed onion to make a salad of "wilted" greens.

If you're looking for a simple way to serve your garden vegetables hot, consider cooking any of them quickly by stir-frying in a small amount of oil in a very hot skillet or wok. Again, pick them young and small, wash

Some Tips on Using Tomatoes

Versatile Tomato Stuffing

Chopped, cubed, or diced fresh tomatoes can be mixed with a variety of other ingredients to make a very interesting and delicious stuffing. What gets stuffed? Almost anything: zucchini or yellow squash, meat loaf, egg boats, pasta shells—you name it!

The simplest stuffing starts with sautéing fresh bread cubes in butter until crisp and golden brown. Remove from heat and add peeled, cubed, fresh tomatoes. (The easiest way to peel a tomato is to drop it in boiling water for 10 to 30 seconds. It won't cook, but the skin will shrivel and split so you can remove it easily.) Season to taste and fill the hollowed-out portion of a summer squash or add to the center of a meat loaf. Bake as usual for that dish. The flavor of the fresh tomato and the crispness of the bread cubes add a new taste to any dish.

A Tip for Freezing Tomatoes

You can freeze whole tomatoes, tomato slices, or just the juice, but don't expect whole or sliced tomatoes to look whole or sliced when defrosted—they won't. However, they'll still have the taste of fresh tomatoes and can be used for cooking. Wash the tomatoes; remove stems. If you are slicing them, slice into rounds ¼ inch thick and put freezer paper between each layer of slices in your freezer container. Or, like many people, you can cook up a basic tomato sauce and then freeze it. It takes up a lot less room in the freezer, but does require a lot of cooking when your harvest is abundant.

and dice or slice thinly with the skins on. Cook quickly by constantly stirring. Mix any combination, add any seasonings you like, and you have a delicious side dish fresh from your garden—quick and easy and, of course, very inexpensive. Add some ground beef or diced ham, or top with some Parmesan cheese for a main dish treat. The last thing to add, just before serving, is ½ cup of mixed vegetable juice. Try it and you'll be having it often.

Putting Up a Smaller Harvest

Even though your square foot garden will not be producing one-time harvests on a grand scale, there may be days when you just can't eat everything fresh, and you'd like to put up some of those good vegetables to enjoy in winter. The two most-used methods of preserving food are canning and freezing. Which way is best? Like everything else in life there is no simple answer to this question. It all depends on your purpose, equipment, and interest. For large quantities of food, canning is probably the cheapest and most satisfying from a homemaker's point of view. For small quantities and without spending a lot of time and effort, freezing is by far the best.

The directions for canning are well known and available from many sources, so I won't go into them here. But I'd like to tell you about a new and different idea in freezing. Actually, it's as much an attitude toward using vegetables as it is a way to use your freezer effectively.

The secret of putting up good-tasting vegetables is the same as serving them fresh from the garden: harvest them when small, young, and tender and use them as soon after harvest as possible. Don't get in the habit of letting fresh vegetables sit around very long, particularly in the sun or in a hot kitchen. If you can't serve or put them up right away, store them in a cool, dark place like a cellar or refrigerator. To get the most flavor and nutrition from fresh vegetables, you should think in terms of hours, not days, from garden to table.

My ideas about using the garden's output took shape one autumn a few years ago, when my wife broke her leg and was confined to bed for some time and I inherited the dubious opportunity of shopping, cooking, and serving meals. After getting very tired of dealing with leftovers, some for the third time, a new idea hit me (new to me, at least). Why not treat leftovers as a basic ingredient for a new dish rather than serving them warmed up again?

Since there were usually small quantities of each item, I had to figure out what dishes they could be used in as basic ingredients. The answer was simple—soups, stews, casseroles, and pot pies. The next step was to learn how to do it.

As you know, all vegetables deteriorate with age—cooked or raw—but if you freeze them the deterioration process is practically stopped. I decided to freeze the vegetables in combinations that could be used in various dishes.

I now realize that this idea would work equally well with fresh vegetables picked that day, or with leftovers from each meal. When preparing dinner, cook all the vegetables you harvested whether you are serving them that night or not. The ones not served (as well as leftovers) will be ready for freezing with very little extra work, eliminating all those dishes and containers in the refrigerator that get pushed to the rear and only get noticed when their odor says, "Hey—I'm still here!" It also means that tomorrow night's dinner doesn't have to start with monotonous leftovers, but can be something new and different. Now you can see why this is really an attitude toward how to use small quantities of different vegetables (or meat, for that matter) as well as a different way to serve them. We found this method worked very well for us that year.

Recycled milk containers or regular plastic freezer jars are ideal for this method. After every meal, instead of storing the leftovers in the refrigerator, take out the container, add the new vegetable as another layer, cover, and replace the container in the freezer. Keep doing this until

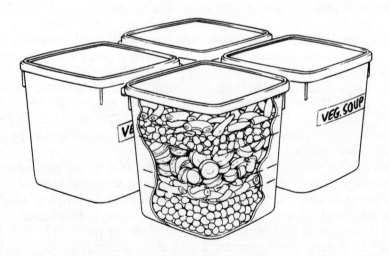

Leftover vegetables can be frozen in layers, according to the kinds of dishes you will use them in. This is a convenient way to freeze the small amounts of leftovers you'll have throughout the summer.

the container is filled. You can fill the containers with the same vegetable or mix each layer.

Use a large indelible marking pen to draw a line at the new level and label the ingredients as you add them—or don't bother, and just be surprised when you're ready to use the filled container. You could even decide ahead of time and label each container for a different dish, so as to build the layers or ingredients more in keeping with a recipe for the final dish. This way you will have several freezer containers being built up at the same time and have a choice each time you have a vegetable or meat to add. That sounds almost too well organized, doesn't it?

The other type of container to use is a plastic bag or similar airtight product which seals itself. Use these for meal-size portions of each vegetable and remember to label them with the large marking pen. Since the bags and contents will freeze into any shape, tuck them into a shallow box or container for freezing into a neat, square shape for easy storage and stacking later.

Chapter 15
⊠ Extending the Growing Season

In most parts of the continental United States, the average growing season runs from May to September—a season of 5 months. More serious gardeners may start in April and end in October—a growing season of 7 months. But that means most of us grow vegetables during an average of 6 months out of a possible 12. If those 6 months could be extended by an additional 2, that would mean a 33 percent increase in the growing season; a 3-month extension would provide a 50 percent increase. These are worthwhile goals, and they can be achieved easily and inexpensively. Gardeners would gain a great sense of accomplishment from these increased yields and homesteaders and food preservers would find them an absolute blessing.

To accomplish this extended-season growing all you basically need is an understanding of which plants to grow and when, and how to make use of the special structures described in chapter 9.

The obvious way to extend the garden year is to start earlier than you normally would and to keep the plants growing later. To do this it's important to know what can and cannot be grown in the off-season and how to provide these crops with a little extra protection from the elements. Cool-weather crops, for example, can be grown in two extra plantings for a longer season. The first planting is made in earliest spring to mature in the cool weather of late spring, and the second crop is planted in late summer to mature in the fall. Since early spring and late fall can bring some rather severe weather, it's important to provide extra protection for the plants. You can cover the plants every night or grow them in an enclosure. Covering is a nuisance and a lot of work. Enclosures, however, are not, and they come in many shapes and sizes from simple plastic tents to sophisticated and expensive heated greenhouses.

Usually the elaborateness of the enclosure determines the ease of use, convenience, and amount of protection it offers. If you want to grow warm-weather crops out of season, you must provide an expensive, energy-consuming heating system. It's much simpler and less costly to grow cool-weather crops for an extended season, using a solar-heated system which allows some frost and an occasional freezing but protects the plants from the most severe weather fluctuations. The sun box and plastic-covered cages described in chapter 9, along with the tunnels for vertical crops described in chapter 8, will do just that.

Crops can be started in the sun box to get a jump on the spring season.

Many gardeners tend to forget that they can grow two full crops of cool-weather vegetables every year. The fall planting is actually more rewarding from a production standpoint. However, the average gardener's interest and enthusiasm is highest during spring and early summer, therefore that is when most gardens are planted. By mid and late summer, when the fall crop should be planted, most gardeners have gone on to other interests and left the garden to the weeds and pests.

From the plants' standpoint, however, fall is absolutely the best time of the year for cool-season crops. Think of a lettuce or cabbage plant's requirements: the seed needs warmth and moisture to germinate; lots of sun, warm soil, and moisture to grow quickly; then cool weather and less sunlight to keep it from bolting to seed when it is mature and ready for harvest. You can see that a summer planting maturing into fall fulfills those conditions much better than a spring planting maturing into summer. Lettuce planted in springtime will take a fairly long time to grow to harvestable size, but will then mature almost overnight. It will start to get bitter and bolt to seed because of the hot weather and long days of early summer just when it's maturing. Just the opposite is true of a fall crop of lettuce, which sprouts and grows quickly in its early stage (August–September), but slows down to a long period of harvest, without bolting (September–October). In fact, almost all cool-weather crops virtually stop growing in late fall and just sit quietly, not presenting any demands. In addition, there is little competition from weeds, few insects, and virtually no watering problems. Plants grow very slowly so your harvests are not large, but they are sure.

Actually you can extend your harvest by growing many types of crops out of their normal season if you give them a little extra protection. The first planting of all types of cool-weather crops can be started at least a month earlier than normal so you can have two spring crops. After the first fall crop is under way, a second fall crop can be planted in order to also extend that harvest. In addition, all of the summer or hot-weather crops can be started two to three weeks earlier than normal and they, too, can be extended up to a month beyond their normal season. Furthermore, an extra planting of lettuce and radishes can be grown during the hot summer months which are normally considered out of season for these two crops. The extra protection and special techniques vary with the season and the variety of vegetable, but are quickly learned and easily practiced. Chapter 9 explains the details of how to build a sun box and various kinds of protective cages. Protective tunnels for vertical crops are discussed in chapter 8. These structures make it possible to moderate the climate in your garden so you can stretch your growing season at both ends.

Understanding the Climate Needs of Crops

Most garden books divide vegetables into two categories, "warm weather" and "cool weather," and I've found the easiest way to remember which is which is to memorize the hot-weather crops. Then the cool-weather group will simply consist of everything else. Sounds backward, but it really works because the hot-weather group consists of most of our favorite garden vegetables: tomatoes, cucumbers, eggplant, peppers, squash, corn, beans, and melons.

All the rest are cool-weather crops. I divide them into three basic groups to make it easier to remember them: root vegetables, leaf crops, and head types. There are a few unusual individuals that resist this classification, such as peas, celery, and kohlrabi, but they are nonetheless also cool-weather crops.

Getting an Early Start in Spring

After your garden plan is completed in midwinter and you've decided where you want your peas, the rest of your spring crops, and finally the summer vegetables, including tomatoes and squash, you can plan to use

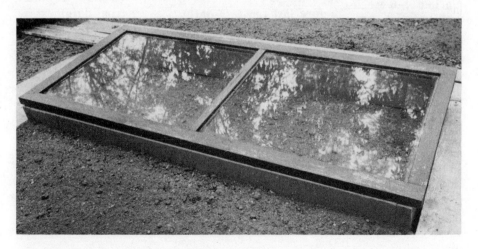

A one-level sun box with a glass cover can be placed over the ground before crops are planted in spring, to warm the soil.

your sun box or plastic-covered cages and tunnels to start all of these crops from two to four weeks early.

Because the sun box is made up of separate modular units each frame, or "level," of the box can be placed on the ground and covered with a storm window to serve as a nursery for your early spring crops. By the time the plants outgrow the single-level frames, the weather will be warm enough to transplant the crops into open garden squares, or you can leave them to grow where they were planted. A protective cage or tunnel is simply removed from the squares. The spring crops can be grown from seeds or from transplants started indoors ahead of time.

About four weeks before it's time to plant your seeds, set up one level of the sun box with a storm window cover over any garden block where you'll be planting an early crop so the sun will start warming the soil. Or use several cages or tunnels. One of the best aids for growing a good crop is a rich organic soil, with lots of humus or peat moss. It's best to prepare the soil the fall before, but if you didn't get around to it, you can prepare the soil as soon as it thaws and dries out slightly in spring.

CROPS FOR EARLY PLANTING OUTDOORS

Very Early Spring (4–6 weeks before last frost date)	Early Spring (0–4 weeks before last frost date)	Spring (on last frost date)	Late Spring (0–2 weeks after last frost date)
🌿 Broccoli	◯ Beets	◯ Beans	◯ 🌿 Cucumbers
🌿 Cabbage	◯ Carrots	◯ Corn	🌿 Eggplant
🌿 Cauliflower	◯ 🌿 Swiss chard	◯ 🌿 Summer squash	◯ 🌿 Muskmelons
◯ 🌿 Lettuce	◯ Radishes	🌿 Tomatoes	🌿 Peppers
🌿 Onions			◯ Winter squash
🌿 Parsley			
◯ Peas			
◯ Spinach			

◯ Plant seeds
🌿 Plant transplants

It takes a little experience to learn how to control the heat and moisture inside your frame. Your only means of control are the opening of the cover to provide ventilation, and the amount of your watering. Heat builds up quickly in the boxes on sunny days. As the weather warms up, slide the cover open a little farther each week until you can remove it entirely. A light frost won't hurt most of the cool-weather crops, but too much heat will cook them.

Watering is best done with a bucket since the area is rather small. You must check your sun boxes every few days in sunny weather. If you notice that plants are beginning to wilt, or if the soil dries out to a depth of 1 inch, it's time to water.

In addition to giving you a jump on the season's seed starting, the sun box can also warm the ground in perennial beds. For example, in early spring you can place a frame over half of your asparagus bed to stimulate growth and produce an extra-early picking of that favorite crop.

Extending the Season for Warm-Weather Crops

As the spring season progresses it will be time to give some summer vegetables such as beans, squash, and cucumbers an extra-early start. For earlier harvests, try starting the seeds for these warm-weather crops right in their permanent location, in your sun box or under a protective cage or tunnel, two weeks ahead of the time you'd normally plant them. They will be much hardier and stronger than seedlings grown on the windowsill. When all danger of frost is past, remove the covers. If you're using a sun box, the wood frames can be removed a few days later.

Another one of the frustrations of gardening is that just when all of the good summer salad vegetables (like tomatoes, cucumbers, and peppers) are ready, the lettuce and radishes are all gone. In the hot, long days of summer, these spring crops bolt to seed, becoming bitter and unappetizing. However, there is a way to get around this and still "have your salad and eat it, too."

If you're the type of person who doesn't like hot, sticky weather, and you literally wilt under the hot noonday sun, then the obvious solution is to move into the shade and drink as many cool liquids as possible. Well, lettuce and radishes are no different. If you can provide that same shade for these spring crops, along with a little extra water, you will be able to harvest throughout most of the summer. Cover the square with a shade cage and give the plants plenty of water—as a general rule, water them twice as often as you normally would. You might also provide the soil in that particular square with extra humus, vermiculite, and peat moss. When you're making the initial planting, a little extra of these water-holding materials would help to keep your lettuce growing right through the hot weather. The shade cage will admit enough light for proper growth, but will keep the temperature down considerably. A thick mulch will also help to moderate soil temperatures.

You might also make use of natural shade or sun screens by locating a planting of spring crops behind (to the north of) your vertical growing frames.

In selecting varieties of cool-weather crops to grow into summer, look for words like "long standing," "slow to bolt," and "heat resistant" in the seed catalogs. In addition to lettuce and radishes, you might also try growing spinach and even cabbage out of season in the early summer. I've also read of gardeners growing peas during the hot weather by using lots and lots of water as well as some shade. I've never tried it, but I'll bet it works.

Extending the Season for Fall Crops

Your sun box will come in handy again in summer, when you can start an early fall crop. One or two decks with a screen cover provide an ideal nursery for starting flowering perennials and fall vegetables. The seedlings are protected from birds and rabbits while being slightly shaded from the hot summer sun. You'll also find seed starting much easier when it's done in a concentrated area. We tend to pay more attention to a "special" area than to just another corner of the garden.

Once fall has arrived, it's always a constant battle to outwit nature and protect all of the summer vegetables from that first killing frost. Many gardeners wonder sometimes whether the extra effort involved in protecting summer crops into the fall and winter is worthwhile. I think it certainly is if you want an extra two or three weeks' worth of harvest from your tomatoes, cucumbers, squash, eggplant, and peppers. Knowing that most of these crops have a six- to eight-week harvest season, the extra two to three weeks you can gain begins to amount to quite a bit—more than a 25 percent extension of the season. Quite often the first frost is followed by two or three weeks of clear, warm weather before the next frost. If you can protect your garden from that first killing frost, you can enjoy green plants and fresh vegetables during one of the most pleasant periods of the year—mid-autumn.

To find out approximately when to expect your first killing frost, look up your area on the frost map in chapter 6. Remember that the date varies not only from year to year but even from area to area. Frost occurs when there is an accumulation of cold air at ground level and it drops to 32°F, causing a freezing of plant material. Since hot air rises and cold air falls, a frost can and does occur in low areas while the hill and slopes right next to them might be frost free. If a body of water is nearby, it will greatly reduce the occurrence of frost.

In general, frost usually occurs in the very early morning hours, particularly after a still, calm night when the weather is dry. The chances of frost are also better following the passage of a cold front, indicated by an intermittent and changing weather pattern of broken clouds and occasional precipitation rather than the steady or continuous rain and the heavy, low-hanging clouds that accompany a warm front. Your best bet is to catch the nightly weather forecast, particularly from a local radio station. When frost is predicted, be ready in your garden. One year I recall an extra-early frost followed by four weeks of beautiful weather, a rather unusual turn of events, but it was certainly well worth the effort to protect my crops from that first frost. What to protect and when depends a lot on your particular weather patterns, but knowing a few basic definitions helps.

Light frost is indicated by a white covering on the lawn in very early morning. It will touch or blacken the outer leaves of most summer flowers and vegetables. Fruit is still harvestable if eaten shortly thereafter, certainly within a few days.

Hard frost is indicated by a crunchy feel to the ground and a thin film of ice on the birdbath. This will kill off all summer flowers or vegetables and can be a very disheartening experience for gardeners who come out in the morning to find that the garden has been devastated. Plants that were bushy and colorful the day before are now just droopy skeletons with blackened leaves hanging like rags from the stems. This is the time when most gardeners declare an end to the season, but if you quickly clean up the garden your spirits will be lifted and you can go on to enjoy an autumn garden. If you have planted some colorful fall-blooming plants (mums, asters, and some hardy daisies) along with the fall crop of vegetables, your garden will still look attractive and inviting after a hard frost.

During a *light freeze* the ground stays firm and frozen on the surface, and all standing water has a thin crust of ice. Most fall crops can withstand a light freeze if they are covered, and it's still possible to dig in the soil because only the top inch is frozen and hard. Warm or sunny days erase all traces of a light freeze.

After a *hard freeze* the ground stays firm and hard while ice stays on the driveway puddles and in the birdbath. Not much work can be done

CROPS FOR A FALL HARVEST

Summer Crops Still Growing (harvest continues until first frost)	New Outdoor Plantings in Midsummer (5–10 weeks before first fall frost)	New Outdoor Plantings in Late Summer (0–5 weeks before first fall frost)
Beans	🌱 Broccoli	🌱 Lettuce
Swiss chard	🌱 Cabbage	⬭ Radishes
Corn	🌱 Cauliflower	
Cucumbers	⬭ Beets	
Eggplant	⬭ Carrots	
Muskmelons	⬭ Lettuce	
Summer squash	⬭ Spinach	
Winter squash		
Tomatoes		

⬭ Plant seeds
🌱 Plant transplants

in the garden, as digging is difficult and nonproductive. Only the hardiest or best-protected crops will remain after this stage.

How to Protect Your Plants from Frost

If you have all of your summer crop growing in the same area, it's much easier to protect it from frost. All you need is a large sheet of plastic or cloth, or light blankets. Even newspapers will do. The low-growing crops can be readily protected with a loose covering of hay (which is easily removed the next morning). Fasten down the corners of the sheets of cloth or plastic so they don't blow off during the night. A set of 18-inch metal garden stakes or pins is particularly handy for this.

Another way to provide a protective covering without the constant

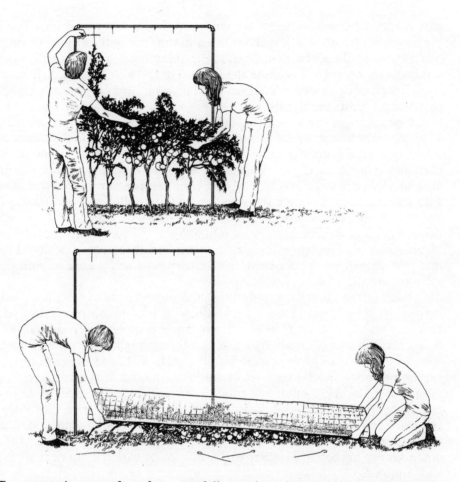

To protect vine crops from frost, carefully cut the strings and lay the plants gently in their planting trench. Cover them with a tunnel made of wire-reinforced plastic.

on-and-off of temporary covers is to install a plastic-covered cage over all squares of peppers, eggplant, and bush beans. For vertically grown crops, you can form some wire-reinforced plastic into a tunnel shape to cover the plants. If you're using string or netting for your vertical growing, the easiest way to protect these crops is to cut the strings or unfasten the netting and lay it down (with the plants still attached) carefully along the base of the frame. Line the ground with dry straw beforehand and be very careful as you're laying down the plants. It's best to have two people so that you don't crush or break the vines too much. They may look like a tangled mess, but they will still be alive and the fruit will continue to ripen while the tunnel covers them from the evening cold. You can still water if it becomes necessary, because the vertical crops were originally planted in a trench (as described in chapter 8). Harvest is also easy to accomplish by reaching in under the tunnel.

Once you get the knack of watching out for frost and then covering your plants when it threatens, you will begin to see the advantages of selecting a garden on the top or south side of a slope rather than at the bottom of a low area, if you have any choice. On a cold night you can walk around your property and actually feel the temperature difference. The cold air virtually rolls down the slope (in fact, it's called cold air drainage) and settles in the low areas. Surprisingly, this will happen even where there is not a great difference in elevation. You will also see the advantage of grouping your crops according to their weather requirements. This makes it simpler to protect them from either frost or freezing in both the spring and fall.

Temperature is not the only thing that determines which plants will survive. Wind and rain have a lot to do with how much protection you should provide and what effect it will have on keeping your harvest. Gardeners who are particularly ambitious (some might say foolhardy) and want to continue to grow something all winter will need even additional special protection and a very select variety of plants. If you can keep the ground from freezing solid, and provide sunlight in just a small area, you can grow special varieties of lettuce and spinach along with hardy leaf crops such as kale and a number of oriental vegetables all winter long in many areas of the country. It's also possible to plant some members of the onion family in the fall in order to get a large or earlier crop next spring and summer.

With experience, you'll learn which vegetables can withstand your particular climate. Lettuce can survive some frosts; spinach, especially Winter Bloomsdale, will hold up through several freezes; and of course, kale loves all the snow and ice you can give it. Carrots can freeze in the ground without any harm—it's just very hard to dig them. The advantages of using a sun box all winter are that most of the cool-weather crops will continue growing a little; you can find everything easily; and your harvest will be protected from the hungry pests around a garden.

Of course, all of this effort is only worthwhile if you enjoy the challenge of growing out of season, or feel the necessity, or want the nutritional value of your own freshly picked vegetables. For most of us, reading a good garden book is about as close as we want to get during the cold, snowy, winter months.

A Winter Salad Garden

A sun box can provide you with fresh salad every week of the winter without a greenhouse. Here's how: first, pick the sunniest, most sheltered spot you can find to locate your winter garden. It doesn't have to be in the main garden; next to the house or garage is even better, particularly if you have a white painted brick or stucco wall (it will reflect quite a bit of heat into your miniature garden). If the area is sheltered from the strong winter winds you'll have twice the growth of any other spot. If it also gets the maximum winter sunlight, you're in good shape. Remember that the sun is very low in the sky during the winter, and that what might have been in shadow during the summer could be very sunny in the winter. Don't place the sun box under the roof or gutterline or you'll risk the chance that snow will fall on it.

Prepare the soil as you would for a normal garden block (as described in chapter 5), but add a little extra compost, peat moss, sand, and vermiculite. Install your sun box and start your planting. Since the plants will grow very slowly compared to spring and summer, and you'll be harvesting every leaf almost as it is ready, you can plant closer than the normal spacing, even as close as one half the recommended distance.

Try to select fast-growing vegetables for your winter garden. You could try any of the hardy salad greens and root crops, but look for special cold-tolerant varieties. Every seed company offers different varieties, but look through the catalogs and select those that are recommended for cold and winter growing. See the chart on Crops for a Fall Harvest on page 228 for some additional suggestions.

To get a quicker start and earlier growth, always presprout your seeds indoors. Transplant them when very young into individual containers, and before the plants get too large, harden them off before planting them in your enclosure.

To insulate the sun box, bank the outside with soil or place bales of hay all around it or line the outside with Styrofoam panels. To keep the soil and air from losing all their heat at night provide a tight-fitting cover, or make a double-layer cover with glass or plastic. You can even cover the entire box with a quilt or tarp on extra-cold nights.

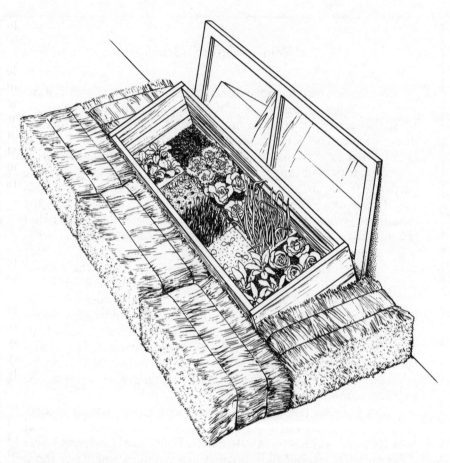

If properly insulated, the sun box can house a salad garden all winter long.

Extending the Harvest by Storing It

Storing a fall harvest of vegetables is not only the cheapest but also the most rewarding method of extending your garden harvest into the winter months. The flavor and nutritional values of each vegetable are greater than if they were frozen or canned, and the work and money involved is almost zero.

The only secret of successful storage for crops is to know what conditions each vegetable likes best and then to provide them. This is actually very simple, once you understand that there are really only two groups of vegetables requiring two conditions of storage: cold and moist or cool and dry. Before we learn which vegetables fall into each group, let's discuss methods of picking and preparing for storage that apply to both.

The most important thing to remember is to handle the fruit as little as possible and as gently as you can. Treat each vegetable as if it were an egg, as any bruise or cut will be the first spot to spoil. Don't pile the vegetables all together but lay each one separately in a box of sawdust or crumpled newspaper. Do not wash off or scrub any vegetables. For root crops, do not cut off the bottom of the roots, and be sure to leave at least an inch of the tops on. For others, leave as much of the stem on as you can. Pick only your most perfect vegetables for storage and eat the others now.

Vegetables for Cold and Moist Conditions

This group includes all root crops (carrots, beets, turnips, white potatoes, and winter radishes), as well as cabbage and cauliflower. It also includes fruit, especially apples.

The best storage temperature is as close to freezing as you can get without actually freezing—35° to 45°F is ideal. The simplest way to store all your root crops is not to dig them up at all, but to roll a bale of hay over the square. This will break the tops and stop them from growing any more but will keep the ground from freezing. In the winter, you merely roll the bale over, dig up a few vegetables, and replace the bale.

Experiment a little with leaving different root crops in the ground to see what lasts through your fall and winter, so you know what to expect the following year. For example, you'll find that regular radishes won't hold up too long in freezing weather, while the winter radish will last almost indefinitely. Carrots and leeks also do quite well through the entire winter.

The only problem with using hay bales as winter mulch is that they provide a cozy nest for ground mice and voles, who love to eat those crunchy root crops. So keep an eye out for them and the damage they do. If they do infest your winter storage plot, it's best to harvest everything and store it in a different place.

Other storage methods for root crops include burying a container in the ground and packing your vegetables in layers of moist sawdust, peat moss, or sand. You can sink a wooden nail keg or a plastic or metal garbage can straight into the ground, keeping the top a few inches above the surface. Be sure you have a tight-fitting cover, and then pile at least 12 inches of hay or leaves over the top. Keep everything dry by then covering it with a plastic or canvas tarp. (You might also use your sun box if you cover it well with mulch.) The ground will not freeze under or around this container, and your vegetables will be maintained in a very even and moist condition. The only problem could occur if the container leaks and ground water seeps in, so watch out for that condition. Locate the storage container on high ground if you can.

Cabbage and other leaf and head crops can also be stored in the garden, but they won't do well under a solid bale of hay. They like a loose, fluffy covering, whether it be straw or leaves. Lettuce, spinach, kale, cabbage, and brussels sprouts all can withstand a great deal of cold if the weather has gotten gradually colder, rather than in a quick freeze and cold snap. This is especially true of lettuce. Kale and brussels sprouts are very tough, and even unprotected, they may still be harvestable at any time. Like salsify, kale tastes better after frost. To keep the wind from blowing a loose covering of leaves around, you might want to place a 2-foot-high fence of chicken wire around that particular block or space, anchoring it at each corner with steel garden pins.

Remember, though, to draw a diagram of what's still in the garden and where, so you won't be frantically digging up all the corners some cold winter afternoon looking for the carrots or the cabbages. Once the snow covers everything it's very easy to forget exactly where things were before this blanket of white made the entire garden look the same.

Vegetables for Cool and Dry Conditions

This group is easy to remember because there are only a few vegetables that should be stored this way—onions, pumpkins, and winter squash. The temperature should be from 50° to 60°F and humidity fairly low, about 50 percent.

The ideal location is a cool corner of your basement or garage where it won't freeze or go over 60°F. These vegetables should have lots of air circulation around them, so don't stack them up in a big pile, but spread them out on a shelf (not on the floor). If your corner might either get too warm or freeze at times, you could build two walls to enclose that corner and, with some insulation, provide an even-temperature fruit closet. Just remember to allow plenty of air circulation.

Chapter 16
▨ End-of-Season Activities

Many gardeners are tempted to hang up their tools and walk away from their gardens once frost has killed most of their plants, but serious gardeners know there are still things to be done. Late in the fall is the best time of the year to prepare your garden soil for next spring. There are several reasons why. First of all, if you want to plant early crops in your garden next spring, you can get a two- to four-week head start if you do a few things right now before the ground freezes solid. The weather and soil conditions during the late fall are just the opposite of what they are going to be next spring. The soil in the fall is still warm, fairly dry, and easily dug. However, in the springtime the soil is cold, wet, and difficult to work. The advantages of fall preparation (adding humus and fertilizer and turning over the soil) seem so obvious that it's difficult to understand why everyone doesn't do it. I suppose that after we've been planting, growing, and harvesting all spring, summer, and fall, most of us are now ready for something new. By next spring you will be all enthused and anxious to start the garden anew, but then the weather and soil conditions will keep you waiting. However, you can get a jump on the spring season and have a better garden if you prepare your soil in the fall. Pick one of those beautiful, crisp, cool fall days when it's a joy to be outside.

235

As soon as the frosts have killed all your summer crops, you can start the winterization process. It's easiest to tackle one 4-foot by 4-foot garden block at a time (if you have more than one). After clearing away all the plant residue (be sure to place all diseased or insect-infested material into the trash for removal, while placing all other plant material on the compost pile), turn over a few spade fulls of earth to look at your soil. Notice the color, texture, organic matter content, and depth of tillage. Then make a pH test and if necessary add lime if the soil is acid or sulfur if it's alkaline in order to bring the pH between 6 and 7. Peat moss can be added to adjust soil that is only very slightly alkaline, while wood ashes can adjust a slightly acid soil. A little-known fact is that lime takes up to six months to react and change the pH of the soil. The traditional time to add lime to gardens and lawns has always been in spring. But you can see that it won't be of much value in the garden until well into summer if it is applied in March or April—another very important reason for doing your soil preparation in the fall.

The importance of a pH test cannot be overemphasized. If your soil isn't in the proper range of 6 to 7, most vegetables and flowers cannot use the nutrients of any fertilizer you've added, and won't grow well. If you're not too sure of the proper test or corrective procedure, review chapter 5 on soils again.

Once your pH corrections have been made it's time to add humus to your garden. How much? All you can get! Your compost or leaf mold pile from the previous fall should be completely decomposed by now and ready for use after the hot summer. If it's not, try to get some decomposed animal manure. Horse manure is usually available in most areas of the country. As a last resort, buy some peat moss. But plan to add a layer at least 3 inches thick of some organic material; the more the better, even up to 6 inches or so. Since your garden is small, a little compost will go a long way. Remember that organic matter is always decomposing, so you must replenish the supply after every crop you grow in that soil.

Since you won't be growing any plants in these blocks until next spring you could also dig in some manure or leaf mold that hasn't decomposed completely. It will continue to break down over the fall and winter. Don't add fresh or green material, however; it may not decompose completely by spring and would make the soil in your growing beds rough and coarse, which you want to avoid.

Next add some fertilizers high in phosphorus and potassium, or potash, such as bone meal and wood ashes or rock powders, along with some compost or manure. Or add any of the other fertilizers described in chapter 5.

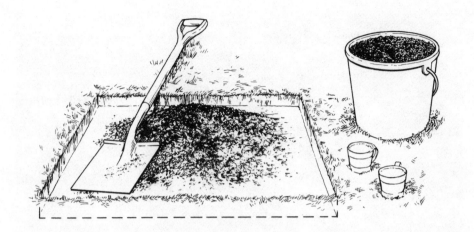

Soil preparation should always be done in fall. Layers of organic matter and fertilizer are added to each garden block, along with lime if that's needed.

Because a square foot garden is small, you can turn over your soil by hand; you don't need to rent or buy power equipment. A garden fork, shovel, or spade is all you really need. Each person has his or her favorite tool, so use whatever you have handy or particularly like. Many gardeners prefer to use a fork for turning over the soil, but if your soil is soft and loose, you'll find that the fork just slips through. A spade will be much easier to use and will do the job adequately. Dig as deep as you can. Again, each person has physical limitations and although deeper is better (up to 12 inches), you will still grow a good crop if you use the square foot method, even though you can't dig that deep.

Next break up any large clods, remove any stones, sticks, or man-made debris, level the block, and rake it smooth. It is now ready for planting.

To keep it that way through the winter with all its harsh weather, freezing and thawing, rain, sleet, and snow, cover the block with a 3-inch layer of hay, leaves, pine boughs, or similar material. Quite often if you use hay or finely chopped leaves, you'll find that the earthworms will keep working much of the time, and your soil will be in even better condition for the spring planting. Since no one is going to walk on it all winter, it will still be loose and friable when you remove the cover in February, March, or April, depending on when you want to start and what part of the country you live in.

Cover your garden blocks with a thick layer of mulch to protect your soil from the ravages of winter weather.

The extra work you do in fall will make your life much easier in spring, when you will be able to go out and just rake off the mulch cover and start planting. Chapter 15 described how to get off to an extra-early start by uncovering a block and placing a protective device over it a few weeks before your first planting to allow the soil to warm up extra fast. This will allow the sun to warm the soil, and will also keep the chilling, drenching rains and snow off the garden.

You might notice something else that's going to happen automatically: the block you're getting ready for early spring crops was the one used for growing hot-weather crops. You're practicing crop rotation without any elaborate plans or figuring ahead of time. The only thing you have to keep in mind perhaps if you're planning to start this block extra early, is to keep the entire block planted in vegetables that have similar requirements and that mature or finish at about the same time. The other blocks in your garden which might still have fall crops growing in them will be in use most of the fall and winter, and then won't be used again until next year for the summer crop. Since that won't be planted until early summer, you can safely and conveniently prepare that soil after it has warmed up and dried out in late spring. This not only splits up the demanding spring chores, it also divides the real hard work of gardening between fall and spring.

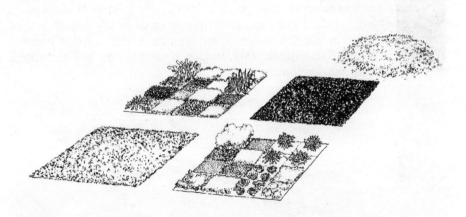

You'll find as you get the soil ready for next season that crop rotation is occurring automatically in your garden. The blocks that held summer crops are the ones that will be ready for fall soil preparation and early planting next spring. Blocks that still hold fall crops won't be ready for planting until next summer, so the same crops will not be planted in them.

After the first few light frosts, you should take steps to protect all of the hardy crops so you can continue your harvest well into the late fall, and even early winter in some parts of the country. Each vegetable requires a little different procedure, but basically you want to protect them from the extremes of weather and still make the harvest accessible and easy, despite snow, ice, and frozen soil.

Planting a Cover Crop

Here's another idea that not only will improve your soil, but also will make your winter garden look pretty (particularly if you don't have a lot of snow in your area), and at the same time make even more use of your growing soil. In those blocks that are growing a fall crop, as you harvest each square, whether it be lettuce, carrots, beets, or cabbage, and rather than leave the square bare all winter, sow a stand of winter rye grass. Since this space won't be needed until late spring for the planting of next summer's crop, you can grow a beautiful green cover all winter and spring. The use of a cover crop of annual grass is an old organic practice. When the grass is at its lushest green in the spring, it is turned under to add nitrogen-rich organic matter to the soil. The nice thing about winter rye is that it will sprout and grow even in the coldest of weather. On very warm or sunny days, it grows just a little and by spring, it's off to a nice start and adds a wonderful, lush, green color to your garden. If it's planted in the early fall, you'll have a beautiful patch of color all winter in that spot. When sown in late fall, a plastic-covered cage (described in chapter 9) will help get it off to a quick start. In fact, a cage left on will encourage more growth all winter long.

A winter cover crop of rye grass looks attractive and adds vital organic matter to the soil when it is tilled under in spring.

Putting Away Those Tools

One of the last steps of any hobby or activity is putting everything away until the next time you need them. Our natural tendency is to do just that, put it away and forget about it. Fall is usually a less hectic time than spring, and it's not a bad idea to take care of your garden tools before storing them away. Of course, this applies to everything in life. How many times have you unpacked the Christmas tree lights and found them a tangled mess with half of the bulbs burned out? That's not the time to have to go shopping for new ones. How much easier it would have been to buy new bulbs last year (especially at the half-price sale most stores have after the holidays), and then pack the strings—all in working order and rolled up neatly, ready for the next year. But that's too well-organized, and most of us don't do things that way; at least I don't, even though it's fun to write or talk about how it should be done. One of these days I'm going to follow my own advice and put everything away cleaned, oiled, and ready for use the next season.

Hand tools and shovels should all be sharpened and oiled before storing them away, a simple but fun project if you have the right tools. Two sizes of files with good handles, a pair of heavy gloves, and an oil-soaked rag are all that is needed. Of course, a well-lighted work area with a sturdy vise is important for safety's sake. If you don't think a sharp spade is half the work of digging, ask any professional nurseryman. Most of them carry a file in their back pocket when doing a lot of digging.

Another autumn chore is repairing tool handles. They always seem to need repair and fall is also a good time to work on them. I used to put them aside thinking I'd fix broken handles all at one time in the winter, but you know what happens. I have six shovels of various sizes, all with broken handles, and not a good one on the rack ready for use.

Storage of all your supplies is also a good fall project. Most fertilizer, lime, peat moss, and other garden products can be successfully stored over the winter, but only if they are kept dry and tightly sealed. If you're storing them on concrete in the garage make sure you lay down some heavy plastic first, as the cold dampness will seep up through the bags and ruin the fertilizer before spring. Better yet, put the bags on some boards which have been placed over the plastic. If you do have any old bags of material that you are not sure is still usable, or that has become lumpy, the compost pile is a good place for them. There's no need to waste or throw them out, just sprinkle or spread the material lightly on each layer of leaves as you add it to the pile.

Since in the square foot garden you use just a few seeds from each packet and store the remainder for following years, fall is also a good time to make sure that the seed packages are all tightly closed and stored away properly in the refrigerator. (See chapter 10 for details.)

Record Keeping

The end of the growing season is also a good time to catch up on your records and notes you wanted to jot down. It's a good idea to keep track of the successes and failures of the past season, which varieties turned out the best, and which were disappointments. Seed varieties have a habit of changing, new ones are introduced every year and older ones are discontinued, or sometimes the seed companies even change the names. Since you will be keeping your seed packets for many years, you might find that the description and pictures of some of your varieties will no longer be included in the catalog. In that case, if the packet doesn't tell you everything you want to know about that variety, you're going to be at quite a loss for information. So it's a good idea, along with your record of what went well and not so well each year, to consider making notes right in your seed catalogs, and then keeping them for future reference. Of course, this approach is only practical if you buy seeds from just one or two companies, otherwise your stack of old catalogs gets quite large. Another way would be to combine the idea of a notebook for your records along with cut-out pictures and descriptions from the seed catalog pages.

Take a looseleaf notebook and assign one page for each vegetable. You can start a personal gardening book this way by jotting down any interesting or pertinent facts that you might have heard or read about under the entry for that particular vegetable. I started this way and still use and refer to my notebook very often. It contains the best ideas of all the authors and experts I've ever heard or read. Also included on each page would be the cut-out picture and description of those vegetable seeds you've purchased, along with a yearly record of how well the variety did. You will soon have a reference of unusual value to your gardening. The notebook is also a good place to record dates of first and last frosts, planting time for each variety, quantities of harvest, and so on.

You might also want to add pages for soil preparation, fertilizer, mulch piles, various pests, and even one for cooking methods and favorite recipes. Since no one book has everything a person wants in it, this way you can create your own reference book, tailored specifically to you and your garden.

Chapter 17
🌱 Special Gardens

Square foot gardening is adaptable to all sorts of gardening situations, and in this chapter we'll take a look at just a few of them. Your square foot garden can be small or large; it can be located in an open field, a shady lawn, a flower bed next to the house, or even indoors. It can be in the form of a movable planter for a patio or rooftop, or it can be raised off the ground for wheelchair access. You can grow many kinds of crops, or you can concentrate on raising different varieties of one vegetable. And you can have a square foot garden in whatever type of climate you live.

In this chapter I'd like to show you some ideas for different kinds of square foot gardens. I hope they will inspire you to create the special kind of garden that will fit your particular needs.

A Children's Garden

Kids love gardening, but they are impatient and restless. A garden for children should contain plants that are easy and quick to grow, and colorful and interesting to look at. At first you might think that those are impossible requirements, but the garden world has lots of candidates for you to consider. Just go through your favorite seed catalog and look for

243

vegetables and flowers with these characteristics—there are many to choose from.

In addition to the above considerations, children need to work with seeds that are big enough to be easily handled; those that sprout quickly and do not require any special treatment. In fact, the entire garden should be able to grow almost on its own. Since children aren't as tall as grownups and can't reach as far, make their garden 3 feet by 3 feet instead of the standard 4-foot by 4-foot block. Put up a vertical frame at one end of the garden, but make it only 5 feet tall instead of 6 feet. Remember to locate the frame on the north side of the garden.

In the three squares next to the vertical frame, plant one tomato plant in the first, two cucumber seeds in the second, and eight pole beans in the third. You could also hang some extra strings to make it easier to support the plants. The plant varieties selected should produce abundant amounts of fruit. Any of the vine-type cherry tomatoes would be good varieties for a child's garden. (Don't get dwarf or patio kinds; they won't climb the strings.) Or choose any heavy-bearing variety, like Sweet 100 or Early Cascade. These varieties bear cluster after cluster of little tomatoes that are fun to pick. The best cucumbers for kids to grow are pickling varieties. Although their fruit is smaller than slicing cucumbers, each vine produces an abundance of fruit. Another spectacular cucumber is the Burpless or China cucumber, which grows long, thin fruits. For beans you can't beat Kentucky Wonder, or Blue Lake. Just make sure you select a pole bean for the vertical frame. If your children want to grow climbing flowers instead of one of the vine vegetables just mentioned, I would suggest morning glories. The seeds need to be soaked overnight before planting and you should nick each one with a sharp knife to help it break out of its hard shell. Morning glory vines are a little scrawny, but the blossoms which open daily are quite beautiful.

To fill the remaining six squares of the garden, radishes are an obvious first choice. But show your child how to plant only four seeds each week so that he or she will get a nicely staggered harvest. Of course the garden needs at least one square of leaf lettuce: Oak Leaf, Salad Bowl, Summer Bibb, Black-Seeded Simpson, and Ruby are all good varieties. Don't plant head lettuce because it takes too long to grow. The remaining square can contain a combination of beets (any good variety), onions, (plant sets of any variety rather than seeds), Swiss chard (the red type is the most colorful but the white type stands up straighter and is a little neater), and it wouldn't hurt to have a square of yellow bush beans. They're fast and easy to grow, produce a good crop, and provide a nice visual contrast to your green pole beans.

A garden for children should contain an assortment of colorful, easy-to-grow plants to encourage them to develop a lifelong interest in gardening.

Pretty flowers are a must for this garden, and dwarf marigolds are by far the best. Buy plants for instant color or plant seeds of these quick-growing flowers. You should have on hand a few small vases and encourage your child to pick a flower to decorate the table at every meal.

Remember to show your young gardener the basic techniques of square foot gardening, such as how to stay off the soil, how to weed and water weekly, and how to help the vine crops up their strings.

Don't let your child's first gardening experience end in frustration and boredom; never give in to the temptation to plant too large a garden. Remember, a child's enthusiasm and desire to start too big and too early is even greater than ours. Give your children the guidance they need to make their first garden a success and they'll come back for more every year and will retain their love of growing things throughout a lifetime of gardening. You can give a child or grandchild no better gift in life.

A Patio Garden

If you want a garden right on your patio, there's no reason why you can't have one, large enough to make it really worthwhile. Remember, a 4-foot by 4-foot garden block can provide enough salad vegetables to feed one person all season. The basic difference between the patio garden and a block in your regular garden is the soil. To contain the soil in the patio model, build a planter as described in chapter 9. Remember before putting in the soil to locate the planter in a spot that gets good sunlight for at least six hours every day.

The soil for this particular garden must be the very best growing soil you can provide. In a container of this sort, the soil will tend to dry out quickly and the frequent watering required will wash out many of the nutrients. So your soil must contain lots of organic matter, vermiculite, and peat moss. You can mix your own following the formula given in chapter 8. *Do not use* regular garden soil or potting soil no matter how good you think it is. In a container it will pack down too easily and won't hold moisture as well as a specially prepared mix.

What plants to grow will depend a lot on why you want the patio garden, and how dependent you are going to be on its harvest. Is the garden just for looks? If so, put in lots of flowers, useful herbs, and the most colorful and spectacular vegetables you can find, lots of leafy lettuce, bright red radishes, and a few unusual but attractive plants, such as red Swiss chard. Any shallow-rooted vegetable with attractive leaves or colorful fruit is a candidate for the patio garden; consider yellow wax beans, for example, or frilly parsley, or red onions. Sugar snap peas will look

A patio can be brightened with a garden growing in a wood planter with a vertical frame attached to one end.

great on your vertical frame if you're not going to grow tomatoes and cucumbers. If you grow tomatoes, stick with the vining types or small-fruited varieties like Early Cascade or Early Girl. If you're going to grow peppers, choose small, unusual varieties like yellow banana peppers or hot red chilis rather than the standard green bell peppers everybody grows. You can even grow carrots in this garden; just select the short- or round-rooted types that don't grow very deeply.

Use the same plant spacings as you use in the regular square foot garden. Make watering easy for yourself by keeping a bucket of water nearby. Try to get in the habit of refilling it right after you water. Usually one bucket full will be enough for the garden unless it's very dry. The only other maintenance you need do is to watch for pests, pinch off all yellow or dead leaves, and help the vine plants up the strings.

If your patio gets very hot or windy in the summer, take a few extra precautions to guarantee success: water more often, and plant more of the vegetables and flowers that can withstand hot weather—beans, Swiss chard, peppers, parsley, chives, marigolds, petunias, and zinnias. Wait until cooler weather to plant lettuce, beets, and carrots.

A Rooftop Garden

The patio garden just described is equally suited for a rooftop or balcony if a few extra precautions are taken. If you're going to move the garden about, it's better to nail on a plywood bottom rather than the stapled plastic suggested before. Use outdoor-rated plywood that is at least ½ inch thick; ⅝ inch is even better. In addition, rooftops are windier than ground level patios, so consider that when selecting your crops. Stay away from plants that grow tall, have delicate stems, or that might be blown over when they are mature and filled with ripening fruit. That would rule out bush tomatoes, eggplant, and peppers. Be sure all your vine crops are securely tied to or twisted around the strings. Provide some extra support for the vertical frame. Although it wouldn't look as nice, you might consider installing guy wires or strings to make sure the frame can't blow over. You should also consider the wind when you're locating your garden. Try to pick a sheltered spot away from the wind. The wind can be unmerciful to a plant; it whips the leaves about and can dry out the plant in short order.

The other big consideration for rooftop growing is heat buildup. Many roofs are either painted white or coated with black tar; the white roof bounces a tremendous amount of heat off its surface, and the black roof collects heat until it becomes almost unbearable. These conditions

The same type of planter used for a patio garden can also accommodate a garden on a city rooftop. Be sure to use a very lightweight, porous soil mix with a good proportion of vermiculite, and anchor the vertical frame with guy wires to secure it against heavy winds.

naturally affect both the frequency and amount of watering the garden will need. In many cases, you'll need to water once a day, so try to take this into account ahead of time. In addition to keeping the garden away from the wind, try to locate it where it will get some shade, too. The soil in your rooftop garden should be as light and porous (yet still water retentive) as possible. Mix in lots of vermiculite and peat moss. Make the planter box as deep as you can afford to in order to help slow evaporation of moisture from the soil. A good mulch will also help to keep the moisture in the soil, and will moderate the soil temperatures as well.

I've been talking so far about the special precautions needed during hot summer weather, but the strong winds and cold exposure can also cause problems in early spring and late fall. At those times you may want to provide special protection by installing wire and plastic sides or even covers on your small garden. One easy solution is to build a simple wire or wood frame and cover it with plastic. Or more simply, buy a roll of the wire-reinforced plastic material called "instant greenhouse" to make an easily removed cover. The plastic cover will not only keep out the wind, but will also warm up the soil much quicker in the spring.

A Truly Gourmet Garden

If you've always wanted to grow those baby, finger-size carrots, tiny beets, and young, tender beans that are the true gourmet's delight, here's your chance. These succulent vegetables have to grow rapidly, so they need the very best environmental conditions. That means a rich, well-drained, well-fertilized, loose, and friable soil with lots of organic matter. They need plenty of even, regular watering and lots of sunlight. In addition, they must be protected from pests and have absolutely no competition from weeds or other plants too close by. That's a tall order to fill, and there are very few gardens that can do it.

Many gardeners think that eating the thinnings from the garden is the same as having succulent baby vegetables, but it's not really true, at least not for the real gourmet. Thinnings may taste better than tough, overgrown vegetables that are harvested late. But they have usually been grown in poor soil without proper watering, and have been crowded in among all the other crops. A truly gourmet vegetable should be carefully nurtured under ideal conditions; it is not simply consumed as an alternative to throwing out young thinnings. The conventional row garden is not suited to this type of meticulous growing, because it cannot be monitored or controlled carefully enough. But using the square foot system you can easily create a perfect environment with all of the best conditions for a really gourmet harvest.

Your gourmet garden should be located in a sunny spot with well-drained soil. Make sure it's very close to your kitchen door. To prepare a first-rate soil, it wouldn't be too extreme to build a slightly raised bed for your special garden. After preparing the soil as described in chapter 5, nail together a 4-foot square frame of 1 by 4s, place it over the spot and fill it with the lightweight soil mix recommended for the patio garden. Be sure to add a cup of lime and your basic fertilizer mix to the soil and then turn it under lightly with a garden fork or trowel. Mix the light soil slightly with the garden soil below, but keep most of the special mix on top.

Now divide the space up into 16 squares and plant your favorite vegetables or herbs. Plant as much as you need to prepare your special dishes. You might have to plant 2 or more squares of some vegetables to give you enough. If pests are any threat, cover the entire block with chicken wire to keep out cats, rabbits, and squirrels. Or make a cover out of large-mesh wire and drape insect netting or fine screening over the wire frame to keep out insects. Watering is another basic key to success. If you water a little each day (with lukewarm water) you'll encourage continuous, rapid growth. The danger is that you will also encourage plant roots to stay near the surface, so if you miss a few days of watering during a very hot spell, your plants will suffer. You might wish to water with a weak solution of manure tea every third day or so, to keep plants well supplied with nutrients.

Remember, this is *not* a conventional garden. You're pampering these plants, but they will reward you with the most tender, delicious vegetables you could imagine. The varieties to grow in the gourmet garden depend on your taste. Search the seed catalogs for superior varieties. You might also write your favorite seed company and ask their recommendations after telling them what you're doing.

A Weekend or Vacation Garden

Would you like a garden you have to tend only once a week? Then try a few garden blocks of low-maintenance plants, along with some special, easy-care provisions. First select varieties that don't require constant harvesting. That means don't plant summer squash. Zucchini can grow several inches in a few days, and if you don't keep up with the harvest the plants will stop producing. Winter squash and pumpkins are different, because you don't harvest them until the plants die in the fall. A weekend garden is also not a good place for peas and beans; they also can grow astonishingly fast. Corn is another poor choice. Cucumbers can grow very quickly, but are worth a try. Tomatoes seem to be able to hold

A garden can be left untended for a week at a time if it contains low-maintenance plants and is covered with netting to keep out birds and animals.

on the vine longer, and the plants don't shut down as fast as the summer squashes and beans if the fruit isn't picked right away.

The best crops for a low-maintenance garden are root crops like beets, carrots, onions, and winter or white radishes (red radishes mature too quickly); and most leaf crops, including lettuce, cabbage, Swiss chard, parsley, spinach, and kale. Some members of the cabbage family can mature very fast in hot weather but are excellent in the fall. These would include broccoli and cauliflower. In fact, most vegetables will hold up longer and better during cool fall weather than in the warm spring or hot summer.

In addition to growing only low-maintenance crops, you should take extra precautions against pests, weeds, and drought. Make sure you have a good rabbit fence up all around each block. Hammer a metal or wood stake into the ground at each corner of the block, then wrap the fence around all four sides, bending the bottom 4 inches outward as a skirt. Drape a bird netting across the top with a few clothespins. Now *no one,* stray cats, hungry rabbits, or curious neighbors, will bother your garden. If you want to keep out insects, you could also drape insect netting over the top and down the sides for a really pestproof garden.

Weed control and moisture conservation are accomplished by the same procedure—use a mulch! And use it early. The mulch should be thick and impenetrable. If you're going to use hay or dried grass clippings, make it at least 4 inches, or better still 6 inches, thick. If you use newspaper or cardboard, put on several layers. Sprinkle a *lot* of soil on top of the newspapers to weight them down. You don't want to come back a week later and find the newspapers blown all over the yard. Pieces of carpet probably work best for weed control and keeping moisture in the ground. The one precaution you have to remember with most mulches is that they also soak up rain or water from a bucket and keep it from getting down to the soil, so make sure you water thoroughly every week.

A Wheelchair Garden

The person who can't bend over or who is confined to a wheelchair can also have a square foot garden. By building a patio model, but with a plywood bottom, the entire garden can be placed up on sawhorses at the necessary height to allow a wheelchair to slip underneath. Because the garden is small and accessible from all sides, the gardener will be able to reach all parts of the garden easily and comfortably. A vertical frame can also be attached to the garden, but to keep the vine crops from growing

A 4-foot by 4-foot planter box elevated on sawhorses can be tended from all sides by a person in a wheelchair. A 1-foot by 4-foot planter box resting on the floor at one end of the garden can contain a vertical frame for growing vining crops.

too tall and out of reach it would be easier to start them all in their own patio planters at ground level. Once the plants start to grow, most of the work of grooming them and picking the vegetables will be up higher, at lap or shoulder level.

Soil and plants can be similar to those used in the patio and rooftop gardens. Of course, the garden should be located on a patio or paved area that's easy to wheel over, and you might want to take the same precautions against excessive winds and heat as explained in the Patio and Rooftop sections.

A Waist-High Garden

If you have trouble bending over or can't kneel, you might want to consider a garden raised to waist level. It can easily be made either permanent or movable. You can build a planter in the garden and install it on sawhorses as described in the Wheelchair section (but at standing height instead of sitting height), or you might want to consider a permanent installation. The planter could remain 4 feet by 4 feet, or you might consider a pathway lined with 2-foot by 4-foot boxes. They, too, can be set on sawhorses, or could be placed on a more permanent post installation. A combination of both the vertical frame planters with the patio-type boxes would make a very attractive installation. These could be worked on the patio or even on a rooftop. The size and arrangement will be limited only by your imagination. Regardless of the layout, the planting and care will still be easily accomplished by the square foot method.

An Indoor Garden

When cold weather comes, there's no reason why you can't move your patio or rooftop planter right indoors, and continue growing fresh vegetables all winter. If you're a confirmed indoor gardener, you might even want to build a special planter just for use indoors. All you need is a movable planter with a good, strong plywood bottom at least ⅝ inch thick (make sure you use outdoor-rated plywood). It's best to build the planters in 2-foot by 4-foot sizes so they can be carried through doorways easily. Then you'll be able to bring them indoors with no trouble when really cold weather threatens in the fall. In early spring, the indoor garden can serve as a nursery for plants for the outdoor garden. Or you can just plant your patio garden extra early and when the weather is warm enough

A patio planter can be elevated for a waist-high garden that can be cultivated without bending over.

You can keep gardening all winter long if you bring a planter box (minus the vertical frame) indoors and position it under fluorescent lights.

you can carry the garden-in-progress right out to its summer location. Not only will your neighbors be amazed by your "instant garden," but you'll get an earlier harvest, too. The construction of the planter box, type of soil to use, and spacing requirements of the plants are all the same as for the patio garden. However, plants will grow a little more slowly indoors because of the poorer light conditions. The easiest way to provide enough light for your garden is to arrange a support so you can hang a two-tube fluorescent fixture right over the box. Don't use incandescent bulbs or even the kind that are designed as grow lights. I've found they are tricky to use because they heat up the soil and plants too much, eventually resulting in wilting and drying out. Stick with fluorescent lights and you'll have much better luck. Try a mixture of cool white and warm white tubes suspended from 6 to 12 inches above the plant tops. The light fixture should be adjustable, and the easiest way is to hang it on chains from the ceiling. Install eye hooks in both the ceiling and the fixture itself. Cultural information can be found in any good indoor gardening book. Space the plants according to the appropriate square foot spacings described in this book.

Leaf and root crops grow better indoors under lights than do sun-loving and warm-weather vegetables like beans or tomatoes. Summer crops are not impossible to grow indoors, but they are difficult. Try to choose plants that grow to approximately the same height, so some aren't too close to the light fixture while shorter ones are too far away.

Locate the garden someplace where dripping water or spilled dirt won't harm the floor or rug. You might want to put it in the basement. If the garden gets little or no light besides that shed by the fluorescent lights, you'll need to keep the lights on for at least 14 hours a day. If the garden is in a sunny room, lights will only be required for about 8 hours, part in the morning and the rest in the evening. The only problem in a sunny room is that the plants will tend to bend toward the window, searching for the maximum light.

If your indoor garden is located in an unheated area, it's simple enough to install a heating cable or mat in the bottom of the box. These come furnished with automatic thermostats that turn them on when the soil temperature drops below 70°F and turn them off when it exceeds 74°F. Cool-weather plants will not be harmed if the air temperature in the room dips down at night into the 40s, just as long as it doesn't freeze. If your garden is in a garage or sun porch where freezing temperatures are possible, you could provide a cover for the garden as described in chapter 15.

A Winter Garden

You can continue growing all winter very easily in your square foot garden. Winter gardening is not to be confused with extending the season as described in chapter 15. The methods described in that chapter are aimed at holding crops that are already mature in order to prolong the harvest in cold weather. It doesn't matter if this winter garden block is located in your garden or on the patio. The first step in the wintering process is to provide some shelter from really cold, windy, and wet weather. This can be done with a simple cover of plastic over a wood or wire frame installed over the garden. The next step is to prevent the ground from freezing hard. The easiest way to do that is to install a heating

A garden block will continue to grow all winter if it is covered with plastic and a heating cable is installed to keep the ground from freezing.

cable or heating mat at the bottom of your patio planter, or about 6 inches deep in the garden. If it's in the garden, dig out your soil to a depth of 6 inches, install the cable, cover with a wire mesh so you won't accidentally dig into the heating wires, and fill the bed with your best growing soil. To make a more elaborate setup you might even install Styrofoam panels in the very bottom and along the sides of the garden block to hold in the heat without wasting energy. The bottom sheet of Styrofoam should be covered with an inch or two of sand or soil before the heating cable is installed, just so the two don't touch.

The winter garden is maintained pretty much the same as the regular square foot garden except that the plants will need very little water during the winter, and you must select only cold-tolerant varieties to grow. Almost all of the root crops are good, and so are the leaf and head crops. There are some very durable varieties of spinach (such as Winter Bloomsdale), and lettuce (Arctic King), and other vegetables like corn salad and Swiss chard are very hardy if given a little protection. Check the seed catalogs for crops that are especially adaptable to cold-weather growing. I've grown a full block of vegetables right through the coldest of winters in New York state with nothing more than the heating cables and a single-layer plastic cover. It helps to mulch heavily, too. Loose hay is especially good to pile up around the plant tops, but don't pile it so high that it blocks out the light coming in.

An Herb Garden

An entire square foot garden of nothing but herbs is a very attractive and worthwhile project. Because you're working with a basic square shape, you can create many different and interesting patterns. You can create a checkerboard effect by sticking to the basic 16-square planting pattern, or you can vary the design by planting in geometric freeform shapes within the block. Plan out your basic design before you select the plants. Try to select herbs with a variety of colors and leaf shapes. Put compact and low-growing varieties like thyme in the borders of the planting, and taller plants like dill toward the back. Most herbs are undemanding and don't need a very rich soil.

An All-Lettuce Garden

A complete garden of nothing but lettuce and leafy vegetables is a real eye-catcher. The accompanying illustration shows some of the most at-

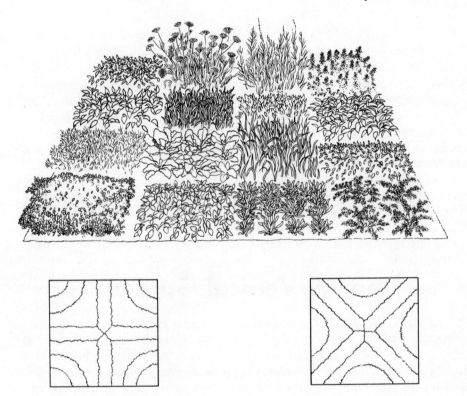

A garden of all your favorite herbs can be planted in squares, or in an interesting geometric pattern.

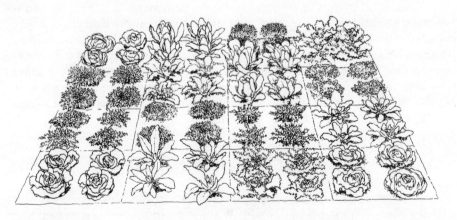

Real salad-lovers will enjoy a garden of many different kinds of lettuce. A combination of varieties like Oak Leaf, Salad Bowl, Ruby, Black-Seeded Simpson, and others provides an appealing array of contrasting visual textures in the garden.

tractive varieties to include. Don't worry about planting for a staggered harvest in this garden. The best visual effect will be produced if all the plants mature at the same time. This garden would make a strong entry in a big flower show. You can arrange the lettuce squares in almost any order; the different subtle shades of green will provide a delicately contrasting pattern. You'll find that by just mixing the lettuces throughout the block, you'll get an astonishing variety of not only colors, but also leaf textures, shapes, and growing habits.

In addition, a garden containing several kinds of lettuce will guarantee a summer full of interesting salads. From the crisp crunchiness of Black-Seeded Simpson and Ruby to the mellow, succulent tenderness of Oak Leaf or Bibb, an all-lettuce garden will provide you with a range of tastes and textures that mean your family's daily salads will never be dull.

An All-Vertical Garden

If you're not much for vegetable gardening except for your favorite summer tomatoes and cucumbers, you might want to try an all-vertical garden, or you might just want to erect a vertical garden in a separate area from your regular garden. Perhaps there is an area of your property that gets lots of sunshine but either has poor soil or is someplace where you don't want a full garden. Then a vertical garden where you can have a separate frame or section of fencing for each different variety of tomato and cucumber is just the thing.

Your frames can be placed in any arrangement or configuration—fancy, or straight down the aisle. Just make sure you provide good labels, because visitors will want to know what each different variety is. Adding some melons and winter squash or gourds will make the garden even more interesting. The nice thing about this all-vertical garden is that it takes very little work once the frames are up and the plants are in the ground. If you follow my advice and use the trench method as described in chapter 8, you'll produce a good crop with little work.

Desert Gardening

Obviously the biggest gardening problem in the arid regions of our country are the hot sun and dry soil. Watering can become a never-ending chore, but if you add extra peat moss and vermiculite to your soil and mulch heavily you can grow a good crop of vegetables right through the hot summer in almost any region using the square foot method. The

Vertical frames can be arranged in many different ways to add beauty and diversity to your landscape.

condensed size of the garden makes it easier and less expensive to provide the kind of soil and water plants need to thrive in the arid desert environment. You might also consider installing a sun shade over the garden during the hottest, most intense portion of the day.

Southern Gardening

Folks in the South are lucky to be able to start gardening nice and early in the spring, but they run into problems in the hot summer. Many plants won't grow well in the heat, and the same precautions recommended for desert gardening must be taken. By using the same methods as desert gardeners many southern gardeners could grow a larger variety of vegetables all summer. In addition, employing the season-extending techniques explained in chapter 15 can enable the warm-climate garden to remain active the entire 12 months of the year, providing fresh vegetables year-round. This is certainly a worthwhile accomplishment.

Western Gardening

The West Coast is a garden paradise, blessed with good growing weather all year long and fertile soil. To those of us in the rest of the country, the problem of our western colleagues in deciding what to grow next seems hardly a problem at all. But soil in constant use can become worn out quickly, and when there's no break in the garden year, it can become monotonous just like anything else. So the western gardener probably needs new methods of crop rotation and soil building more than anyone else, because the garden is such a continuous process. The space limitations of the square foot garden seem ideally suited to someone who has no restrictions on sun, soil, water, or growing season. How else could you control your urge to plant too much? In addition, the square foot method allows the vegetable garden to be well cared for and attractive at all times, so that it can be incorporated into the landscaping plans of an entire yard. No longer does the vegetable garden have to be hidden away "out back"; it can be right next to the pool or even by the front entrance. Certainly it can become part of the planting around the patio. The vertical frames are especially suited to meticulous landscaping plans in an area with a long growing season.

Short-Season Gardening in the North

If your frost-free growing season is very short you can avoid a lot of frustration by selecting fast-growing vegetable varieties that mature early. Since this information is to be found mostly in seed catalogs rather than at a nursery or garden supply center, you should do most of your shopping by mail and plan on starting a lot of your own seeds. You want to avoid jumbo, late-season varieties of tomatoes and other hot-weather crops. Instead, concentrate on early-season varieties. The number of summer crops you can grow will be limited, but on the other hand, you have an advantage over other parts of the country in that you can probably grow most of the spring or cool-season crops all summer. Long after most gardeners' lettuce has bolted to seed you'll still be picking crisp, succulent leaves for your summertime salads.

Invest in some seed-starting equipment, at least a heating cable or mat, build a few sun boxes, and experiment with starting your own plants. Don't make the mistake of planting too much, and you'll do all right in your cold zone.

Chapter 18
⊠ A Guide to Growing Crops by the Square Foot Method

This chapter is intended as a quick reference to the basic considerations for growing 22 favorite garden crops by the square foot method. The box at the beginning of each entry provides basic botanical information, which will be of help to you in achieving a better understanding of the characteristics of each crop. You'll find a brief description of each crop, a spacing diagram, and a summary of the necessary planting and cultural information. The basic and high-nitrogen fertilizers called for here are explained in chapter 5. There's also a list of pest and disease problems to which each one may be susceptible. There are directions for harvesting, and I've shared some of my favorite ways to serve each vegetable. I've also included some of the questions I'm most often asked about these crops at my lectures.

All the methods for planting, growing, maintaining, and harvesting crops in the square foot garden are detailed elsewhere in this book. Consult the appropriate chapter for further information.

Use the following key to interpret the cultural information chart which accompanies each vegetable:

Planting Key:	◯ Plant Seeds	⚘ Plant Transplants	🧺–🧺 Harvest Period
---Indoor Growing Time	——Outdoor Growing Time		

Beans

At A Glance

Botanical Information:

Pulse family
Vine (pole) or bush, 12 to 18″ tall
Annual, frost tender

Spacing: Bush type—9 plants per square; pole type—8 plants per square

Growing Season:

Spring: no
Summer: yes
Fall: no
Winter: no

Seed to Harvest: 8 weeks

Seeds Store: 3–4 years

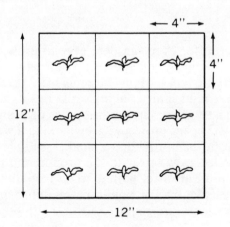

Bush Beans

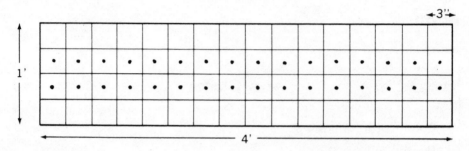

Pole Beans

		Weeks Before	Last Spring Frost	Weeks After		Weeks Before	First Fall Frost	Weeks After
		10 8 6 4 2	0	2 4 6 8		8 6 4 2	0	2 4 6 8
Bush beans (8 wks. to maturity)	Indoor Seed Starting		Do not transplant well					
	Earliest Outdoor Planting							
	Additional Plantings		Plant a new crop every 2 to 4 weeks					
	Last Planting							
Pole beans (9 wks. to maturity)	Indoor Seed Starting		Do not transplant well					
	Earliest Outdoor Planting							
	Additional Plantings		Not needed					
	Last Planting		Not needed					

Description

An excellent crop for every garden; easy to grow, very productive. Many varieties of different kinds and colors, growth habits basically divided into bush and pole types. Many gardeners feel that pole varieties are better tasting, with a mild, nutty flavor, while bush varieties have more of a "green bean" taste. However, new varieties of bush beans are better tasting than ever. Pole beans grow and grow, taking a week or two longer to start producing, but then providing a small, steady harvest all summer and fall. Bush varieties grow lower to the ground and produce basically one large main crop all at once, with a second smaller crop two weeks later. Therefore, one planting of pole types is sufficient, but additional plantings of bush varieties are required for a continuous harvest.

Starting

Location: Full sun. Bush varieties in any garden square. Pole varieties under a vertical frame.

Soil: pH 5.5 to 7.0; light, well-drained soil (seeds sprout poorly in a wet, clayey soil).

Seeds Indoors: No.

Transplanting: Do not transplant well.

Seeds Outdoors: Presoak seeds two to four hours. Plant nine bush or eight pole variety seeds 1 inch deep in a square. Make a slight depression around each seed for future waterings. Water soil and cover square with a chicken-wire cage to keep out birds. Remove cage after two weeks. Seeds sprout in five to ten days.

Growing

Watering: Weekly, ½ cup per plant; twice weekly in very hot weather. Beans must have regular waterings. Do not allow the soil to dry out but keep the leaves dry.

Fertilizing: Feed monthly if desired with basic fertilizer mix.

Maintenance: Weed weekly; mulch during hot weather.

Harvesting

How: Break or cut each stem holding the bean pod (no harm done if bean breaks and stem with part of pod stays on the vine). Do not pull on the plant when harvesting.

When: Pick when still small and tender. *Do not* allow to get big enough so pods bulge with seeds or the plant will stop producing.

Preparing and Using

Wash and refrigerate if not using immediately. Beans do not store well so try to use them the same day they are picked. There's no need to string them as in the old days when they were called string beans. Present-day varieties are called snap beans; they do not form strings unless you let them get too large and tough.

Beans can be eaten raw when small or cooked at any size; the smaller, the more tender. Beans contain lots of vitamins A, B, and C, as well as calcium and iron. There are probably as many ways to fix and serve them as there are varieties in the seed catalogs. Raw beans can be served either whole with a dip or cut into pieces for addition to a salad. They can be steamed, boiled, or stir-fried, then served individually with a little butter, grated cheese, parsley, or mixed with just about any other cooked vegetable. Excellent for addition to soups, stews, or mixed vegetable dishes. Leftovers are easily marinated for addition to a salad or use as a relish. I've even heard of people adding marinated beans to a sandwich, along with lettuce, tomato, and cheese.

Problems

Aphids, Japanese and Mexican bean beetles, birds, rabbits, wood-chucks, and deer; blight, rust, and mildew.

Questions and Answers

Q. Should I turn my bush bean plants under after their final harvest?

A. You can bury them right in the same square you grew them in for additional nitrogen-rich humus, but it is a little messy unless you chop them up first with a hedge clipper. Otherwise remove the vines and roots to the compost pile.

Q. Our first planting of bean seeds often comes up poorly. Why?

A. Bean seeds need a warm soil that's not too wet at first. You might be planting too early (never plant before your last spring frost date); the cold spring rains might be the culprit in your area. Try placing a plastic-covered cage over the square one week before planting (to warm up the soil), and leave on two weeks after planting (to keep out cold rains and birds.)

Q. What is the black powder my neighbor uses to cover bean and pea seeds before planting, and is it worthwhile?

A. Yes, it increases your crop and helps the pea and bean plants pull more nitrogen from the air into the roots, thus fixing nitrogen in the soil for future crops (this is one reason it's good to plant lettuce or another leafy crop following your bean crop in the same square). The material is a special preparation of bacteria or nitrogen inoculant powder sold in garden centers. The plant roots need a certain bacteria in the soil to help them pull nitrogen into the plant from the surrounding air. This material merely insures that there's enough of that bacteria present for the plants to do just that.

Q. I've been told you should never water beans from above, or work around the plants when the leaves are wet. Why?

A. Bean foliage should not be touched when wet because the leaves can carry several mildew diseases which are spread when wet.

Q. What can I do when my pole beans reach the top of my 6-foot-high support?

A. Just cut off the tops that are waving in the breeze. The plant will then force out new side branches farther down the plant for later harvests.

Q. What causes my bean pods to be fat at one end but shriveled up at the other?

A. You probably let the soil dry out, and the plant stopped growing, then started up again. Make sure you water regularly as recommended.

Beets

At A Glance

Botanical Information:

Goosefoot family
12″ tall
Biennial, frost hardy (spring and fall)

Spacing: 16 plants per square

Growing Season:

Spring: yes
Summer: yes
Fall: yes
Winter: no

Seed to Harvest: 8 weeks

Seeds Store: 4–5 years

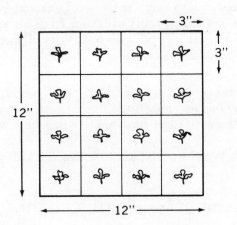

		Weeks Before	Last Spring Frost	Weeks After		Weeks Before	First Fall Frost	Weeks After
		10 8 6 4 2	0	2 4 6 8		8 6 4 2	0	2 4 6 8
Beets (8 wks. to maturity)	Indoor Seed Starting		Do not transplant well					
	Earliest Outdoor Planting							
	Additional Plantings		Plant a new crop every 2 to 4 weeks					
	Last Planting							

Description

An excellent, easy-to-grow vegetable; both the greens and roots are edible. Relatively free from pests and disease. Hardy to both spring and fall frosts, although the root gets tough when grown in the hot summer weather.

Starting

Location: Partial shade or full sun.

Soil: pH 6.0 to 7.5; deeply dug, friable, loose soil. Lots of humus required, but no manure.

Seeds Indoors: No.

Transplanting: Do not transplant well.

Seeds Outdoors: Each seed in the packet is actually a cluster of two to five individual seeds, so several sprouts will come up from each seed cluster that's planted. Plant one presoaked seed cluster in each space ½ inch deep three weeks before your last spring frost. For a continuous harvest plant a new square every three weeks except in the hottest part of the summer. Two to four sprouts will come from each seed cluster; after they are about 1 inch tall cut off with a scissors all except the strongest plant in each little space.

Growing

Watering: Weekly, ½ cup per plant; twice weekly in hot weather. Plants need even, constant moisture.

Fertilizing: Heavy feeder; feed once, when half grown, with basic fertilizer mix.

Maintenance: Weed weekly; keep damaged leaves picked off; mulch in hot weather.

Harvesting

How: Pull up entire plant with the largest top. If not sure of bulb size dig around the root with your finger to uncover the top portion to check the size. To harvest greens, individual leaves can be cut at any time; don't take more than one or two from each plant.

When: Roots are most tender when half size, so start pulling when the roots are approximately the size of a ping pong ball and continue until they are full size. Leaves are usable at any size.

Preparing and Using

Use greens whole or chopped in fresh salads, or cook them like spinach. Roots are rich in iron and B vitamins. Serve hot, boiled or steamed. Marinate leftovers for next day's salad or relish. Try cooking shredded raw beets quickly in butter and serve hot, or try cooked and chilled (shredded, sliced, or diced) in salads or mixed with cottage cheese. Sliced small whole beets can also be cooked and served with an orange sauce, or add just butter or a spoonful of sour cream.

Autumn Growing

Plant seeds in early fall; mulch heavily and enclose in sun box for winter growing. Harvest leaves occasionally; pull the roots anytime. For winter storage cover with a thick mulch, and dig any time until December.

Problems

Cutworms, slugs and snails, leaf miners, rabbits, woodchucks, and deer. Relatively disease free.

Questions and Answers

Q. My beets always seem to be cracked and are very tough.
A. Watering was probably irregular. Beets need a steady supply of moisture to keep up continuous growth.
Q. When should I plant a crop of fall beets?
A. They require at least 12 weeks to grow, so subtract 12 weeks or 3 months from your first fall frost date, and plant the seeds then. Beets won't grow much after frost, but keep well in the ground even after they become large.

Broccoli

At A Glance

Botanical Information:

Mustard family
18 to 24" tall
Biennial, partially frost hardy

Spacing: 1 plant per square

Growing Season:

Spring: yes
Summer: no
Fall: yes
Winter: no

Seed to Harvest: 16 weeks

Seeds Store: 5–6 years

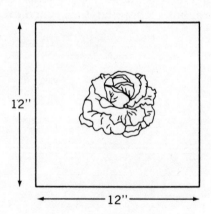

12"

12"

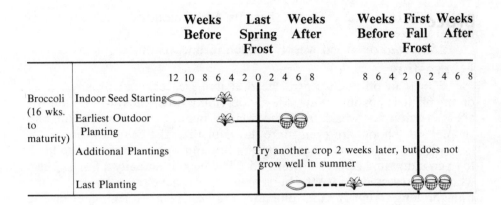

		Weeks Before	Last Spring Frost	Weeks After		Weeks Before	First Fall Frost	Weeks After

Description

Although it takes a lot of room and a long time to grow, it's well worth the effort for this flavorful plant. A member of the mustard family, it suffers from the same pest and disease problems. But all of that pales when the first head is harvested, cooked, covered with a cheese sauce, and placed on the table. Although broccoli doesn't grow well in the hot summer, it is very frost hardy and both a spring and a separate fall crop can be grown.

Starting

Location: Needs full sun. Don't plant in the same square where any other mustard family member has grown for the past 12 months.

Soil: pH 6.0 to 7.5; rich, loose soil with lots of humus. Add a little extra lime (¼ cup per square) to discourage club root disease.

Seeds Indoors: Plant five to ten seeds in a cup of vermiculite, or place one seed ¼ inch deep in potting soil in each individual compartment of a seedling tray, approximately 12 weeks before your last spring frost. Will sprout indoors in 5 to 10 days at 70°F. Keep warm (70°F) until sprouted; move to full sunlight as soon as first shoots appear.

Transplanting: Plant out approximately five weeks before the last spring frost.

Seeds Outdoors: Not satisfactory, as season is too short before hot weather arrives.

Growing

Watering: Weekly, one cup per plant; twice weekly during hot weather. Like all of the cabbage group, you're growing leaves and flowers which need a lot of constantly available moisture. Never let the plant dry out or wilt.

Fertilizing: Heavy feeder; benefits from monthly applications of basic fertilizer mix.

Maintenance: Weed weekly; mulch in hot weather.

Harvesting

How: Cut off main central head at its base, leaving as many leaves on the plant as possible. New side-shoots (miniature heads) will then form and grow in a few weeks from the original plant. Some people claim the smaller side-shoots are even more flavorful than the central head.

When: As soon as a head appears full and tight, but before it starts to open individual cells or flower buds. The head is actually a flower head which is harvested before the buds open. If you have several plants don't wait too long to cut the first one after the heads start forming, even if it looks a little small. It's still very edible when small.

Preparing and Using

Broccoli contains vitamins A, B, and C, as well as calcium, phosphorus, and iron. Wash under running water and soak in cold salt water for two hours, if there's any chance that a green cabbage worm is present in the head. Refrigerate if you're not using immediately. Broccoli can be served fresh and raw with mayonnaise, or any dip; or can be chopped fresh into a salad. To cook it, you can steam, boil, or stir-fry. Try it plain with just a little butter, sour cream, or topped with a cheese sauce. Leftovers or extras can be marinated after cooking for additions to future salads or relishes. It's an excellent addition to any stir-fried dish; mix it with any other interesting combination of meat and vegetables.

Autumn Growing

Can be protected for two- to four-week extension of the harvest into late fall by covering with a hay mulch.

Problems

Cutworms, root maggots, green worm, cabbage worms; club root.

Questions and Answers

Q. I was told you can eat the stem and leaves of broccoli—is it true?
A. Yes, they are usually tender enough if you have grown them properly and cooked them soon after harvesting. However, the more stem and leaves you cut from the main plant the fewer side-shoots will be produced for a second harvest.

Q. My spring broccoli burst into beautiful yellow flowers; can I eat them?
A. I never have, but there is no reason why not. One gardener told me he cooked the flower head after it blossomed and it tasted just fine. What happened is that you let the head go too long to harvest, and it flowered. Pick the others sooner, before the buds start to swell.

Cabbage

At A Glance

Botanical Information:

Mustard family
12 to 18″ tall
Biennial, frost hardy (spring and fall)

Spacing: 1 plant per square

Growing Season:

Spring: yes
Summer: no
Fall: yes
Winter: no

Seed to Harvest: 16 weeks

Seeds Store: 5–6 years

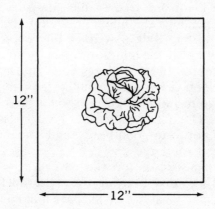

12″

12″

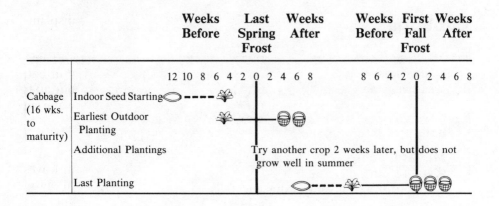

		Weeks Before	Last Spring Frost	Weeks After		Weeks Before	First Fall Frost	Weeks After
		12 10 8 6 4 2 0 2 4 6 8				8 6 4 2 0 2 4 6 8		
Cabbage (16 wks. to maturity)	Indoor Seed Starting							
	Earliest Outdoor Planting							
	Additional Plantings	Try another crop 2 weeks later, but does not grow well in summer						
	Last Planting							

Description

A fairly popular, easy-to-grow vegetable in most gardens, cabbage is nondemanding and very hardy to frosts. However, it does take up a lot of growing room and is prone to some troublesome pests. Cabbage contains lots of vitamin C and is delicious either raw or cooked.

Cabbage comes in a range of sizes, shapes (round or flat heads), colors (red or various shades of green), and leaf textures (smooth or crinkled), as well as early- to late-season varieties. As is true of most vegetables, the early-season varieties are smaller and faster growing, while the late or long-season types are the really big ones. All require cool spring or fall weather for best growth.

Starting

Location: Full sun.

Soil: pH 6.0 to 7.5; fertile soil with lots of humus.

Seeds Indoors: Plant one seed ¼ inch deep in potting soil in each individual compartment of a seedling tray 12 weeks before your last spring frost. Seeds sprout in 5 to 8 days at 70°F. For a second crop in the fall repeat the above anytime in the middle of June, (or subtract 16 weeks from your first fall frost date). In most places you can usually start seeds of a new crop as soon as you've harvested your spring crop. Keep warm (70°F) until sprouted; move to full sunlight as soon as first shoots appear.

Transplanting: Don't let transplants get too large before planting them out. They do not form good heads, and sometimes flower the first year if allowed to get too large.

Seeds Outdoors: Season is too short to plant seeds directly in the garden for this spring crop. Starting the fall crop from seed outdoors would tie up too much valuable garden space that could be more productively used. Start all seeds indoors in individual containers for transplanting into the garden.

Growing

Watering: Weekly, one to two cups per plant; twice weekly in hot, dry weather. Cabbage needs lots of water to head up properly, but after the head is formed and while it grows to full size cut back on watering or the head will grow too fast and split.

Fertilizing: Heavy feeder; benefits from monthly applications of basic fertilizer mix.

Maintenance: Weed weekly; cut away any extra-large bottom leaves if yellowed. If large lower leaves are spreading to other squares, cut away any portions that are "over the line." This will not hurt the plant.

Harvesting

How: Cut off entire head.

When: Anytime the head starts developing and feels firm. If you have several plants, don't wait until all the heads are really large. They may all split in hot weather, and you'll be left with nothing.

Autumn Growing

Plants are cold tolerant and can be carried into the fall before harvesting. Cover entire plant with a thick layer of loose hay, and extend your harvest right on through December.

Problems

Slugs and snails, aphids, cabbage worms (worst enemy).

Questions and Answers

Q. My cabbages start splitting just after they grow to a nice size.
A. This is caused by too-rapid growth in hot weather, and sometimes too much water. What's happening is that the inside of the head is growing faster than the outer leaves can open and the head is splitting to keep up with the growth. The solution is to stop the rapid growth by slowing down the water, or by actually root pruning. This can be done easily by grasping the heads and giving them a half-turn twist so that you break most of the roots. The plant will stay in the ground but will slow down its growth. Usually when the heads start splitting it's best to harvest and store them.

Q. Many of my transplants went to flower before forming heads.
A. This sometimes happens if the transplants are too large, or if they've been exposed to a constant cold temperature (50°F) for over two weeks.

Q. What's an easy way to store the fall crop if I want to clean up the garden?
A. Pull the entire plant, root and all, stuff a plastic bag around the roots and tie at the stem to keep the head clean. Then hang upside down in a cool, dark garage.

Carrots

At A Glance

Botanical Information:

Parsley family
12″ tall
Biennial, frost hardy (spring and fall)

Spacing: 16 plants per square

Growing Season:

Spring: yes
Summer: yes
Fall: yes
Winter: yes, with protection

Seed to Harvest: 10 weeks

Seeds Store: 3–4 years

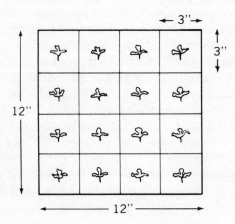

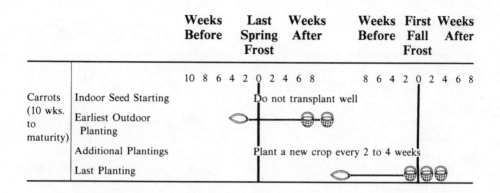

		Weeks Before	Last Spring Frost	Weeks After		Weeks Before	First Fall Frost	Weeks After
		10 8 6 4 2	0	2 4 6 8		8 6 4 2	0	2 4 6 8
Carrots (10 wks. to maturity)	Indoor Seed Starting		Do not transplant well					
	Earliest Outdoor Planting							
	Additional Plantings		Plant a new crop every 2 to 4 weeks					
	Last Planting							

Description

Related to the familiar eastern wildflower Queen Anne's lace, carrots come in many shapes and sizes. The long, thin ones are beautiful, but can only be grown in deep, loose, friable soil; the short, stubby, or round-rooted varieties are better suited for a heavy clayey soil. Make sure you pick a shape and size suited to your garden. Carrots are very easy to grow once you get the seedlings started, but planting is a tedious chore because the seeds are so small.

Starting

Location: Full sun, but can stand partial shade.

Soil: pH of 5.5 to 7.0; loose, friable, deeply dug soil, free from stones or dirt clods. Don't add manure within six months of planting time, or roots may be deformed. Prepare soil with a little extra potassium.

Seeds Indoors: No.

Transplanting: Do not transplant well.

Seeds Outdoors: Sprout in two to three weeks outdoors. Seeds are very small; try pelleted seeds if preferred. Plant one or two seeds in each of the 16 spaces in a square. Cover with vermiculite or sifted compost. Water soil and cover square with a plastic-covered cage. Keep the ground moist at all times, even if it means daily spraying in hot sunny weather.

Growing

Watering: Weekly, ¼ cup per plant. Carrots must have constant moisture until almost mature to grow quickly and continuously, without any stops. Then slow down on the water so the carrots don't crack from over-rapid growth.

Fertilizing: Light feeder; may benefit from occasional applications of basic fertilizer mix.

Maintenance: Weed weekly; otherwise relatively work free.

Harvesting

How: Pull up those with the largest tops. If not sure which are biggest, dig around the plant with your finger to test the size.

When: Pick them early, when only half size and at their sweetest and most tender stage.

Preparing and Using

Scrub with a vegetable brush, don't peel. Most of the vitamins are in the skin or close to the surface. Rich in vitamin A and thiamine, carrots also contain vitamin B_1 and calcium. Carrots are delicious fresh and raw —shredded, sliced thinly, or cut into sticks for snacking. They can be cooked by steaming or boiling. They can be served in a variety of dishes, or added to soups and stews, but seem best by themselves served with butter, a dab of sour cream, or sprinkled with parsley and grated cheese. Carrots are so versatile you can even make a wonderfully moist cake with them.

Winter Growing

Mulch heavily enough to keep the ground from freezing to protect your planted carrots for a late winter harvest.

Problems

Carrot rust fly, rabbits, woodchucks, deer, and voles. Virtually disease free.

Questions and Answers

Q. My carrots are all stumpy and misshapen.

A. You probably have rough, stony soil, so the roots cannot grow straight. Take a square and lift out the soil so the hole is about 9 inches deep, then fill with a special soil mix of equal parts of peat moss, vermiculite, sifted topsoil, and sand, along with ½ cup of lime. Space according to the square foot method, and water weekly, and you'll have the best carrots you've ever seen. Rotate the next planting to another square, and before you know it you'll have many squares of super soil for all your plants.

Q. My large carrots are all split.

A. They had *too* much water at the very end of the growing cycle, causing the centers to grow and swell faster than the outside rim and producing the splits. This sometimes happens when large carrots are stored in the ground in late fall when there's a lot of rain. Withhold water near the end or cover with a plastic-covered cage to keep excess rainwater off the plants.

Q. The tops of all my carrot roots are greenish brown.

A. They probably were exposed to daylight with their tops sticking out of the ground. When that happens, cover them with an inch of screened compost, or mulch a little more thickly to keep the light out. Cut off the discolored portion before eating.

Cauliflower

At A Glance

Botanical Information:

Mustard family
18 to 24″ tall
Biennial, semi-frost hardy (spring and fall)

Spacing: 1 plant per square

Growing Season:

Spring: yes
Summer: no
Fall: yes
Winter: no

Seed to Harvest: 14 weeks

Seeds Store: 5–6 years

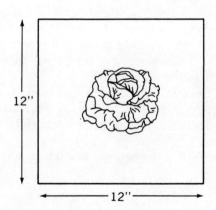

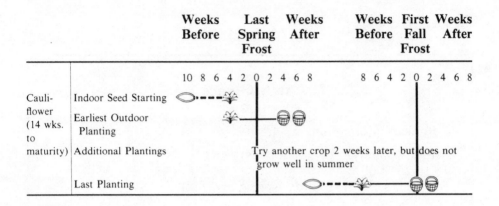

		Weeks Before	Last Spring Frost	Weeks After		Weeks Before	First Fall Frost	Weeks After
		10 8 6 4 2	0	2 4 6 8		8 6 4 2	0	2 4 6 8
Cauli-flower (14 wks. to maturity)	Indoor Seed Starting							
	Earliest Outdoor Planting							
	Additional Plantings		Try another crop 2 weeks later, but does not grow well in summer					
	Last Planting							

Description

A temperamental member of the cabbage group, cauliflower is not as cold hardy as other members (broccoli or cabbage), and is much more susceptible to heat. A spring and fall crop is possible but not always successful. Fall is by far the best season because the plant will mature in the cool weather which it likes.

Most popular varieties are white, but the purple head is said to be more flavorful, and more tolerant of heat. Growing time varies from 14 to 15 weeks for the white varieties, and up to 19 weeks for the purple varieties.

Starting

Location: Full sun, but will tolerate partial shade.

Soil: pH 6.0 to 7.5; rich, loose soil with lots of humus; add an extra ½ cup of lime to each square to discourage club root disease.

Seeds Indoors: Will sprout in five to ten days at 70°F. Plant five to ten seeds in a cup of vermiculite, or plant one seed ¼ inch deep in potting soil in each individual compartment of a seedling flat ten weeks before the last spring frost. For a second crop in the fall repeat the above anytime from June 15 to July 1. Keep warm (70°F) until sprouted; move to full sunlight as soon as first shoots appear.

Transplanting: Set out in the garden four weeks before the last spring frost. Place a cutworm collar around the stem, water, and provide a shade cage. Be extra careful when planting; cauliflower suffers more from transplanting than any other cabbage group member.

Seeds Outdoors: Not satisfactory; season is too short before hot weather arrives.

Growing

Watering: Weekly, one cup per plant; twice weekly in hot weather. Never let the plant dry out.

Fertilizer: Heavy feeder; benefits from monthly applications of basic fertilizer mix.

Maintenance: Weed weekly; mulch in hot weather. For white varieties that are not self-blanching, when heads start to form, bend or break large leaves over the top, tie or hold with a rubber band to cover and protect the head from exposure to the sun, which can turn the head yellow.

Harvesting

How: Cut off the entire head at its base with a sharp knife or clippers.

When: As soon as the head enlarges, is firm and a nice white color; before the buds separate or open. Do not delay harvest, as the head will grow fast and pass the harvest point in just a few days.

Preparing and Using

Serve florets fresh and raw with any salad dressing or dip. Excellent chopped up in tossed salads. Cook by steaming, boiling, or stir-frying. Serve hot with cheese sauce, melted butter, or just sprinkled with grated cheese. Excellent addition to any soup or stew. Cauliflower soup is superb and quite unusual. Marinate any leftovers for addition to salads or relishes.

Problems

Cutworms, root maggots, occasionally cabbage worms and cabbage loopers; club root.

Questions and Answers

Q. After cutting the central head, will the plant develop side-shoots like broccoli does?

A. No.

Q. I keep reading that broccoli and cauliflower should be rotated in the different spaces, but it never says why.

A. The reason is to prevent a buildup of the disease, club root, which is quite disastrous to the mustard family. It affects primarily this family of plants, so the bacteria can be present in soil but will not affect other plants. Club root has a life span of several years, so it is important to keep moving the mustard family plants into fresh soil. A telltale symptom of club root is wilting of the plant when it is near maturity. If you continue to water and the plant still wilts on hot days, it means that the plant no longer has the capacity to bring water up from the ground into the leaves, and water is evaporating too fast from the leaves, thereby causing the wilting.

Swiss Chard

At A Glance

Botanical Information:

Goosefoot family
12 to 18″ tall
Biennial, frost hardy (spring and fall)

Spacing: 4 plants per square

Growing Season:

Spring: yes
Summer: yes
Fall: yes
Winter: yes, with protection

Seed to Harvest: 8 weeks

Seeds Store: 4–5 years

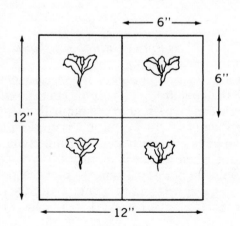

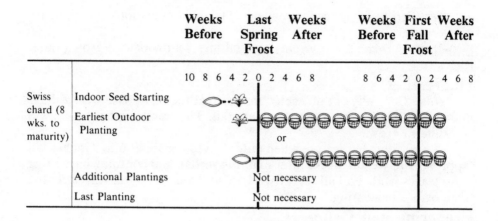

		Weeks Before	Last Spring Frost	Weeks After		Weeks Before	First Fall	Weeks After
		10 8 6 4 2	0	2 4 6 8		8 6 4 2	0	2 4 6 8
Swiss chard (8 wks. to maturity)	Indoor Seed Starting							
	Earliest Outdoor Planting			or				
	Additional Plantings		Not necessary					
	Last Planting		Not necessary					

Description

One of the easiest vegetables to grow in any part of the country, a tall, erect relative of the beet. Chard is grown both for its vitamin-rich leaves and its succulent stems. Grows in sun or shade, all spring, summer, and fall, for a continuous harvest all season long. It can even be carried over the winter in most climates. A must in every garden, virtually pest and disease free. Available in white- or red-stemmed varieties with smooth or crinkled leaves.

Starting

Location: Does best in full sun, but can grow in partial shade.

Soil: pH 6.0 to 7.5; extra lime is beneficial. Does well in almost any soil, but likes lots of humus.

Seeds Indoors: Plant ten seeds in a cup of vermiculite, or place one seed ½ inch deep in potting soil in each individual compartment of a seedling tray seven weeks before your last spring frost. Seeds will sprout in five to ten days at 70°F. Keep warm (70°F) until sprouted; move to full sunlight as soon as first shoots appear.

Transplanting: Plant into the garden three weeks before the last spring frost. Water and cover with a plastic-covered cage.

Seeds Outdoors: Plant presoaked seeds ½ inch deep in each square three weeks before your last spring frost. Seeds sprout outdoors in two to three weeks. Water and cover with a plastic-covered cage.

Growing

Watering: Weekly, one to two cups per plant; twice weekly in hot weather. Like all leaf crops, Swiss chard needs lots of water for luxurious leaf growth.

Fertilizing: Light feeder; may benefit from applications of high-nitrogen fertilizer.

Maintenance: Weed weekly; cut off any yellow or overgrown outer leaves.

Harvesting

How: Carefully cut off each outer stem at the plant base with a sharp knife when the leaves are 6 to 9 inches tall. The smaller inner leaves will continue to grow.

When: Start harvesting when outer leaves are about 6 to 9 inches tall (approximately eight weeks after planting seeds), and continue harvesting outer leaves (stalk and all) every week or so. Don't let outer leaves get too large before harvesting.

Preparing and Using

Both leaf and stem are edible. The stalks can be cooked and served like asparagus; the leaves are used fresh or cooked, and are similar to but milder in taste than spinach. After harvest, rinse off and pat dry like lettuce or spinach, refrigerate if not using immediately. Leaves are very rich in vitamins A and C, calcium, and iron. Cut out central stalk and use the leaves as fresh greens for salads, or boil or steam as you would spinach. Add freshly chopped greens to any appropriate soup for a garden-fresh taste. Chop central stem or stalk into convenient-size pieces and boil or steam like asparagus or cooked celery. Serve with melted butter, bread crumbs, or grated cheese. Marinate leftover stalks overnight for next day's salad or appetizer on a toothpick.

Winter Growing

Swiss chard will withstand several frosts even when unprotected, for a fall harvest. If mulched with loose hay it can be harvested right into the winter in most climates. With a complete mulch cover it will also winter over and resprout the second year for a very early spring harvest. Gradually remove the mulch in early spring and be rewarded with the first fresh greens from your garden. Plants will only produce crop in early spring the second year; later they will go to seed, so start new plants every year.

Problems

Slugs and snails, cutworms, leaf miners; occasionally rabbits, woodchucks, and deer. Free of most diseases.

Questions and Answers

Q. My Swiss chard leaves are nice and big, but don't taste tender.
A. You're either not watering regularly enough or you're letting the stalks get too big before cutting. Harvest the outer leaves before they get more than 9 inches tall.

Q. My plants don't grow very fast despite constant waterings.

A. You probably need to add more nitrogen to your soil for better leaf growth.

Q. I read that you should break off chard stalks rather than cutting each stalk with a knife. Is that true?

A. You can give each outer stalk a sideways pull, but it's very easy to pull the entire plant out of the ground that way. You must use one hand to hold the base of the plant. Therefore, I always advise cutting each stalk at the base with a sharp knife, being careful not to cut through to the next stalk.

Q. One of my neighbors told me the correct way to harvest Swiss chard is to cut the entire plant off about 2 inches above the crown, rather than cutting individual leaves.

A. Many gardeners use this method. The advantage is that you get a few of the more tender, smaller leaves from the center along with all of the larger stalks. But in volume the amount is such a small percentage of the total harvest that it hardly seems worthwhile. The plant will sprout new center leaves if you don't cut it off too low (always a danger if you're not sure where to cut). But the plant looks rather unsightly when it's cut straight off. So for all those reasons I usually advise cutting just the outer leaves and leaving the smaller center stalks, which will then grow into the next harvest much sooner than if you cut off the entire plant.

Q. Is the entire leaf edible? Someone told me the fleshy stalk was poisonous.

A. Both the stalk and leaf are very edible and delicious. Your friend was probably thinking of rhubarb where only the stalk is edible. The rhubarb leaf is slightly poisonous if eaten. That's one reason you see only the stalks bound up for sale in the grocery store.

Corn

At A Glance

Botanical Information:

Grass family
5 to 6' tall
Annual, frost tender

Spacing: 1 plant per square

Growing Season:

Spring: no
Summer: yes
Fall: no
Winter: no

Seed to Harvest: 9–13 weeks

Seeds Store: 1–2 years

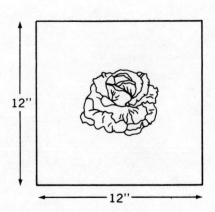

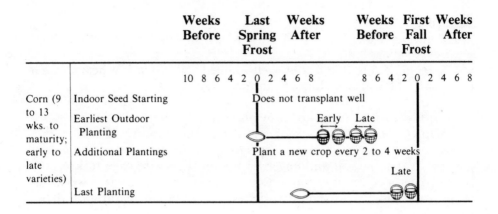

		Weeks Before	Last Spring Frost	Weeks After		Weeks Before	First Fall Frost	Weeks After
		10 8 6 4 2	0	2 4 6 8		8 6 4 2	0	2 4 6 8
Corn (9 to 13 wks. to maturity; early to late varieties)	Indoor Seed Starting			Does not transplant well				
	Earliest Outdoor Planting			Early Late				
	Additional Plantings			Plant a new crop every 2 to 4 weeks				
							Late	
	Last Planting							

Description

The square foot method is an easy way to grow corn. Always a favorite crop, corn takes a lot of room, is difficult to protect from pests, and the yield is very low (one or two ears per plant) compared to other vegetables. Despite all of that, many gardeners love to grow it. The taste of store-bought corn cannot compare with the flavor of corn freshly picked from your garden. Corn requires a very long season of hot weather, so only one crop can occupy the same garden space during the main season.

Corn comes in many varieties and colors, divided generally into early, midseason, and late-season crops. The early varieties are very popular, but are not considered as good tasting as the later ones. There are also new varieties called "extra sweet." These are exceptionally good, and they hold their sweetness longer after being picked. But most of these new varieties must be grown separately from all others so as not to cross-pollinate and lose their special sweetness. Golden yellow is the most familiar color, but white and bicolor corn are considered the sweetest and best tasting of all. The early varieties grow the shortest, approximately 4 to 5 feet tall, and they can be spaced fairly close together, about 8 inches apart. The plants average just one fairly small ear per plant. Midseason varieties grow taller, 5 to 7 feet, and the late- or main-season crop gets to be 7 or 8 feet tall, and should be spaced about 12 inches apart. They produce about two large ears per plant when grown properly. The difference in time to maturity varies from 6 to 7 weeks for the early varieties up to 8 to 10 weeks for the midseason varieties and 12 to 13 weeks for the late crop.

Starting
Location: Full sun; locate corn where it won't shade other crops because it gets so tall.

Soil: pH 5.5 to 7.0; fertile, well-drained soil. Corn is a heavy feeder so prepare the soil with lots of humus.

Seeds Indoors: No.

Transplanting: Does not transplant well.

Seeds Outdoors: Sprout in five to ten days outdoors. Plant each pre-soaked seed 1 to 2 inches deep, depending on the weather, at the proper spacing. Water the soil and cover with a chicken-wire cage to keep out birds. To get a continuous harvest, plant a new crop every two weeks, or plant at the same time several varieties with different maturation dates.

Growing
Watering: Weekly, one cup per plant; twice weekly in very hot weather.

Fertilizing: Heavy feeder; benefits from monthly applications of basic fertilizer mix.

Maintenance: Weed weekly; remove chicken-wire cage when corn is 6 inches tall. Place raccoon-proof fence around your blocks when the ears are starting to form.

Harvesting
How: Use two hands to harvest—one to hold the stalk and the other to pull down and break off the ear—otherwise you may break the stalk. If there are no other ears left on that stalk it's best to cut it down to the ground. Don't pull it out or you may disturb the roots of the remaining stalks.

When: Check the ears daily when the silk first browns and the ears feel full and slightly bumpy. The final test of each ear before harvesting is to peel away a small strip of the husk to expose the kernels. They should be plump and full. To see if the ear is ready, puncture a kernel with your thumbnail. If milky juice squirts out, it's ready; if juice is clear, corn is not quite ready to pick.

Preparing and Using
Corn loses its sweet taste very quickly after being picked, so try to cook and eat it as soon as possible. If you can't use it immediately, husk it and refrigerate it. Up to 50 percent of the flavor is lost in the first 12 hours of storage, more if it's not refrigerated. If you harvest more than you eat, either freeze the leftovers after cutting the kernels off the cob, add them to a relish dish, or serve warm with butter and parsley. Of course, corn is excellent added to any kind of soup or stew.

Problems

Probably more than any other garden crop, including corn borer, ear worm, birds, raccoons, and squirrels. Relatively few diseases that bother the home gardener.

Questions and Answers

Q. The leaves of my corn stalks curl in very hot weather, yet I water regularly.

A. It's a normal occurrence and nothing is wrong, as long as they uncurl after the sun goes down.

Q. My neighbor said I should cut out the side suckers growing on each plant.

A. Don't. Repeated tests have shown they actually help production rather than sapping the strength as was once thought.

Q. My father said your planting space is too close and you won't get as many ears per plant as with his spacing of 12 inches in a row with 3-foot spacing between rows.

A. He's right on one account—the individual plant production is slightly less using my method. But you can fit so many more plants into the same space that the harvest per square foot is far greater than with the conventional single-row method, and that's what most gardeners are interested in.

Q. Can corn be started early indoors and transplanted?

A. Some gardeners have been successful doing this if the roots aren't disturbed when it's transplanted. However, corn likes it very warm for growing, and setting out young plants early in the season is not often worth the effort.

Q. I've had trouble with full pollination of our corn. We have a very windy garden site.

A. Corn is pollinated when pollen falls from the tassels down to the silk on each ear. Remember to plant in a block pattern so that no matter which way the wind is blowing some pollen will fall down to all of the tassels. If you have a constant wind in one direction it's then possible that the pollen is floating down and not getting into all of the silk on the upwind side. It would be advantageous for you to help the pollination along by going out on a calm day and shaking the plants so that the pollen is helped to fall straight down into the silk of each ear.

Cucumbers

At A Glance

Botanical Information:

Gourd family
Vine
Annual, frost tender

Spacing: 2 plants per square

Growing Season:

Spring: no
Summer: yes
Fall: no
Winter: no

Seed to Harvest: 9 weeks

Seeds Store: 5–6 years

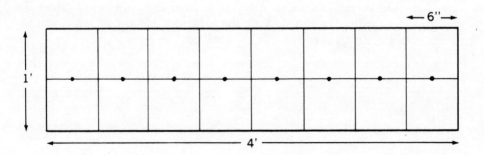

		Weeks Before	Last Spring Frost	Weeks After		Weeks Before	First Fall Frost	Weeks After
		10 8 6 4 2 0 2 4 6 8				8 6 4 2 0 2 4 6 8		
Cucumbers (9 wks. to maturity)	Indoor Seed Starting							
	Earliest Outdoor Planting							
		or						
	Additional Plantings							
	Last Planting	Not needed						

Note: Sometimes the plants stop producing or die from wilt disease so an additional planting is advisable.

Description

A popular, easy-to-grow warm-weather vegetable; should be grown on vertical frames for maximum space efficiency using the trench method of soil preparation.

Cucumbers vary in size from long and thin to short and fat. There are varieties for pickling, slicing, eating, and even long slender varieties called burpless. Slicing varieties grow larger and are more often used for salads; pickling varieties are picked much smaller, and although they can be eaten fresh they are usually grown for the pickle jar.

Starting

Location: Full sun, although the vines will tolerate some shade.

Soil: pH 5.5 to 7.0; does well in almost any soil. Try adding any kind of well-rotted manure to your trench for vigorous, rampant growth.

Seeds Indoors: Sprout in four to eight days at 70°F; will sprout even faster at 80°F. Plant one seed in individual paper cups filled with potting soil mix. Punch holes in bottom for drainage. Keep warm (70°F) until sprouted; move to full sunlight as soon as first shoots appear.

Transplanting: Plant cup and all in the ground at the proper plant spacing. If the cup is waxed cardboard or a heavy paper, tear away the bottom carefully. Avoid disturbing the roots. Water and cover with a shade cage. To facilitate watering make sure the entire trench is depressed about 2 inches.

Seeds Outdoors: Sprout in five to ten days; place presoaked seeds at proper spacing, water, and keep soil moist until seeds sprout.

Growing

Watering: Weekly, two cups per plant; twice weekly in hot weather. Never let the soil dry out. Avoid wetting the leaves, as this spreads any fungus disease that may be present. Cucumbers have the highest water content of any vegetable, so plenty of moisture is required for proper growth.

Fertilizing: Heavy feeder; benefits from monthly applications of basic fertilizer mix.

Maintenance: Weed weekly; keep vines on the trellis; watch out for beetles; mulch in hot weather.

Harvesting

How: Cut (don't pull) stem connecting the fruit to the vine.

When: Continually! Never allow any cucumbers to become yellow or overly large, or the plant will stop producing. Keep picking even if you have to toss some on the compost pile because you can't use them. Don't try the old practice of eating the large cukes and leaving the smaller ones on the vine, because in only one or two days the little ones will be big. Instead, compost the very large cucumbers and eat the smaller ones.

Preparing and Using

Wash and scrub with a vegetable brush. Serve long, slender burpless varieties with the skins left on. Peel the fatter varieties before slicing, cubing, or cutting into long sticks. Serve fresh, sliced on sandwiches with onions and mayonnaise, or marinate for relish. Many gardeners like cucumbers simply soaked in vinegar overnight and served with lots of pepper. They also go well in any salad or arranged around a spoonful of cottage cheese.

Problems

Cucumber beetles; mildew, wilt, and mosaic.

Questions and Answers

Q. My cucumber plant just started blooming and yet no cucumbers have formed.

A. Don't worry, they will. Usually the plant produces a rush of male flowers at first, then a mixture of both male and female. Remember the male and female blossoms are separate. You can identify the female flowers because they will open on the end of a miniature pickle that has formed before the blossom opens. The male flower is on the end of a long stem and has no pickle shape before it. Some new varieties of cucumbers have been developed to have all female flowers and therefore produce a larger harvest. But they do need a male-flowering plant nearby for pollination.

Q. Is there any way to cook cucumbers?
A. One way is to treat thick slices of a large cucumber like eggplant and fry them after dipping them in beaten egg and bread crumbs.

Q. Why are my cucumbers bitter?
A. You are probably picking them too large. As they get older and larger they lose their crisp, sweet taste and become more bitter. Constant moisture is also important for good flavor.

Q. My plants just seem to wilt overnight and die; what causes it and what can I do to prevent it?
A. They were probably infected with bacterial wilt disease, probably spread by the cucumber beetle. There is nothing you can do to cure them once they are infested. In the future keep a watch out for the beetles, and hand pick them. Second, if it's not too late in the season, plant another crop of cucumber seeds right away. Remember they grow to harvest size in just eight to nine weeks, especially when the seeds are started in the hot summer. In the future (and this is a good idea for most gardeners) plant two crops of cucumbers, one in late spring at the proper time just after the last spring frost, and another crop two months later. You might plant cucumber seeds in the space vacated by your vertically grown peas.

Q. The leaves of my plant wilt on very hot days; is this normal?
A. Yes, as long as they perk up at night and look okay the next morning. In the future add more humus to the soil for better moisture-holding capacity.

Q. My vines get too bulky for the vertical frames when I put two plants in a 12-inch square.
A. Some varieties produce larger and more vigorous vines than others, so you could space them a little farther apart. Or control the growth by cutting out side-shoots as they grow so just the main vine grows to the top of the frame. When it does reach the top, simply cut off the top of that vine and new side-shoots will develop all along it.

Eggplant

At A Glance

Botanical Information:

Nightshade family
24 to 30″ tall
Annual, frost tender

Spacing: 1 plant per square (will expand to encroach on surrounding plants)

Growing Season:

Spring: no
Summer: yes
Fall: no
Winter: no

Seed to Harvest: 19 weeks

Seeds Store: 5–6 years

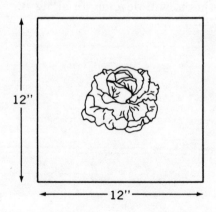

12"

12"

		Weeks Before	Last Spring Frost	Weeks After		Weeks Before	First Fall Frost	Weeks After
		10 8 6 4 2	0	2 4 6 8		8 6 4 2	0	2 4 6 8
Eggplant (19 wks. to maturity)	Indoor Seed Starting							
	Earliest Outdoor Planting							
	Additional Plantings		Not needed					
	Last Planting		Not needed					

Description

A very popular summer vegetable that is easy to grow and produces a large harvest. Since time to maturity is almost five months, seeds must be started indoors in spring or transplants bought at a local nursery. Eggplant has a distinctive taste and is used extensively in cooking.

Most varieties produce large, egg-shaped fruit that is a glossy, purple-black color, but there are other newer varieties that are white, yellow, or brown with fruit in small, round, or elongated shapes.

Starting

Location: Full sun and lots of heat; pick your sunniest spot for eggplant.

Soil: pH of 5.5 to 7.0; fertile, well-drained soil with lots of humus.

Seeds Indoors: Sprout in 12 days at 70°F, but only 6 days at 85°F; won't sprout below 65°F. Sprinkle five to ten seeds ¼ inch deep in a cup filled with vermiculite 7 weeks before your last spring frost. Keep warm (70°F) until sprouted; move to full sunlight as soon as first shoots appear; then pot up in seedling trays as soon as plants are large enough (usually one to three weeks). Keep a careful watch over the plants, especially after transplanting them into seedling trays, because any check or stoppage of the growth will affect the ultimate bearing capacity of the plant.

Transplanting: Plant into the garden two weeks after the last spring frost. Disturb the roots as little as possible, water, and cover with a shade cage. Since eggplant is so vulnerable to cold weather, if it is at all chilly at that time of the year you should cover the wire cage with a clear plastic cover as well as a sun shade to provide a greenhouse atmosphere. In a few days the sun shade can be removed.

Growing

Watering: Weekly, two cups per plant; twice weekly in hot summer weather. Eggplant needs constant moisture, especially when fruits are forming and enlarging.

Fertilizing: Heavy feeder; benefits from monthly applications of basic fertilizer mix.

Maintenance: Weed weekly; add a thick mulch when hot weather sets in. Provide a wide mesh, open-wire cage support when half grown so the plant can grow right through it, and will be supported when full grown without staking.

Harvesting

How: Always cut the fruit from the bush with clippers; watch out for sharp spines on the stem and fruit.

When: Edible at almost any time after fruit turns dark and glossy (about 6 inches) so don't let them get too large. If they turn a dull color they are overripe and the seeds will become large and hard.

Preparing and Using

Peel and slice or dice, then stew, fry, stir-fry, or bake; add to casseroles, or bread and fry by itself. Mixes especially well with tomatoes and onions. If you're not going to use the eggplant right away, don't refrigerate it, but store it on the kitchen counter and enjoy its good looks. Handle carefully or fruit will bruise.

Problems

Cutworms, flea beetles; Verticillium wilt.

Questions and Answers

Q. I've read where you should pinch out the growing tip and remove all flowers after four or five fruits are set, then pinch out all further side-shoots. Does this help?

A. It will probably help you more than the plant if you're trying to lose weight with all that bending over. In all fairness, this will control the plant and allow it to put all its energy into producing four good fruits. But personally I think it's too much work. The pinching out of the center shoot does encourage the plant to branch out laterally and form a shorter, bushier plant that doesn't require as much staking. But this advantage is negligible in the square foot garden because plants are fully supported by wire cages.

Q. Are there any plants that shouldn't grow in the same soil as eggplant in future years?

A. Yes, any of the other plants in the nightshade family, including tomatoes, potatoes, and peppers, as well as eggplant again. When you do that you take a chance of spreading Verticillium wilt disease in the same soil. So rotate your plants every year.

Lettuce

At A Glance

Botanical Information:

Composite family
6 to 12″ tall
Annual, frost hardy

Spacing: 4 plants per square

Growing Season:

Spring: yes
Summer: possibly, with protection
Fall: yes
Winter: some varieties, with protection

Seed to Harvest: 7 weeks

Seeds Store: 5–6 years

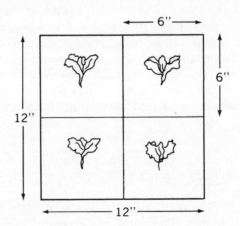

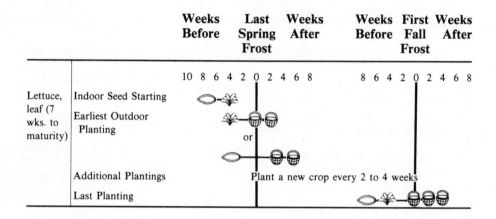

		Weeks Before	Last Spring Frost	Weeks After		Weeks Before	First Fall Frost	Weeks After
		10 8 6 4 2	0	2 4 6 8		8 6 4 2	0	2 4 6 8
Lettuce, leaf (7 wks. to maturity)	Indoor Seed Starting							
	Earliest Outdoor Planting			or				
	Additional Plantings		Plant a new crop every 2 to 4 weeks					
	Last Planting							

Description

Probably the most suitable, easy to grow, and satisfying crop for the home gardener. It is fast growing and very productive for the space used, and is probably the prettiest vegetable in the garden. Grows best in the cooler spring and fall weather, yet is cold tolerant and withstands enough heat to be "almost" grown year-round.

There are basically four types of lettuce: the solid head usually found in supermarkets; the loose head or bibb, which is a smaller and faster-growing head type; leaf lettuce, which is composed of many leaves (and is by far the best choice for home gardens); and romaine or cos, which is a loose, upright head with a much sharper and coarser texture than the leaf and bibb varieties. I do not recommend the solid head types for home gardens. They take too long to grow, don't head up well in hot weather, and most are not as good tasting as the leaf and bibb varieties. There are so many excellent varieties of bibb and leaf lettuce, and they grow so fast, that every garden should have at least four different varieties growing at all times. All do best as a spring and fall crop. With protection they can be grown in summer and even winter in many parts of the country. Choose special varieties that are advertised for their adaptability to either summer or winter growing.

Starting

Location: Full sun to partial shade; shade is welcomed in the hot summer. As with all leafy vegetables, the stronger the light, the higher the vitamin C content will be.

Soil: pH 6.0 to 7.5; loose, light, friable with extra humus and nitrogen in the upper 4 inches. The plant has a skimpy, shallow root system that doesn't spread far. Needs constant soil moisture and nutrients close to home.

Seeds Indoors: Sprout in two to three days at 70°F. Start five to ten seeds of several different varieties in cups filled with vermiculite seven weeks before your last spring frost date. Keep warm (70°F) until sprouted; move to full sunlight as soon as first shoots appear; then pot up in seedling trays as soon as plants are large enough (usually one to three weeks).

Transplanting: Move plants into the garden anytime until they are half grown. Plant a new square or two of lettuce every other week until early summer. The hot weather, long days, warm nights, and dry soil of summer cause lettuce to bolt to seed. Plant special varieties sold as heat or bolt resistant. After summer is over you can start planting the same varieties you did in the spring.

Seeds Outdoors: Sprout in five to ten days. Seeds sprout quickly outdoors and grow fairly rapidly. However, this method is time-saving but space-consuming. If space is your concern, start all seeds indoors or off to the side of the garden and move plants into the garden when half grown. However, transplants seem to bolt to seed more easily than direct-seeded plants, so plant the summer crop directly in the garden. Plant one or two seeds in each space; water daily until they sprout.

Growing

Watering: Weekly, one cup per plant; twice weekly in hot weather. Try not to wet the leaves; you may spread fungus disease. Don't water at night; morning is the best. Noon or even late afternoon is better than the evening.

Fertilizing: Heavy feeder; benefits from monthly applications of high-nitrogen fertilizer.

Maintenance: Weed weekly; don't let any weeds grow. Lettuce has such a shallow root system it can't compete with weeds. Provide shade covers for plants in summer.

Harvesting

How: Cut individual outer leaves or the entire plant. If you're going to cut outer leaves you can start when the plant is half grown. This makes a surprisingly large harvest combined with a few leaves of beet, spinach, and Swiss chard. When you take just one leaf from each plant you can still harvest a lot and hardly notice that you've been in the garden.

When: Leaf varieties, seven weeks; bibb varieties, nine weeks, or you can harvest outer leaves from either one when the plant is half grown. You can also cut the entire plant at any time; it doesn't have to grow to full size to be edible. If you wait until all your plants reach full size you will have to harvest almost all of them at once or they will go to seed.

Preparing and Using

Rinse under cool water, spin or pat dry, and store in refrigerator in plastic bag until ready to use. Lettuce will stay fresh and crisp for several days, although it's even better to harvest almost daily for maximum nutritional value. Lettuce contains vitamins A and B, also calcium and iron (especially the dark green outer leaves).

Problems

Slugs, cutworms, sow bugs, wire worms, rabbits, deer, woodchucks. Not many diseases to be concerned about unless the lettuce is quite wet at ground level.

Questions and Answers

Q. My lettuce always tastes bitter; why?
A. Probably because you didn't give it enough water while growing.
Q. My lettuce leaves are turning yellow.
A. The soil probably needs more nitrogen.
Q. The bottom leaves of my plants are all gray and molded and rotten.
A. You probably transplanted them a little too deep, causing the bottom leaves to be in contact with the soil. Plant at the same depth as the plant grew in its original container.

Muskmelons

At A Glance

Botanical Information:

Gourd family
Vine
Annual, frost tender

Spacing: 1 plant per square

Growing Season:

Spring: no
Summer: yes
Fall: no
Winter: no

Seed to Harvest: 12 weeks

Seeds Store: 5–6 years

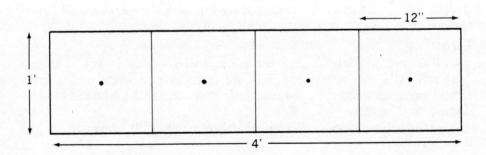

		Weeks Before	Last Spring Frost	Weeks After		Weeks Before	First Fall Frost	Weeks After
		10 8 6 4 2	0	2 4 6 8		8 6 4 2	0	2 4 6 8
Musk-melons (12 wks. to maturity)	Indoor Seed Starting							
	Earliest Outdoor Planting							
			or					
	Additional Plantings		Not needed					
	Last Planting		Not needed					

Description

These heat-loving plants take a fairly long time to grow (three months of hot, dry weather), don't produce a great deal for the space they occupy, and take up a lot of space. But melons are oh, so rewarding when the harvest finally comes in that it all seems worthwhile. They should be grown vertically on frames to save space and mature earlier.

Starting

Location: Full sun; grow on a vertical frame.

Soil: pH 6.0 to 7.5; loose, humus, soil not too high in nitrogen. Use the trench method; prepare soil two weeks ahead of planting time and cover with a clear plastic tunnel to warm up the soil.

Seeds Indoors: Sprout in five to ten days at 70°F; the hotter the better, even up to 90°F for sprouting. Plant seeds singly in individual paper cups. Plants do not transplant well so don't start them until two weeks before planting out.

Transplanting: Plant outdoors two weeks after the last frost date. Sink the entire cup in the ground after tearing off the bottom.

Seeds Outdoors: Will not sprout in soil below 65°F; takes five to ten days in 70°F soil. Plant one presoaked seed in each square, one week after the last frost date. Cover with a plastic-covered cage.

Growing

Watering: Weekly, 2 cups per plant; twice weekly in hot weather. Mulch heavily in hot weather. Cut water to ½ cup when melons are almost ripe to develop their sweetness. Keep the leaves dry to avoid fungus diseases and mildew.

Fertilizing: Heavy feeder; benefits from monthly applications of basic fertilizer mix.

Maintenance: Weed weekly; support the half-grown melons in slings; pinch out all new, small melons near the end of the growing season so that all the plant's strength goes into ripening the larger melons already set.

Harvesting

How: Twist the melon with one hand, while holding the stem with the other. If it resists parting the melon is not ripe.

When: Whenever it has a strong melon odor, and the netting pattern on the rind (if a cantaloupe) becomes very prominent on the melon. Stem will slip easily off when the melon is rotated. If each melon is held in a sling it won't roll around and accidentally part by itself when ripe.

Preparing and Using

Some people like it warm, some chilled. Just cut melon in half and scoop out the seeds and cut into wedges, or serve an entire half filled with ice cream, blueberries, or custard. Can also be scooped out as balls or cut into cubes and mixed with or added to a fresh fruit salad. Excellent for breakfast or served as a dinner dessert.

Problems

Cutworms; mildew and wilt disease.

Questions and Answers

Q. My melons are poorly flavored.

A. Either your weather was too cool or too humid, or you didn't provide constant soil moisture. Also be sure melons are fully ripe before picking.

Q. Is black plastic mulch okay to use for melons?

A. Yes, it has proved successful for many growers. However, by growing your melons vertically, you eliminate the need to prepare a large area of soil and lay down a lot of sheets of plastic. You can mulch your trench with black plastic, hay, or any good mulching material. This will provide a more uniform soil moisture content which is good for the melons.

Q. I've been told that since the melon and cucumber are in the same family, they will cross-pollinate and the melons will have a cucumber taste.

A. No, they will not cross-pollinate, and if they did it would affect the seeds only and not the taste of this year's crop.

Q. I read where excessive rain at maturity will cause poor flavor, yet you advise constant soil moisture.

A. Anything used to excess has a bad effect. Watering should be sufficient to keep the soil moist, not soggy. In addition, you'll notice that cultural directions for melons do indicate a lessening of water when the melons are starting to ripen. Here's where a lot of humus added to the soil plays an important part, because it can hold moisture without causing the soil to be soggy. If you have a lot of rain near harvest time, try covering the trench with plastic so most of the rainwater runs off.

Onions

At A Glance

Botanical Information:

Lily family
12″ tall
Biennial, frost hardy

Spacing: 16 plants per square

Growing Season:

Spring: yes
Summer: yes
Fall: no
Winter: no

Seed to Harvest: 20 weeks

Seeds Store: 1–2 years

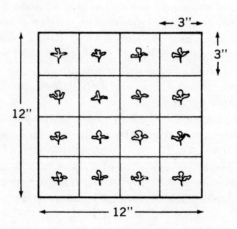

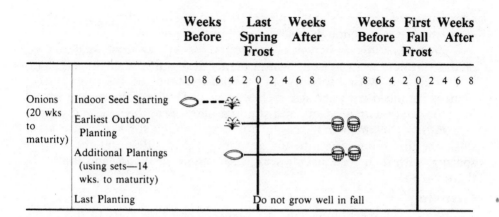

		Weeks Before	Last Spring Frost	Weeks After		Weeks Before	First Fall Frost	Weeks After
		10 8 6 4 2	0	2 4 6 8		8 6 4 2	0	2 4 6 8
Onions (20 wks to maturity)	Indoor Seed Starting							
	Earliest Outdoor Planting							
	Additional Plantings (using sets—14 wks. to maturity)							
	Last Planting			Do not grow well in fall				

Description

A fun-to-grow vegetable, easy and undemanding, although a little unsightly near the end of the season as the tops all fall over and turn brown. But that's a sign that the onions are maturing and will be ready for harvest soon.

There are innumerable varieties of onions: yellow, white, or red; big fat ones, little golf-ball-size ones; some specially for storing, others for immediate use; scallions, and green bunching onions.

To add to the confusion, onions can be planted from either seeds, plants, or sets. Since onions take 20 weeks to mature, growers start the seeds for you and sell them as 2-month-old plants or sets (which were started from seeds the previous year and partially grown). Since the onion plant matures near the middle of summer (the summer solstice in June starts the process), the size each bulb can attain depends on the length of the growing season before that date. If your growing season is short, don't fool around with seeds; buy and plant sets. If you have a very long growing season you might want to try seeds.

Starting

Location: Onions like a sunny spot, but will tolerate some shade.

Soil: pH 6.0 to 7.5; well-drained soil with lots of decomposed manure mixed in for large growth. Firm soil before planting by pressing down on the soil with the top of a rake or back of a shovel after you're finished turning it over.

Seeds Indoors: Sprout in 5 days at 70°F. Sprinkle about 20 seeds of each variety desired into cups filled with vermiculite 8 to 12 weeks before your last spring frost. Keep warm (70°F) until sprouted; move to full sunlight as soon as first shoots appear; then pot up in seedling trays as soon as plants are large enough (usually one to three weeks).

Transplanting: Four weeks before the last spring frost, shake most of the vermiculite from your young plants and gather them together in small bunches. With a scissors cut off both the tops and the roots so the plant is balanced with about 2 inches of each. Drill a hole at each space in your square with a pencil, and slip in a plant, firm the soil, and water.

Planting Outdoors: If season not long enough for seeds, use sets. Push the tiny onion sets into the ground, pointed side up at the proper spacing, with their tops just showing above the soil. Water, and that's all there is to it.

Growing

Watering: Weekly, ¼ cup per plant. When tops start to fall over, withhold water.

Fertilizing: Light feeder; may benefit from applications of basic fertilizer mix.

Maintenance: Weed weekly; when bulbs start expanding use your finger to remove some of the soil around each bulb and partially uncover it. This makes it easier for the bulb to expand. It will not hurt if you can actually see the top of every bulb.

Harvesting

How: Pull the onions out of the ground and place on chicken wire or a window screen laid out in the sun for several days. The tops, roots, and outer skin of each onion will then dry thoroughly. Brush them off and clean off any loose skins, dried tops, or roots by rubbing them between your palms. Then store for later use. Any onions with green or thick tops should not be stored but used immediately.

When: About in the middle of the summer you'll see your onion tops turning brown and falling over. When the majority have fallen, bend over the remaining ones with your hand. In a short while, the tops will dry up while the bulbs attain their maximum size.

Preparing and Using

You'll find homegrown onions much milder and sweeter than store-bought ones. This makes them more useful, especially for those folks who must be careful of eating too many onions. For a real treat try an onion sandwich—thin slices of onion with mayonnaise and lots of pepper on your favorite bread. Or add fresh, crisp cucumber slices to the sandwich for a delightful combination. Hang dried onions in a mesh bag in a cool, dry area for storage all winter.

Problems

Onion fly maggot. Resistant to most diseases.

Questions and Answers

Q. What is a green onion?

A. That refers to a regular onion planted as a seed or set, but pulled when it is very young. It looks similar to a scallion in that the bulb has not yet formed, and the neck is white while the top is green. It's eaten just like a scallion.

Q. What are boiling onions?

A. Same as green onions, but grown a little longer and then harvested when the bulb has enlarged a little bit, but while the top is still green. In other words, a half-size onion. As you can see, onions can be eaten at any size and at any stage; the confusing part is that they have different names for different sizes.

Q. My onion tops never got brown and we didn't get any bulbs.

A. Your soil probably contained too much nitrogen; it kept the tops growing, but didn't allow the energy to go into the enlargement of the bulbs.

Q. Is garlic an onion or an herb?

A. It's a member of the same family as onions, the lily family, which also contains chives, shallots, and leeks. All are grown the same as onions except chives are grown for their leaves, leeks for their enlarged stems, and garlic and shallots for the bulbs.

Q. Can you raise your own onion sets?

A. Yes, very easily if you start the year before you want to plant them. Sprinkle 20 to 40 seeds in a square, or half that amount in half a square if you don't need that many, along about July or August. Water and weed but don't thin. In two months rake the tops over and let the small bulbs form. After the tops are brown and dry, pull the plants, dry them in the sun for a few days, and store the sets for next spring's planting. This is a very good way to get sets of special varieties that are sold only as seeds.

Parsley

At A Glance

Botanical Information:

Umbellifer family
6 to 12″ tall
Biennial, frost hardy

Spacing: 4 plants per square

Growing Season:

Spring: yes
Summer: yes
Fall: yes
Winter: yes

Seed to Harvest: 14 weeks

Seeds Store: 2–3 years

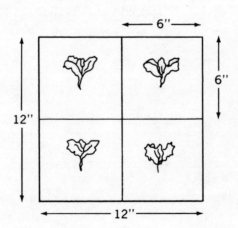

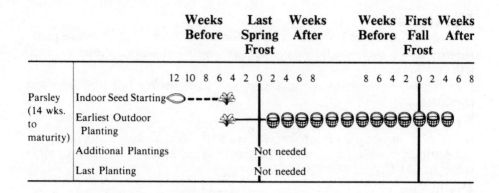

		Weeks Before	Last Spring Frost	Weeks After		Weeks Before	First Fall Frost	Weeks After
		12 10 8 6 4 2	0	2 4 6 8		8 6 4 2	0	2 4 6 8
Parsley (14 wks. to maturity)	Indoor Seed Starting							
	Earliest Outdoor Planting							
	Additional Plantings		Not needed					
	Last Planting		Not needed					

Description

An excellent herb that's nondemanding, good looking, high yielding, and very nutritional. Pest and disease free, it's almost a perfect addition to every garden. There are several varieties of parsley, basically curly-leaved and flat-leaved. Curly-leaved plants are more attractive, but the flat-leaved type is said to taste better.

Starting

Location: Full sun to partial shade.

Soil: pH 5.5 to 7.0; will do well in almost any type of soil.

Seeds Indoors: Sprout in 10 to 15 days at 70°F. Seeds are *very* slow to germinate, should be soaked in lukewarm water for 24 hours before planting. Sprinkle ten presoaked seeds in a cup filled with vermiculite 12 weeks before last spring frost. Keep warm (70°F) until sprouted; move to full sunlight as soon as first shoots appear; then pot up in seedling trays as soon as plants are large enough (usually one to three weeks).

Transplanting: Move outdoors five weeks before the last spring frost or anytime plants are large enough; plant them at the same depth they grew in the pot.

Seeds Outdoors: Better to start indoors, because seeds are slow and difficult to germinate.

Growing

Watering: Weekly, one cup per plant. Never let parsley dry out completely for it becomes tough and bitter and may bolt to seed in the first year.

Fertilizing: Heavy feeder; benefits from monthly applications of high-nitrogen fertilizer.

Maintenance: Weed weekly. Mulch heavily for continual harvest in winter, and for early-spring growing the following year.

Harvesting

How: Cut outer leaves as needed; for large harvest cut off entire plant slightly above tiny middle shoots. Either way plant will continue to grow with no harm.

When: As soon as the plant gets 3 to 4 inches tall and anytime thereafter.

Preparing and Using

Good in soups, casseroles, stews, with fish or any kind of meat; excellent over boiled vegetables, particularly potatoes. Very high in vitamins A and C.

Problems

Relatively free from pests and diseases.

Questions and Answers

Q. Is it true that pouring boiling water over parsley seed helps it to germinate?

A. This is supposed to help if the hot water is poured over the outdoor seed furrow after the seed has been planted, rather than soaking the seeds in boiling water. I've never tried it because outdoor seed starting in early spring takes four to five weeks. I'd rather start seeds indoors at 70°F temperature where they sprout in two weeks.

Q. Can parsley be dried?

A. Yes, it is very easy to dry, although it does lose some of its flavor and vitamins. Since it's so easy to winter over in the garden or pot up for the house, though, you can have fresh parsley year-round.

Peas

At A Glance

Botanical Information:

Pulse family
Vine
Annual, frost hardy

Spacing: 8 plants per square

Growing Season:

Spring: yes
Summer: no
Fall: yes
Winter: no

Seed to Harvest: 10 weeks

Seeds Store: 3–4 years

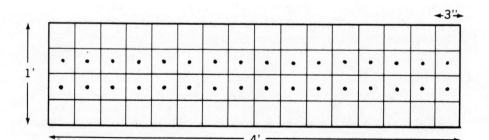

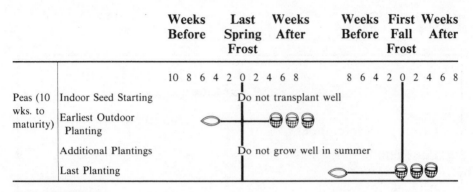

		Weeks Before	Last Spring Frost	Weeks After		Weeks Before	First Fall Frost	Weeks After
		10 8 6 4 2	0	2 4 6 8		8 6 4 2	0	2 4 6 8
Peas (10 wks. to maturity)	Indoor Seed Starting		Do not transplant well					
	Earliest Outdoor Planting							
	Additional Plantings		Do not grow well in summer					
	Last Planting							

Description

Almost everyone loves the delightful taste of fresh-picked peas. But until recently it was difficult to grow enough for more than a few meals. Peas take a lot of space, time, and effort to harvest and shell. Somehow when all the peas are shelled it never seems like much of a harvest. But all that's been changed with the introduction of sugar snap peas. The 6-foot-tall vines are very productive, and what really makes this variety so worthwhile is that you eat the entire pod. This makes the harvest about ten times that of regular peas. In addition, sugar snaps are absolutely delicious—sweet, crisp, and juicy. They are edible either raw or cooked. I consider them a must in my garden, and I highly recommend them as the only pea to bother growing. We used to grow edible-podded peas, but they must be picked when the peas are just starting to form inside the pods. This means you have to pick quite a few to make a meal. But with the sugar snap peas you can let the peas grow to their full size, and each pod becomes quite large.

Starting

Location: Full sun in spring; shaded toward summer if possible.

Soil: pH 5.5 to 7.0; rich, humusy, well-drained soil (peas don't like wet feet). Use the trench method and grow on a vertical frame.

Seeds Indoors: No.

Transplanting: Do not transplant well.

Seeds Outdoors: Sprout in 10 to 15 days outdoors. Mix presoaked seeds with legume inoculant powder, then plant 1 inch deep about 5 weeks before the last spring frost. Water and cover with a plastic-covered tunnel.

Growing

Watering: Weekly in cool weather, with 10 to 12 cups per 4-foot-long trench; twice weekly in warm weather. Never let the peas dry out.

Fertilizing: May benefit from monthly applications of basic fertilizer mix.

Maintenance: Weed weekly; keep water off the vines. Keep the vines trained up vertical frame; mulch as weather gets warm.

Harvesting

How: Carefully (with two hands) pick or cut pods off their stems.

When: The beauty of these peas is that you can eat them at any stage of growth. They're just as tasty (raw or cooked) whether their pods are fully mature and bulging with peas, or still thin and barely starting to show the peas inside. A must for every gardener is to munch on a few every time you're in the garden. What a treat!

Preparing and Using

Just wash and they are ready to eat or cook. Try to use them as fresh as possible; store in refrigerator what you can't use right away. Sugar snaps are rich in vitamins A, B_1, and C, with phosphorus and iron. As the pods get nearly full size they do develop a string along each edge, but it's easy to remove. Just snap off the stem end and pull down, and both strings will easily peel off. The pod is still very crisp and tasty even when full size.

If the pods do start to lose their nice pea-green color and turn brown on the vine, they are overripe. Pick them immediately and add them to the compost pile, because if you allow them to grow they will cause the vine to stop producing new peas.

The versatility of these stretches the imagination. Try them raw in salads, with a dip, plain or mixed with other fresh vegetables in vinegar or sour cream dressing, or cook them by boiling, steaming, or stir-frying.

Problems

No pests to speak of, but sometimes prone to powdery mildew, especially during warm weather when the leaves get wet.

Questions and Answers

Q. How does the fall crop of sugar snap peas compare with the spring crop?
A. Unfortunately, it's not as good. The seeds must be started in the hot, dry period of midsummer, and produce most of their growth during the dog days of August and early September. After that the weather gets better and the peas grow better, but they often suffer during that initial period. Try to find a partially shaded location that is protected from the hot summer sun but that gets full sun as fall approaches (the sun is lower in the sky). Remember also to water regularly in hot weather.

Q. I've read where an inexpensive pea support can be made from old dead branches stuck in the ground.
A. I never cared for that practice; it looks terrible and when the vines do cover the branches it's tough to harvest the peas. Stick with the 6-foot-high vertical frame described in this book.

Peppers

At A Glance

Botanical Information:

Nightshade family
12 to 24″ tall
Annual, frost tender

Spacing: 1 plant per square

Growing Season:

Spring: no
Summer: yes
Fall: no
Winter: no

Seed to Harvest: 19 weeks

Seeds Store: 4–5 years

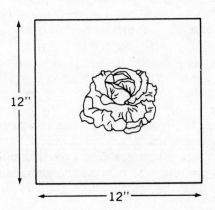

12″

12″

		Weeks Before	Last Spring Frost	Weeks After		Weeks Before	First Fall Frost	Weeks After
		10 8 6 4 2	0	2 4 6 8		8 6 4 2	0	2 4 6 8
Peppers (19 wks. to maturity)	Indoor Seed Starting							
	Earliest Outdoor Planting							
	Additional Plantings		Not needed					
	Last Planting		Not needed					

Description

A very popular summer vegetable with most gardeners. Peppers are good producers for the space they occupy, virtually pest and disease free, and fairly easy to grow. Start your own seeds or buy transplants at a local nursery. They are attractive plants in the garden, and many people grow several varieties just for their decorative touch. If you've always grown green bell peppers, try the sweet yellow banana varieties in addition. They not only taste good but they are also good looking.

Peppers come in a range of colors, from green to red, yellow, and orange. There are also a number of different shapes, from the large block or bell shape to the long, skinny, curved, hot chili peppers. Decide just what kind you want for cooking and then select that variety for your garden.

Starting

Location: Full sun.

Soil: pH 5.5 to 7.0; well-drained, fertile soil. Many gardeners report better luck with a more acid soil of 5.5 to 6.0.

Seeds Indoors: Sprout in 10 to 15 days at 70°F. Sprinkle five to ten seeds approximately 7 weeks before the last spring frost in a cup of vermiculite, cover with ¼ inch more vermiculite. Keep warm (70°F) until sprouted; move to full sunlight as soon as first shoots appear; then pot up in seedling trays as soon as plants are large enough (usually one to three weeks).

Transplanting: Peppers need warm soil so don't transplant until two weeks after the last spring frost.

Seeds Outdoors: Season is too short to start outdoors.

Growing

Watering: Weekly, one cup per plant when young, two or more cups per plant when larger. Don't wet the leaves; this causes fungus and wilt infections.

Fertilizing: Peppers are one crop that responds to a more continuous but weaker application of fertilizer. Try dilute manure tea at every watering instead of monthly fertilizer applications.

Maintenance: Weed weekly; mulch in hot weather; cover half-grown plants with an open-mesh wire cage to support plants without staking. Stems and branches of pepper plants are brittle and break easily, so work carefully among them when harvesting.

Harvesting

How: Carefully cut (don't pull or you'll accidentally break other branches) the fruit from the bush. Leave about 1 inch of stem on each pepper for a longer storage life.

When: At almost any stage of development. Basically, if you want green peppers pick them as soon as they are big enough for your use. You can leave them on the vine and they will turn red or yellow after they become full grown. They can still be eaten; in fact, many people prefer them as their taste is sweeter and not as spicy when they lose their green color. Of course the hot chili peppers should turn color before you use them.

Preparing and Using

Use raw or cooked. Peppers are excellent as a salad or casserole garnish. Cut them into strips, cubes, or thin slices like you would a tomato. This shape is very attractive as a garnish. Peppers stuffed with a meat, rice, or vegetable mixture and baked makes a great summer supper. Peppers are high in vitamins A and C.

Problems

Cutworms and flea beetles. No diseases to speak of except an occasional wilt or fungus problem.

Questions and Answers

Q. Our pepper plants seemed to stop fruiting last summer; why?

A. The blossoms will drop without setting fruit when the daytime temperature goes over 90°F for any period of time, or if the night temperatures remain over 75°F. Quite often you get a nice initial set of growth from your plants, then a period during the summer when no fruit will set. This is nothing to worry about. As soon as the really hot weather is over the plant will return to normal and you'll continue getting fruit in the early fall.

Radishes

At A Glance

Botanical Information:

Mustard family
6 to 12″ tall
Annual, frost hardy

Spacing: 16 plants per square

Growing Season:

Spring: yes
Summer: partially
Fall: yes
Winter: no

Seed to Harvest: 4 weeks

Seeds Store: 5–6 years

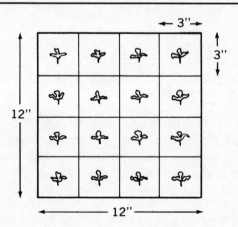

		Weeks Before	Last Spring Frost	Weeks After		Weeks Before	First Fall	Weeks After
		10 8 6 4 2	0	2 4 6 8		8 6 4 2	0	2 4 6 8
Radishes (4 wks. to maturity)	Indoor Seed Starting			Do not transplant well				
	Earliest Outdoor Planting							
	Additional Plantings			Plant a new crop every 1 to 2 weeks				
	Last Planting							

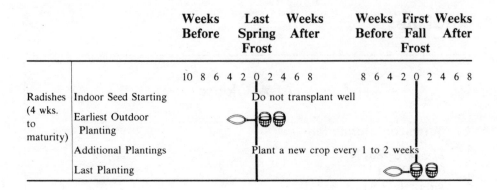

Description

Who can resist a vegetable that can be harvested three weeks after planting the seeds? The only trouble with radishes is that they are so easy to overplant. They don't do well when crowded so my exact spacing and single-seeding methods are perfectly suited to this vegetable. Decide how many radishes you would like to eat each week and then plant double that number (but no more) every other week for a continuous but controlled crop. Radishes are a great crop for all gardeners, beginners and experts alike. They mature quickly, are tasty and add zest to any dish.

Radishes come in a variety of shapes from small and round to long and tapered like a carrot. Colors vary from every shade of red to pink, white, and even black-skinned types. Spring radishes mature in three to four weeks and are usually red and white in color. The fall kinds (called winter radishes) take six to eight weeks to grow and are excellent for storage.

Starting

Location: Full sun to partial shade.

Soil: pH 5.5 to 7.0; a rich, loose soil with lots of compost added to the upper 6 inches is best, but radishes will grow in most any soil.

Transplanting: Do not transplant well.

Seeds Outdoors: Sprout in five to ten days outdoors depending on temperature. Plant five to ten seeds per person every other week for a staggered but continuous harvest. Plant ½ inch deep in spring, 1 inch deep in summer. If you really like radishes a lot, plant some every other week of the growing year, even through the hot weather. The plants will still do fairly well then if you give them some shade, lots of water, and a thick mulch. Winter or long-keeping varieties need two months to mature, so start them at least that long before the first fall frost.

Growing

Watering: Weekly, ¼ cup per plant; twice weekly in hot weather. Don't let radishes stop growing or dry out; lack of water causes hot-tasting and pithy radishes.

Fertilizing: No extra fertilizer needed except for long-growing fall varieties, which may benefit from applications of basic fertilizer mix.

Maintenance: Weed weekly; keep covered with screen-covered cage if root maggots are a problem; mulch in hot weather.

Harvesting

How: Pull up the entire plant; trim off the top. Refrigerate edible portion if not used immediately.

When: As soon as they are marble size up to ping pong ball size. The smaller you pull them, the sweeter they taste. The long fall varieties can be left in the ground until frost, then either mulched to keep the ground from freezing, or pulled and stored in damp peat moss or sand after the tops are removed.

Preparing and Using

Slice, dice, or cut into fancy shapes for eating out of hand or in salads, and for garnishes. If you have too many all at once, twist or cut off the tops and store in a plastic bag in the refrigerator. Radishes will keep for up to a week before getting soft.

Problems

None to speak of, except possibly root maggots.

Questions and Answers

Q. Can I keep the root maggot out of my radishes?
A. Yes, it's very simple. You merely cover each square with a screen-covered cage to prevent the adult fly from laying its eggs in the soil next to each plant.

Q. My radishes are all tops, no bottoms.
A. Probably the plants got too much nitrogen or not enough sunlight.

Spinach

At A Glance

Botanical Information:

Goosefoot family
6 to 12″ tall
Annual, very frost hardy

Spacing: 9 plants per square

Growing Season:

Spring: yes
Summer: no
Fall: yes
Winter: yes, with protection

Seed to Harvest: 7 weeks

Seeds Store: 5–6 years

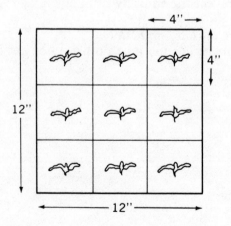

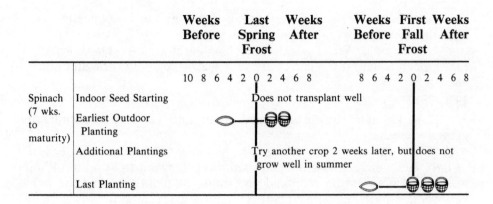

		Weeks Before	Last Spring Frost	Weeks After		Weeks Before	First Fall Frost	Weeks After
		10 8 6 4 2	0	2 4 6 8		8 6 4 2	0	2 4 6 8
Spinach (7 wks. to maturity)	Indoor Seed Starting		Does not transplant well					
	Earliest Outdoor Planting							
	Additional Plantings		Try another crop 2 weeks later, but does not grow well in summer					
	Last Planting							

Description

A very popular plant, but sometimes difficult to grow, spinach usually does well if the spring weather stays cool. It's fast growing, attractive, and fairly productive, as it can be grown in a small space. Spinach can't stand summer heat and bolts to seed very quickly, but a spring and another fall crop can be grown each year. Very cold hardy, spinach winters over in many areas, and can be grown all winter in the milder regions of the country.

There are basically two types of spinach—a smooth-leaved type and a crinkled-leaved kind that is sometimes called savoy. This crinkled type is much more attractive and more popular. Both are grown in cool weather and will not tolerate heat. Some varieties are more frost resistant than others, and are especially good for fall growing, keeping into the winter, and even winter growing.

Starting

Location: Any location is suitable, full sun to partial shade.

Soil: pH 6.0 to 7.5, a neutral 7.0 is ideal. Humusy soil, with lots of nitrogen.

Seeds Indoors: No.

Transplanting: Does not transplant well.

Seeds Outdoors: Sprout in one to two weeks outdoors. Plant seeds ½ inch deep, water, and cover with a plastic-covered cage. Plants can withstand any temperature between 25°F and 75°F, so judge your spring and fall planting accordingly.

Growing

Watering: Weekly, ½ cup per plant; twice weekly in warm weather.

Fertilizing: Heavy feeder; benefits from monthly applications of high-nitrogen fertilizer.

Maintenance: Weed weekly; mulch in warm weather. Don't work in the spinach square if the leaves are very wet—they are brittle and break easily.

Harvesting

How: Cut outer leaves as needed; small inner leaves will continue to grow rapidly.

When: As soon as the plants look like they won't miss an outer leaf or two. Keep picking and the plant will keep growing right up until hot weather. If it's a spring crop and you think the plants are going to bolt very soon, cut off the entire plant for a little extra harvest.

Preparing and Using

Wash carefully; soil tends to cling to the underside, especially of the crinkled leaves. Then spin or pat dry and store in refrigerator just like lettuce. Better yet, eat right away. Serve fresh in salads, cook slightly for a wilted spinach salad, or cook by steaming lightly. Spinach goes great with any meal, especially when garnished with a chopped, hard-boiled egg. It's high in vitamins A, B_1, and C, and is a valuable source of iron.

Problems

Leaf miners and aphids. No diseases to speak of.

Questions and Answers

Q. Can you grow spinach in the wintertime?

A. Yes, in a sun box or other protective enclosure. You can hold over spinach through most winters by just mulching it heavily with hay or chopped leaves. It won't grow, but it won't die either. Then in spring you'll have a head start for a first picking. To do that you must plant the crop in midfall, about a month before your last fall frost. These plants will go to seed much quicker than your spring-planted crop, but you'll get some very early spring harvest for all your effort.

Q. How can I keep out the leaf miners that make a mess of my spinach leaves?

A. They are a nuisance because they ruin every leaf that they get into. The miner is the larva of a tiny black fly that lays little white eggs underneath each leaf. The larvae hatch and tunnel into the leaf, crawling inside and in between the two leaf surfaces (that's how tiny they are). The damage shows up readily, though, as a white or brown spot on the leaf, and all those blotches and tunnels are very unsightly. It usually means cutting away most of the leaf or just throwing the whole thing away. The best way to prevent damage from leaf miners is to screen out the fly. Use a screen-covered cage to cover your spinach square when the plants are fairly small (get the smallest screen opening you can find).

Q. Why can't you grow spinach in summer?

A. It can't stand the heat and bolts to seed, causing a bitter taste in the leaves. But there is a substitute you can grow if you really like spinach that much. It's called New Zealand spinach. The name and the taste (after it's cooked) are all the two plants have in common. New Zealand spinach is not a spinach at all, and it's not even related to the spinach plant. It comes from the carpetweed family. It's a vining plant with small but thick, coarse leaves that grow all summer and love the heat. When the leaves are cooked they taste even better than spinach. When I used to grow vegetables for restaurants, one French gourmet chef insisted I bring him only New Zealand spinach for the spinach soufflé, that's how good it is! And it grows like a weed, too. It will spread out and take over the garden if you let it, so I like to grow it on a vertical frame. Seeds are slow to germinate, so soak them a day before planting them in individual cups about two weeks before your last spring frost. Then plant the young plants one to a square under a vertical frame about four weeks later.

Summer Squash

At A Glance

Botanical Information:

Gourd family
Bush and vining types
Annual, frost tender

Spacing: Vine types—3 plants per 1' × 4' trench; bush types
—1 plant per 3' × 3' space

Growing Season:

Spring: no
Summer: yes
Fall: no
Winter: no

Seed to Harvest: 8 weeks

Seeds Store: 5–6 years

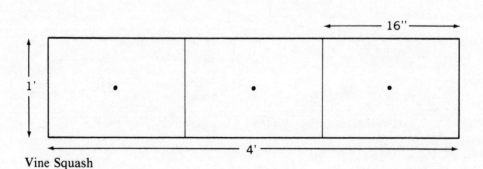

Vine Squash

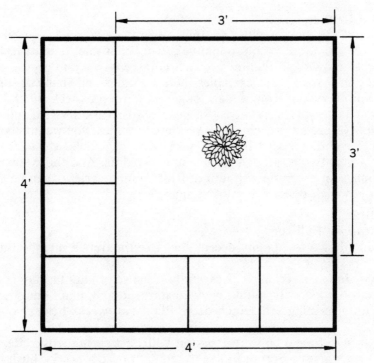

Bush Squash

		Weeks Before Last Spring Frost		Weeks After		Weeks Before First Fall Frost		Weeks After	
		10 8 6 4 2 0 2 4 6 8				8 6 4 2 0 2 4 6 8			
Summer squash (8 wks. to maturity)	Indoor Seed Starting									
	Earliest Outdoor Planting									
			or							
	Additional Plantings									
	Last Planting		Not needed							

Note: The plants are often killed by the squash vine borer, so an additional planting is advisable.

Description

One of the most popular summer vegetables, summer squash takes up a lot of room, but is so productive it's unbelievable. It must have hot weather to grow well. Summer squash is fast and easy to grow.

Like so many other vegetables there's a color and shape of summer squash for everyone—round, flat, long, straight, crookneck. Each has its particular taste, and all are easy to grow. Most varieties sold today are bush types (especially zucchini), so you must decide if you want to commit that much room (almost an entire block) to one vegetable. Most gardeners think it's worthwhile, at least for one or two plants. And those few plants can produce an enormous amount of fruit. Vining varieties can be grown vertically, which does save a lot of space.

Starting

Location: Full sun.

Soil: pH 5.5 to 7.0; any decent soil. Use the trench method for vine types.

Seeds Indoors: Transplant carefully because of long taproot. Best to start seeds outdoors. If you do want to start indoors, plant one seed in a paper cup of potting soil 1 inch deep. Plant two weeks before your last frost date.

Transplanting: Plant outdoors on your last spring frost date.

Seeds Outdoors: Sprout in five to ten days outdoors. For bush types, plant one presoaked seed in the center of a nine-square space. Vine types are placed three to a trench. Make sure you hollow out a dish shape around the seeds in the block to hold plenty of water. Place a plastic-covered cage over the seeds to warm the soil.

Growing

Watering: Weekly, two to four cups per plant depending on size of plant; twice weekly in hot weather. Keep the leaves dry to prevent powdery mildew.

Fertilizing: Heavy feeder; benefits from monthly applications of basic fertilizer mix.

Maintenance: Weed weekly; keep vines trained up vertical frames or within bounds of block.

Harvesting

How: Carefully cut through the fruit stem but do not cut the main vine or leaf stems. Handle the squash gently as their skins are very soft and easily damaged by fingernails or if dropped.

When: As soon as the blossoms wilt, and until the fruits are 6 to 9 inches long. Don't let them grow any longer. Sometimes you have to harvest at least three times a week, they grow that fast. Squash loses flavor as the seeds inside mature.

Preparing and Using

Rinse lightly and serve sliced or cut into sticks with a dip, or just as an appetizer any time of the day. Cook lightly by steaming or stir-frying, in any number of dishes or combinations. Serve by itself or with other vegetables seasoned with a little butter, grated cheese, or chopped parsley. High in vitamins A, B_1, and C.

Problems

Squash vine borer and squash bug; powdery mildew.

Questions and Answers

Q. What are the various methods to eliminate the dreaded squash vine borer?

A. If your plant wilts overnight you have a bad infestation of them and the only solution is to cut open the stem along its length with a very sharp knife. Don't cut crosswise. Look for the white grubs that have hollowed out the stem, causing the wilting. There will be more than one, I guarantee. You must handle the stem very carefully, obviously, or it may break in two. After you have found all the grubs that you can, lay the stem down on the ground and mound soil over the cut portion. The plant may root along its stem and possibly survive after your radical surgery. However, after many discouraging years spending hours digging out these critters, my favorite method now is to plant a second crop of summer squash two months after the first. Then, if one becomes infested and wilts I just pull it up and have a new crop coming along to take its place. Of course you need a lot of room to do that, as each plant takes up almost a full garden block when mature. Other methods of control include wrapping the stems with foil or plastic to prevent the squash borer moth from laying its eggs in the first place.

Q. I've heard that squash blossoms are edible. How are they prepared?

A. Pick the male flowers just before or as they are opening, and wash them. Sautéed in butter they are delicious. I've even had them stuffed with a meat filler—really scrumptious. They can also be dipped in a batter and fried.

Winter Squash

At A Glance

Botanical Information:

Gourd family
Vine
Annual, frost tender

Spacing: 2 plants per 1′ × 4′ trench

Growing Season:

Spring: no
Summer: yes
Fall: no
Winter: no

Seed to Harvest: 12 weeks

Seeds Store: 5–6 years

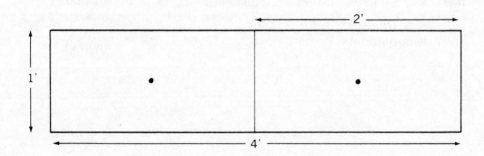

		Weeks Before Last Spring Frost		Weeks After		Weeks Before Fall	First Fall Frost	Weeks After
		10 8 6 4 2 0	2 4 6 8		8 6 4	2 0	2 4 6 8	
Winter squash (12 wks. to maturity)	Indoor Seed Starting		Not worthwhile					
	Earliest Outdoor Planting		⬯⎯⎯⎯⎯			🧺🧺🧺🧺🧺		
	Additional Plantings		Not necessary					
	Last Planting		Not necessary					

Description

A very space-hungry plant, many gardeners resist growing it because of its habit of taking over the entire garden with its huge leaves and trailing vines. Growing winter squash vertically eliminates the usual problems by getting the vines up in the air. The mature squash is harvested in late fall and can be easily stored for use anytime over the winter. It keeps its delicious flavor long after the garden is put to bed.

The most popular varieties are Butternut and Acorn, but there are many others to choose from. All grow with thick skins that harden in the fall, and they are usually harvested after the vines are killed by frost. So your rewards are not given to you until the end of the season, but by then there is little fresh produce from the garden so the squash is most welcome. The flesh is fine grained and of a mild flavor.

Starting

Location: Full sun, but tolerates a little shade.

Soil: pH 6.0 to 7.5; any decent soil will do. Use the trench method for preparing soil.

Seeds Indoors: No.

Transplanting: Do not transplant well because of the long taproot.

Seeds Outdoors: Since the seeds sprout quickly, you might as well start them outdoors. Prepare your trench and plant two presoaked seeds 2 feet apart along the center of it. Make sure you've left a 2-inch depression in the trench to hold lots of water during the season. Cover with a plastic tunnel to warm the soil and encourage fast seed sprouting.

Growing

Watering: Weekly, 10 to 12 cups per trench, depending on the size of the plant; twice weekly in hot weather.

Fertilizing: Heavy feeder; benefits from monthly applications of basic fertilizer mix.

Maintenance: Weed weekly; keep vines trained up the vertical frame.

Harvesting

How: Cut the squash from the vine leaving as long a stem as possible, at least 2 inches. Then set the fruit out in the sun to cure for a few days, protecting it at night when frost is in the forecast.

When: After the first light frost which will kill the leaves and vines, and after the main vine wilts, but before a very hard frost comes.

Preparing and Using

Peel, cut in half, scoop out seeds, and prepare for boiling or baking. Excellent served mashed or in chunks with butter and parsley. Winter squash can even be added to some soups and stews. Butternut can be used for pumpkin pie (many cooks say it's better tasting than pumpkin itself). Store winter squash in a cool, dry place at 40° to 50°F; check often and use if you see any bruised or rotten spots.

Tomatoes

At A Glance

Botanical Information:

Nightshade family
Bush and vining types
Annual, frost tender

Spacing: Bush type—4 plants per 4′ × 4′ block; vine type—1 plant per square

Growing Season:

Spring: no
Summer: yes
Fall: no
Winter: no

Seed to Harvest: 17 weeks

Seeds Store: 4–5 years

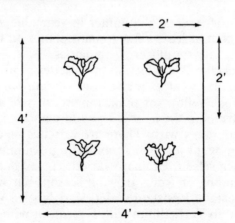

Bush Tomatoes

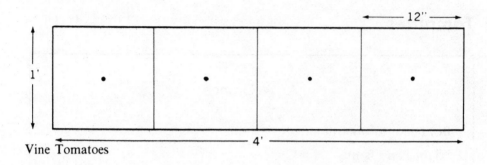

Vine Tomatoes

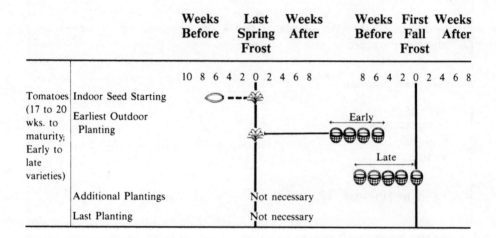

		Weeks Before	Last Spring Frost	Weeks After		Weeks Before	First Fall Frost	Weeks After
		10 8 6 4 2	0	2 4 6 8		8 6 4 2	0	2 4 6 8
Tomatoes (17 to 20 wks. to maturity; Early to late varieties)	Indoor Seed Starting							
	Earliest Outdoor Planting					Early		
						Late		
	Additional Plantings		Not necessary					
	Last Planting		Not necessary					

Description

Tomatoes are the essence of summer in vegetable gardening. Don't plant a garden without at least a few tomato plants. In fact, if you don't plant anything else, you should grow tomatoes.

There is an unbelievable selection of varieties available to the home gardener. You can have early, midseason, or late varieties in various shades of red, orange, yellow, or pink, ranging in size all the way from small marble-size fruits to the 3- and 4-pound giants that everyone loves to have their picture taken with. There are varieties especially suited for juice, cooking, canning, or just plain good eating. An important qualification to look for when selecting tomato varieties is not only how long they take to grow depending on your growing season, but whether they are disease and pest resistant. Resistant varieties are labeled VFN. V indicates the plant is resistant to Verticillium wilt, F means it withstands Fusarium wilt, and N stands for nematodes, an insect infestation of the roots. These special varieties have been bred for protection against these common tomato enemies. Although there are many good, traditionally favorite nonresistant varieties, if you have ever had all of your vines wilt and die almost overnight just at the peak of their harvest season, you'll appreciate the importance of selecting these new resistant varieties. There are many resistant varieties bred today, producing good-tasting tomatoes that mature early, midseason, or late. In general, the early-season varieties are best suited to the short growing season in the northern regions, but if your season is long enough you can grow a few different varieties that mature at different times to have tomatoes throughout the growing season.

As described in chapter 8, tomatoes exhibit two different growth habits—determinate or indeterminate. Determinate tomatoes are bush types that stay short, growing no more than 3 feet tall. Indeterminate varieties grow in long vines, are the most common varieties, usually mature in mid or late season, and will continue growing until frost kills the plant. They produce the largest tomatoes but take longer to mature.

Starting

Location: Full sun.

Soil: pH 5.5 to 7.0; deep, loose, rich soil with lots of humus added.

Seeds Indoors: Sprout in one week at 70°F. Sprinkle five to ten seeds of each variety you want to grow in individual cups filled with vermiculite six weeks before your last spring frost. Just barely cover with vermiculite and water.

Transplanting: Harden-off for one to two weeks, and plant out on or after your frost-free date. Plant four plants per 4-foot trench. Water and cover with a plastic-covered wire tunnel for protection from the cold and wind. Leave the tunnel on until the plants are at least 18 inches tall and pushing at the top.

Seeds Outdoors: Season too short to start outdoors.

Growing

Watering: Weekly, one to two gallons per 4-foot trench, depending on plant size; twice weekly in very hot weather. Keep water off the plant leaves.

Fertilizing: Heavy feeder; benefits from monthly applications of basic fertilizer mix. Also ½ cup of lime per trench each month.

Maintenance: Weekly, prune off side branches (suckers) and twist plant top around string. Prune off lower dead or yellow leaves. Keep adding mulch as the season gets hotter.

Harvesting

How: Gently twist and pull ripe tomato so its stem breaks (if it's ripe it should easily break away), or cut stem so as not to disturb fruit remaining on the vine.

When: If you're not going to wait until they're red and ripe, why grow them yourself? Some gardeners like to pick them just slightly before that point (say a day or two) if they want extra-firm tomatoes for sandwiches or a particular dish. If you leave them on the vine too long they will turn soft and mushy, so inspect daily; it's one of the pleasures you've been waiting for all year.

Preparing and Using

This is a subject fit for an entire book, and in fact many have been written. What can one say in a few paragraphs? Tomatoes can be used in a multitude of ways. You can enjoy plate after plate of sliced tomatoes seasoned with lots of pepper and sometimes a little mayonnaise. Then try pouring your favorite salad dressing over that same dish of sliced tomatoes. Another day soak a plate full in vinegar overnight for the next day's treat. Add thick slices of fresh tomatoes to any casserole and enjoy a flavor not experienced the rest of the year. If you have a lot of tomatoes, use them fresh in cooking instead of canned tomatoes.

Problems

Cutworm and whitefly; various wilt diseases.

Questions and Answers

Q. What should I do with all the tomatoes we have in the fall when frost is imminent?

A. Cover them with a plastic tunnel or pick them for ripening indoors. Pickle the small green ones, fry up the medium-size green ones, and store the larger ones that are starting to turn color. For best storage wash in a solution of 1 part chlorine bleach to 9 parts water, dry and place in a cardboard box or ice chest with a few apples added to provide the ethylene gas needed for ripening. Tomatoes to be stored must be absolutely perfect and free from cracks, splits, and blemishes or they will rot before ripening. Check at least once a week and remove all those that have ripened or started to decay.

Q. Will tomatoes ripen if set on a sunny windowsill?

A. No. Although they may turn pink they usually simply shrivel up and will be bitter tasting. Store in the dark as previously described.

Q. Could I save seeds from a particularly good tomato for growing plants next year?

A. If it was a hybrid, no; if not, it's possible although not usually worthwhile. Seeds are inexpensive, and remember, if you store them properly (cool and dry) they will last for at least four to five years.

Q. Why do my first few tomatoes always seem to have a black rotten spot on the bottom?

A. It's called blossom end rot, caused possibly by too little calcium in the soil, or by uneven water when the tomatoes are forming. Start with a soil that has a pH of about 6.5 to 7.0, and then add a little lime each month with your fertilizer. Never let the soil dry out or let the plants wilt. The rotten spot is caused by too little water while the tomato is enlarging, and then too much water all at once, causing the fruit to grow too rapidly.

Q. Why did our plants suddenly stop bearing tomatoes?

A. The weather probably got too hot (or possibly too cold at night). The blossoms will only set into fruit when the nighttime temperatures are between 55° and 75°F for most varieties, and the daytime temperatures are between 60° and 90°F. Lower or higher temperatures, especially at night, can cause the flower to drop without setting fruit.

Q. I once heard that you should shake tomato plants when they're blooming, but I forgot why.

A. To help spread the pollen so the flower will set fruit. Tomatoes are self-pollinating and don't need bees to spread pollen. Usually the pollen spreads by itself, but if the weather is very still, when the temperature is cool, you can help the pollen spread if you shake or vibrate the plant or its support very lightly. The best time is around noon to early afternoon.

Q: Is it true that you shouldn't smoke when handling tomato plants?

A: Yes, it is true, you should not smoke around your tomato plants or handle the plants without first washing your hands. You can transmit a virus present in tobacco to the tomatoes, causing a disease.

Index